S0-BNW-729

ABOUT THE AUTHOR

Currently Professor of Sociology at Syracuse University, Louis Kriesberg received his Ph.D. from The University of Chicago. He has taught at Columbia University and has been Fulbright Research Scholar at the University of Cologne, Senior Fellow in Law and the Behavioral Sciences at The University of Chicago Law School, and Senior Study Director of the National Opinion Research Center. Professor Kriesberg is an Associate Editor of *Social Problems* and has written many articles and monographs for the professional literature; he is the editor of *Social Processes in International Relations: A Reader.* At the present time, he is conducting research in the areas of social stratification, international relations, and social conflict.

Mothers in Poverty

Mothers in Poverty

A Study of Fatherless Families

Louis Kriesberg

Syracuse University

Aldine Publishing Company: *Chicago*

First published 1970 by
Aldine Publishing Company
529 South Wabash Avenue
Chicago, Illinois 60605

Library of Congress Catalog Number 79-90079
SBN 202-30035
Printed in the United States of America

To
MY MOTHER
AND
DANIEL AND JOSEPH
AND
TO
LOIS

Preface

THIS BOOK is about mothers and children in poor fatherless families. But it is not simply about their plight. It attempts *explanations* of the way of life of poor people and the possible role their way of life plays in the intergenerational transmission of poverty. My purpose in writing this book was to assess basic alternative explanations. Two approaches toward such explanations are examined in detail. One emphasizes the development and maintenance of a subculture of poverty. The other emphasizes the contemporary circumstances that make people poor, keep them poor, and to which the poor respond.

To assess these general approaches more specific questions need to be phrased. This questioning is done in the first chapters of the book. These questions are derived from larger ones, Do poor people develop a distinctive way of life that inhibits their movement out of poverty? Is there a way of life passed on from one generation to the next that keeps each generation poor? Do certain social conditions impose poverty and are the adaptations that poor people make to such conditions readily modifiable if the conditions change?

The assessment is made by seeking to clarify the issues in contention and by bringing relevant data to bear on the contending ideas. The data are drawn from a wide range of work done by others and particularly from a study of families living in and near low-income public housing projects in one city. The study was focused upon certain conditions: marital arrangements, housing and neighborhood, employment, and the public welfare system. The major subject of analysis is one segment of the poor: mothers with young children but without husbands.

The poverty of these mothers is related to their role as women in this society. Insofar as women are and expect to be economically dependent upon men, a marriage broken by death, divorce, or desertion threatens the mother and her children with poverty, unless the government or her former husband or her relatives provide enough money to keep the family out of poverty. Some of this threat would be alleviated if women were expected from childhood to hold jobs, were educated for employment, had equal job opportunities, received equal pay, and had child-care facilities. Such circumstances would also help raise families with husband-fathers out of poverty, as working wives presently often do. Such circumstances might also appear to create new difficulties for the well-being of children and marital stability. The findings and discussion in this book should help realistically to assess these supposed difficulties.

Although focusing upon one segment of the poor, the issues raised and analyzed pertain to poor people generally. Furthermore, given the interrelated nature of the conditions associated with poverty and the responses people make to those conditions, the findings have pertinence to topics such as stratification, marriage, education, blacks, and the urban community. Finally, elucidating the limitations of the subculture-of-poverty approach has important theoretical and policy implications. Those are best discussed after presenting the analysis.

Acknowledgments

THIS BOOK IS BASED UPON DATA collected for the Public Housing and Social Mobility Study. This study was conducted at the Youth Development Center of Syracuse University and supported by funds from the Ford Foundation and the Welfare Administration of the Department of Health, Education and Welfare (grant number 042), and the National Science Foundation (grant GP-1137), to the Computing Center.

Many persons cooperated in the project and I want to use this opportunity to acknowledge their contributions to the overall study.

The Syracuse Housing Authority, under the chairmanship of Jacob Lattiff, granted approval for the cooperation that made the study possible. The cooperation of the Housing Authority staff, notably Fenton Gage, Beatrice McKibbon, and William McGarry, was very great. Robert Hale and William Chiles of the Department of Urban Improvement of the City of Syracuse cooperated in the study of families affected by urban relocation.

Irwin Deutscher was primarily responsible, with the collaboration of Lee J. Cary, for the formulation of the original design of the study. They were assisted by George Freskos, Ronald Ley, and Donald Reeb. During the major data collection phases of the study, Seymour S. Bellin and I were co-directors of the study. Helen Icken Safa aided in the preliminary field work and directed the participant observation phase of the study. Jerome Cohen was field director during the preliminary investigations and helped develop the questionnaires. The study design and questionnaires benefited from the consultations of Robert K. Merton, Marc Fried, David E. Hunt, and John Dopyera.

Several graduate assistants served for varying lengths of time in many capacities. Laurence T. Cagle, Charlotte Mallov, James R. McIntosh, Alphonse J. Sallett, Thelie Trotty, Joan T. Weber, Roland Werner, and Abdel Zikry aided in code construction, card cleaning, and analysis at various stages in the study. The participant observers were David Cumming, George A. Freskos, Elizabeth Lowe, and Mary Reibson.

Virginia B. Brown supervised interviewing the panel of public housing applicants and Dagny Henderson supervised the field operations of the cross-sectional phase of the study. Dean Lindeman supervised the several coding operations of the interview data. Beverly A. McGarry handled many of the problems in the relations between ideas, computers, and data. The Syracuse University Computing Center, under Director Otway O. Pardee, provided the necessary services for processing the data; I am indebted to Dominick Auricchio of the Computing Center for his aid. Crestline Littlefield, Susan Drucker and the Youth Development Center typing staff prepared the many forms used in the study and typed and retyped the working papers, and reports which preceded this book, as well as the revisions of this book.

The writing of this book has benefited from the previous work on the study in collaboration with Seymour S. Bellin and Helen Icken Safa. The preparation of the book has also been aided by the suggestions and comments of Robert H. Hardt, Irwin Deutscher, Lee J. Cary, Howard S. Becker, S. M. Miller, Alexander J. Morin, Alphonse J. Sallett, Elizabeth Thompson, and my brother Irving. My wife, Lois, contributed many insights in the course of my work, some of which I have been able to incorporate in the book.

Most of all, I am indebted to the respondents; their cooperation underlies all the later work.

Contents

1. On Explaining the Life Style of the Poor

THE DEMANDS of the poor in America for more equality and for government efforts to combat poverty have quickened public attention to a fundamental sociological topic: social stratification. Sociologists have studied the ways people rank each other, how people are recruited into different ranks, and how the values, beliefs, and conduct of people in various ranks differ. Most of the studies have described these phenomena, and some have attempted to account for the variations. Government programs against poverty have brought into sharp focus the need to know the causes of poverty and of the immobility of poor people. Programs designed to change poor people or to reduce poverty are based on some beliefs about the significant causal connections.

Some programs are aimed at young children in poor families, presuming that the skills and motives acquired in early life determine later chances to escape from poverty. Other programs aim at providing occupational skills for adolescents and young adults, presuming that changes in children of poverty are still possible and necessary to avoid future poverty. In addition, some programs are directed at expanding the number of jobs available, presuming that if opportunities are available, they will be utilized. Still other programs are aimed at simply insuring a more equitable distribution of available income.[1]

Central to many of these programs is the belief that the way of life of the poor plays a critical role in maintaining poverty, that it impedes the movement out of poverty. On the other hand, it is argued that the poor are made poor and kept poor by circumstances around them. Even granting a critical role to life styles, there is disagreement about the extent to which the poor have a comprehensive and distinctive life style and the degree to which this is an integrated subculture transmitted from one generation to the next.

The vicious circle poor people are ensnared in has been frequently portrayed.[2] That each aspect of poverty compounds the effects of every other one is not hard to understand. An illness that may be worrisome and unpleasant for a family with an adequate income is a disaster for a poor family. Similarly, the likelihood and consequences of being laid off from a job are increased among impoverished families. Recurring disasters make planning difficult and apparently hopeless. In innumerable ways people living in poverty develop attitudes and patterns of conduct that seem to be an accommodation to their circumstances. These accom-

1. For discussions of various programs to counter poverty, see selections in Louis A. Ferman, Joyce L. Kornbluh, and Alan Haber, eds., *Poverty in America* (Ann Arbor: University of Michigan Press, 1965); Herman P. Miller, ed., *Poverty American Style* (Belmont, Calif.: Wadsworth, 1966); Hanna H. Meissner, ed., *Poverty in the Affluent Society* (New York: Harper & Row, 1966); and Leo Fishman, ed., *Poverty Amid Affluence* (New Haven: Yale University Press, 1966).

2. For discussions of various interconnections in the cycle of poverty, see, for example; Oscar Lewis, *Five Families* (New York: Basic Books, 1959); Oscar Lewis, "The Culture of Poverty," *Scientific American*, 215 (October, 1966), pp. 19–25; Frank Riessman, *The Culturally Deprived Child* (New York: Harper & Row, 1962); Allison Davis, *Social Class Influences Upon Learning* (Cambridge: Harvard University Press, 1952); and Walter B. Miller, "Lower Class Culture as a Generating Milieu of Gang Delinquency," *Journal of Social Issues*, XIV (March, 1958), pp. 5–19.

modative ways of thinking and behaving are transmitted to the children of poor families. In addition, the children are subjected to unstable family life, inadequate school environment, and a life of the streets—all of which handicap them in learning how to get out of poverty. What they have learned as children is integrated and imbedded in their personalities and it is resistant to alteration by later experiences.

Compelling as these descriptions may be, they can provide only partial views of the infinite complexity of the life of any category of people. It is true that values, beliefs, and conduct tend toward mutual consistency; they support each other, and they are responses to circumstances they themselves help structure. The meaning of any situation depends on the context provided by other circumstances and the subjective perception and evaluation of the conditions. It is illuminating to point out such interdependence and the resulting integrated set of unique values and practices, but the illuminating beam also casts shadows that obscure other truths.

No category of humans have a way of life completely distinct from other humans. Many experiences are shared by all persons. No human is utterly alien from any other. The shared elements of life are especially important when we compare categories of persons within the same society. It is necessary to recognize that some experiences are shared by everyone, that others are unique to a given category, and still other experiences are shared by some persons in one category with some others in a different category. Furthermore, various aspects of life are changing—at different rates and in response to different sets of conditions. Consequently, no completely integrated set of values, beliefs, and conduct exists for any category of persons. Discrepancies, inconsistencies, and tensions among values, beliefs, and practices are inevitable.

All this suggests another approach to differences in life styles among families of varying incomes. Particular values and beliefs may be shared while others differ as a response to a given situation. Being responsive to particular circumstances, the apparent stability of certain values and beliefs reflects the stability of those circumstances. Under new circumstances, patterns of conduct, beliefs, and values are altered.[3]

These observations are especially pertinent in discussing the heterogenous category of the poor. Families can become poor from loss of income if the family wage earner becomes disabled or too old, or if the market for the wage earner's skills declines. For people reared in families that were not poor, many earlier parental ideas and practices are not appropriate to their new state, and some would be altered, but not all in the same way or at the same rate. On the other hand, many children raised in poor families escape poverty when they grow up. They may have acquired values, beliefs, and practices from their experiences in poverty, but many of these do not persist in changed circumstances, and the persistence varies with the ideas and conduct and the circumstances.

Not only do most of the poor in the United States share many values, beliefs, and practices with the nonpoor, those they do not share are vulnerable to change under changed circumstances, and all together do not constitute an integrated way of life distinctive from that of the nonpoor.

In this book I wish to clarify some of the issues in contention and to present findings pertinent to those issues. I shall consider specific values, beliefs, and patterns of conduct associated with poverty, for example, in regard to the lower educational achievement of children of the poor. I shall examine how these characteristics are affected by prior and contemporary conditions. Such an undertaking should contribute to a sounder explanation of how certain aspects of the way of life of the poor are maintained, perpetuated, resisted, or discontinued.

Fatherless families are the particular subjects of the

3. For discussions of the two approaches and illustrative evidence, see, for example; Louis Kriesberg, "The Relationship Between Socio-Economic Rank and Behavior," *Social Problems,* 10 (Spring, 1963), pp. 334–353; Jack L. Roach and Orville R. Gursalin, "An Evaluation of the Concept 'Culture of Poverty,'" *Social Forces,* 45 (March, 1967), pp. 383-392; and S. M. Miller, Frank Riessman, and Arthur A. Seagull, "Poverty and Self-Indulgence: A Critique of the Non-deferred Gratification Pattern," in Ferman, Kornbluh, and Haber, eds., *op, cit.,* p. 301.

present undertaking. Aside from our intrinsic concern about their plight, we study them as a strategic category in understanding the life of the poor and the perpetuation of poverty. Fatherless families constitute an important segment of the poor. About one-quarter of the poor families in the United States are fatherless, and about 30 per cent of the children living in poverty are in fatherless families.[4] Furthermore, studying fatherless families has several analytic advantages for the issues being considered. In many ways poor fatherless families seem to epitomize the life style of the hard-core poor. The conditions of poverty seem particularly intractable for them and the handicaps of children from such families are particularly severe. Among these families, then, are many that may well exemplify the intergenerationally transmitted subculture of poverty. Yet many fatherless families have fallen into poverty by ill chance: by the death of the husband-father or by divorce, separation, or desertion. The husbandless mothers in many families were raised in a household with an adequate income before the family was disrupted.

Consequently, by comparing fatherless and complete families, it is possible to study the impact of a condition often associated with poverty: the absence of a father in the family. More significantly, we can readily compare the effects of this condition on persons of different social origins and of varying contemporary conditions. At the same time we will assess the consequences of different socioeconomic backgrounds and contemporary circumstances for both complete and fatherless families.

THE SUBCULTURAL AND SITUATIONAL VIEWS

I have sketched out two different approaches to the study of poor families. These two perspectives require further amplification. After discussing each of them in detail, I will

4. Mollie Orshansky, "Counting the Poor: Another Look at the Poverty Profile," XXVIII (January, 1965), Table 11, as reprinted in Ferman, Kornbluh, and Haber, eds., *op. cit.*, pp. 64-65 and Herman P. Miller, *Rich Man, Poor Man* (New York: New American Library, 1965), p. 77.

explain some underlying and cross-cutting issues. The next chapter will present more specific ideas pertaining to poverty and fatherless families.

In examining the subcultural view of poverty, I include research about persons who differ in rank along other dimensions than income. Income, education, occupation, place of residence, and class identification are all highly related to each other. Innumerable studies have been made of people who vary along one, or a combination of several, of these dimensions. Many ideas about the way of life of people in poverty have been drawn from studies made in low-income neighborhoods or of persons with varying occupational or educational levels.

According to the subcultural approach, poor people, like people in every other stratum, possess a mutually consistent and supporting set of values, beliefs, and patterns of conduct. This integrated set of characteristics is shared by members of the stratum and differs in important ways from that possessed by persons in other strata. These characteristics form a way of life appropriate to the recurrent problems the members of the stratum face. The way of life is acquired early in life, and it is perpetuated from one generation to the next.

This view is expounded in many textbooks on social stratification wherein the life styles of different strata in the society are described. For example, Bergel writes,

> Each class has its specific set of values, goals, habits, behavior patterns, its specific "class mentality." Classes live in comparative social isolation; from earliest childhood their members are reared in a specific "class atmosphere," are imbued with specific class values, and thereby acquire specific group traits that set them apart from members of other classes.[5]

Similarly, in studies of a particular stratum, usually the working-class or lower-class strata, researchers report an integrated life style. This has been formulated for persons living in poverty, notably by Oscar Lewis. As he observed, the "culture of poverty" is a catchy phrase and appears

5. Egon Ernest Bergel, *Social Stratification* (New York: McGraw-Hill, Inc., 1962), p. 366.

frequently in the current literature. He explains that he uses the phrase as

> the label for a specific conceptual model that describes in positive terms a subculture of Western society with its own structure and rationale, a way of life handed on from generation to generation along family lines. The culture of poverty is not just a matter of deprivation or disorganization, a term signifying the absence of something. It is a culture in the traditional anthropological sense in that it provides human beings with a design for living with a ready-made set of solutions for human problems, and so serves a significant adaptive function. This style of life transcends national boundaries and regional and rural-urban differences within nations. Wherever it occurs, its practitioners exhibit remarkable similarity in the structure of their families, in interpersonal relations, in their value systems and in their orientation in time.[6]

The culture of poverty as described by Oscar Lewis is similar to the descriptions of lower-class life in urban centers of the United States and of Negro slum dwellers. Variations in the subcultural approach to the study of poor persons will be discussed later. At this point we need only observe that in one approach to the study of poor persons, students may emphasize the interrelationship among values, norms, beliefs, and behavior patterns as they are collectively shaped and perpetuated.

The many pitying, romanticizing, empathetic, condescending, pejorative as well as evaluatively neutral descriptions of the way of life of the poor or of the lower class testify to the interrelations. Poor people are trapped in a vicious circle in which each aspect supports every other aspect. One can start anywhere to note the interrelations. Lacking occupational skills, dependent upon low-paying and unstable employment, they feel cut off from advancement; their situation seems hopeless; they are victims of fate and chance. Their time orientation is shortened and gratifications indulged rather than delayed. Security is found in sharing limited resources with close kin or a network of peers. Work

6. Lewis, "The Culture of Poverty," *op. cit.*, p. 19.

is not valued even when available or cannot be sustained when attempted. Family life is unstable and children grow up without learning the skills and attitudes necessary for employment and a stable marriage. Each spouse maintains close ties with his or her relatives as a refuge, which adds to the brittleness of the marriage. Within the family, activities are clearly demarked between males and females and the mother-child relations are particularly strong and enduring. Female-headed families are common and in some ways represent the epitome of the way of life outlined. Not expecting legal, binding, and faithful marriage nor only legitimate children, legal marriage and legitimate children are not highly valued or normatively controlled.

Several aspects of the subcultural approach can be contested. One point about which there is widespread disagreement is how different are in fact the norms and values of the poor from those of others in the society. Some observers stress the extent to which all members of the society are expected and do indeed share notions of what is desirable. Thus, Merton in his classic essay on social structure and anomie argues:

> Our egalitarian ideology denies by implication the existence of non-competing individuals and groups in the pursuit of pecuniary success. . . . Goals are held to transcend class lines, not be bounded by them, yet the actual social organization is such that there exist class differentials in accessibility of the goals. . . . "poverty" is not an isolated variable which operates in precisely the same fashion wherever found: it is only one in a complex of identifiably interdependent social and cultural variables. . . . when poverty and associated disadvantages in competing for the cultural values approved for all members of the society are linked with a cultural emphasis on pecuniary success as the dominant goal, high rates of criminal behavior are the normal outcome. . . . When we consider the full configuration—poverty, limited opportunity and the assignment of cultural goals—there appears some basis for explaining the higher correlation between poverty and crime in our society than in others where rigidified class structure is coupled with *differential class symbols of success.*[7]

7. Robert K. Merton, *Social Theory and Social Structure* (New York: Free Press, 1957), pp. 146–147.

Thus, too, Hylan Lewis in his study of low-income families in the District of Columbia found that birth in wedlock is an important value, and that low-income parents show conformity to and convergence with middle class family and child-rearing standards in what they say they want for themselves and their children, even if they differ in actual conduct.[8] Similarly, Goode has argued that although common law marriage is widespread in the Caribbean, marriage is the ideal and violators are penalized.[9]

Other arguments have been raised against the subcultural approach. Even if there are differences in some patterns of conduct or in the priority assigned to different values, comparisons between the poor and other segments of the population reveals considerable heterogeneity among both the poor and the other strata; consequently, there is considerable overlap between any comparison groups. In emphasizing the distinctive features of the poor compared to others, the very large similarities among most of the persons in all strata are ignored.

In addition, attention to the existential conditions in which the poor live points to the possibility that what may appear to be profound and deep seated differences in orientations are only accommodations to particular circumstances. Given another set of circumstances, the orientations would be different. Indeed, the same people may exhibit different conduct and different orientations in one situation than in another. Thus, Miller, Riessman, and Seagull, in their analysis of the nondeferred gratification pattern as related to poverty, write:

> we do not view all those who seem to be unable to defer gratification as so psychodynamically constrained that the ability to defer gratification is unavailable to them. For some, this is undoubtedly true. But for others, situations which offer perceived hope do lead to postponement and planning. They may not be

8. Hylan Lewis, "Child Rearing Among Low-Income Families, in Ferman, Kornbluh, and Haber, eds., *op. cit.*, pp. 342–353.

9. William J. Goode, "A Deviant Case: Illegitimacy in the Caribbean," *American Sociological Review*, 25 (February, 1960), pp. 21–30; and William J. Goode, "Note on Problems in Theory and Method: The New World." *American Anthropologist*, 68 (April, 1966), pp. 486–492.

able to overcome all the obstacles which face them, but they are not locked into self-indulgence.[10]

In short, two general approaches to the study of the poor may be distinguished, the subcultural and the situational. On the one hand, some writers emphasize the distinctive set of integrated values, beliefs, and practices shared by the poor and deeply enough embedded in the personality to be relatively stable and perpetuated intergenerationally. On the other hand, some emphasize the variability in circumstances among persons in different strata to account for variations in conduct and, to some extent, subjective orientations.

These approaches differ along many dimensions. It is useful to examine in detail some of these dimensions and the issues inherent in them. By specifying the issues, a more comprehensive and more clearly articulated set of hypotheses about the life of the poor can be attained and the hypotheses can be more successfully tested. For example, the specific role of intergenerational processes in the perpetuation and maintenance of poverty and the way of life of the poor must be clearly distinguished from other processes if the significance of each is to be assessed.

UNDERLYING AND CROSS-CUTTING ISSUES

Distinctiveness of the Strata. One of the major issues between the cultural and situational approaches is the extent to which the poor share a way of life distinctive from other persons. This major issue consists of related subissues: what categories are being compared; what about them is being compared; and how much overlap is there between the categories being compared in any specific regard.

The distinction of any category of persons from any other depends in part upon the categories being compared. Thus, in studies of socioeconomic strata, analyses of the way of life of various strata make it clear that it is necessary to distinguish among a number of manual strata; the lower-lower class, the honest working class, the lumpen proletariat, and the upper-lower class. Similarly in discussions of the poor,

10. Miller, Riessman, and Seagull, *op. cit.*, p. 301.

for many purposes it is necessary to specify whether we refer to urban or rural poor, to the aged or the poor of child-rearing age, or to the poor of one ethnic group or another. Lumping all such categories together may obscure important differences. And generalizing from a description of one type to all others may exaggerate differences. For example, some descriptions of the poor's way of life are extensions based on studies of urban slum Negroes.

We cannot consider the strata being compared without noting the problem of defining the strata. Some writers build into their definitions certain way-of-life characteristics.[11] Thus writers emphasizing a subcultural approach may posit a disorganized family life, reliance upon peer relations, apathy, and giving up efforts at gainful employment as defining characteristics of the poor. Those taking a situational approach are more likely to use some gross objective characteristic, such as income.

Note, however, that in defining the poor partly in terms of their life style, we must acknowledge variations in life style even among the urban poor of child-rearing age. Clearly, all poor persons do not share a common way of life. It is advisable to consider the full range of people in the poverty stratum if we are to account for the variations among persons in the stratum. To attend only to those poor who have a particular style of life, moreover, may incorrectly suggest that all the poor have the same style.

In assessing the distinctiveness of the poor, not only the categories used are pertinent, but also what is being compared. Writers emphasizing a subcultural approach tend to note the distinctiveness of the value and normative systems. If there is anything to the notion of subcultural differences, then values and norms held by persons in poverty should be widely shared and distinctive from those held by the non-poor. Significantly, however, research findings usually

11. For example, see David Matza, "The Disreputable Poor," in Reinhard Bendix and Seymour Martin Lipset, *Class, Status, and Power*, 2nd ed. (New York: Free Press, 1966), pp. 289–302; S. M. Miller, "The American Lower Classes: A Typological Approach," in Arthur B. Shostak and William Gomberg, eds., *Blue Collar World*, (Englewood Cliffs, N. J.: Prentice-Hall, 1964), pp. 9–23; and Herbert J. Gans, *The Urban Villagers*, (New York: Free Press of Glencoe, 1962).

indicate that values and norms of the poor differ less from those of the nonpoor than does the actual conduct of the poor.[12] Even Oscar Lewis in describing the culture of poverty writes,

> There is awareness of middle-class values. People talk about them and even claim some of them as their own. On the whole, however, they do not live by them. They will declare that marriage by law, by the church or by both is the ideal form of marriage, but few will marry.[13]

Observers emphasizing a situational approach to the study of poverty are more likely to note the differences in conduct between the poor and the nonpoor, while noting the similarities in values and norms.

One useful elaboration in this context is suggested by Hyman Rodman in his discussion of the "value stretch." In his words,

> Lower-class persons in close interaction with each other and faced with similar problems do not long remain in a state of mutual ignorance. They do not maintain a strong commitment to middle-class values that they cannot attain, and they do not continue to respond to others in a rewarding or punishing way simply on the basis of whether these others are living up to middle-class values. A change takes place. They come to tolerate and eventually evaluate favorably certain deviations from the middle-class values.[14]

At any given time, then, many lower-class persons may still ostensibly hold middle-class values, but expect deviations and accept them. What they think desirable is not necessarily what they are willing to settle for.

In addition, three methodological problems help account for the continuing disagreement and ambiguity in assertions about the distinctiveness or lack of distinctiveness of the

12. This issue also underlies much of the discussion about juvenile delinquency. See, for example, James F. Short, Jr., and Fred L. Strodtbeck, *Group Process and Gang Delinquency* (Chicago: University of Chicago Press, 1965); and David Matza, *Delinquency and Drift* (New York: John Wiley, 1964).

13. Lewis, "Culture of Poverty," *op. cit.*, p. 23.

14. Hyman Rodman, "The Lower-Class Value Stretch," in Ferman, Kornbluh, and Haber, *op. cit.*, p. 277.

lower class or of the poor. The first problem relates to the method of collecting information, the second to the measurement of values and beliefs, and the third to the decision about how much of a difference is necessary to assert that the poor have a distinctive way of life.

Some of the best work on the life of the poor has been based upon close observation of the way in which poor families live in small communities or neighborhoods. It is natural in this method to study a few networks of families and how the various aspects of their life fit together. Families in the same area who do not participate in this life are less closely observed and figure less in the depictions, and aspects of the activities of even the centrally studied families that do not fit into a coherent picture are likely to be relegated to the periphery of the descriptions. Consequently, a relatively integrated view of the way of life is depicted and variations and inconsistencies downgraded. On the other hand, the use of survey methods, for example, can lead to ticking off a series of percentages indicating similarities and differences on isolated iterms taken out of any meaningful context, though the variations among the poor and any comparison groups will be explicit.[15]

The second methodological problem lies in the assessment of just what it is that people value, what their beliefs are, and what norms they hold. Since mere verbal statements may be suspect, it might seem reasonable to assert that the best measure of what someone wants is to see what he tries to get—what he actually does. But what someone does is obviously affected by the opportunities and constraints he experiences. To argue that a person always does what he wants within the limits and alternatives available to him makes the notion of preference and value meaningless. And to infer preferences from behavior does not allow for the discrepancies we all experience and which may affect behavior in other ways and at other times. If the concepts of value,

15. For a discussion of the differences in findings regarding social networks among different strata derived from ethnographic and survey research methods, see Albert K. Cohen and Harold M. Hodges, "Characteristics of the Lower-Blue-Collar-Class," *Social Problems*, 10 (Spring, 1963), esp. pp. 310–315.

preferences, beliefs, and norms are to have meaning, they must be defined and assessed independently of conduct. They refer to a state of mind which can be assessed only if some attention is given to what people say about the ideas they hold. Obviously the assertions must be carefully considered in terms of their context—to whom made and under what circumstances. While people do talk about their ideas in ways which are obscuring as well as revealing, their verbal gestures must be considered in assessing what they think is good, true, and beautiful.

The third methodological problem relates to deciding how much of a difference between the poor and nonpoor is large enough to speak of a distinctive way of life of the poor. Finding differences between categories of people seems more worth reporting than discovering there is no difference. Furthermore, the magnitude of the differences are often exaggerated in summarization. If low-income persons are less likely than others to engage in a particular activity, it is still incorrect to say the poor do not engage in the activity while others do. Even if the difference is statistically significant, the overlap between categories may be very large indeed. An emphasis upon differences can result in a kind of stereotyping in which members of a category are viewed as much more homogenous than they actually are.[16]

Thus, everyone knows that poor people are less likely to recommend or prefer that their children go to college than are persons with greater income. But if people are asked do they want their children to go to college, most in every income category will say they do. Of course this preference is almost universal among the highest socioeconomic strata and the proportion declines with each socioeconomic stratum. Furthermore, the differences are much greater when actual expectations or conduct of the children are compared.[17] For many other values, beliefs, and patterns of conduct, nevertheless, large differences between the strata being compared coexist with even greater overlap. This is important because

16. Jerome Cohen, "Social Work and the Culture of Poverty," in Frank Riessman, Jerome Cohen, and Arthur Pearl, eds., *Mental Health of the Poor,* (New York: Free Press of Glencoe, 1964), pp. 128–138.

17. Kriesberg, *op. cit.*

if social influences from persons in the same strata are to be important determinants of the values, beliefs, and conduct of each person in the stratum, those characteristics should be commonly held within the stratum but not shared with persons in other strata. Awareness of what the prevailing opinion is in a group depends in large part upon how predominant that opinion is.

Taking into account all these caveats and difficulties, can it be asked, simply, do the poor have a distinctive style of life? It is clear that the question can be answered either negatively or affirmatively, depending upon the categories being compared, what characteristics are being emphasized, and how much difference one considers important, and it therefore becomes necessary to formulate the question more precisely in terms of the extent to which the poor differ from other strata in particular ways.

Relationship between Values and Conduct. As already indicated, persons employing a cultural approach to the study of the poor, compared to those employing a situational approach, tend to believe that the poor generally act in ways which are congruent with their values.[18] It seems reasonable that people will act in terms of their preferences and what they think is proper and desirable, but on the other hand, it is also reasonable to argue that people are not always free or able to do what they want or think desirable and proper. All kinds of circumstances may compel or constrain conduct so that it is not consistent with the desires of the actors.[19] Thus, a man may want to be employed regularly, but will not be if

18. This point of view may be expressed by theorists who assume widespread societal consensus and by those who do not but see values and norms emerging from varying experiences and, at least in the long run, see behavior patterns as expressive of the values and norms of the strata. For example, see writings as diverse as Talcott Parsons, *The Social System*, (Glencoe, Ill.: Free Press, 1951); Talcott Parsons and Edward A. Shils, eds., *Toward a General Theory of Action* (Cambridge: Harvard University Press, 1951); Ralf Dahrendorf, *Class and Class Conflict in Industrial Society* (Stanford, Calif.: Stanford University Press, 1959); and David Lockwood, "Some Remarks on 'The Social System,'" *British Journal of Sociology*, VII (June, 1956), pp. 134-146.

19. For example, see the discussions by Irwin Deutscher, "Words and Deeds: Social Science and Social Policy," *Social Problems*, 13 (Winter, 1966), pp. 235-254; Louis Kriesberg, "National Security and Conduct in the

the only jobs available demand physical strength or technical skills he lacks, or require prohibitive expense in time and money to get to the place of employment.

Furthermore, the factors affecting values are not the same as those which affect conduct. The socialization experiences of childhood, exposure to the mass media, and the evaluations of distant reference groups all affect one's values, but conduct is more directly affected by the immediate situation and the opportunities and constraints immediately confronted. Thus, a man may want the steady income and prestige of regular employment but find that pressures from friends and family or his treatment on the job so interfere that he cannot remain employed.

In addition, the pertinence of some general value to a particular pattern of conduct is always problematic. People hold many values which may be relevant to any given pattern of conduct. An analyst's judgment about which values should be related to some pattern of conduct may not be the same as that of the actor. Thus, a man may want to earn his own way via the conventional labor market but may also value spending time with his family and friends—where the rewards may be greater.

Granting all that, congruence may still be posited as a tendency.[20] Presumably, it distresses people to act contrary to what they desire and think proper. They will try to reduce their distress by increasing congruence, that is, by altering either the conduct or the values. At any given time, however, some people will not have attained this consistency; there is a lag. Sometimes, too, neither values nor conduct can be readily altered, given their somewhat different bases and determinants. In that event, people may use a variety of devices to minimize awareness of the discrepancies. For example, they may compartmentalize, expressing different values at different times and places and to different people.

Steel Gray Market," *Social Forces*, 34 (March, 1956), pp. 268–277: Charles J. Erasmus, *Man Takes Control* (Minneapolis: University of Minnesota Press, 1961); and Dennis H. Wrong, "The Oversocialized Conception of Man," *American Sociological Review*, XXVI (April, 1961), 183–193.

20. Leon Festinger, *A Theory of Cognitive Dissonance* (Stanford: Stanford University Press, 1957).

These remarks also suggest the possibility that analysts may differ in the direction in which they expect movement to occur to bring about congruence. Consider the implications of asserting that values are generally modified so that they are made consistent to behavior or, on the other hand, asserting that changes in behavior result from changes in values. The first assertion implies that the poor are more likely to value steady employment if they have regular jobs; the second implies that they are likely to be able to hold regular jobs if they value steady employment. If proponents of the cultural and situational approaches were narrowly logical, one would expect the cultural proponents to favor the latter position, the situational proponents the former. Actually, some interaction is generally recognized and there is awareness that the outcome depends upon the items being considered and the setting within which the interaction is occurring. Specifying such matters is necessary, then, to assess and integrate the cultural and situational approaches.

Intergenerational versus Contemporary Influences. Another issue underlying the differences between the cultural and situational approaches is the relative importance of intergenerational and contemporary sources of influence. This issue is often only partially made explicit. Sometimes references to the transmission of values, beliefs, habits, and norms from one generation to another are included in the definition of a culture of poverty, but sometimes these references are left implicit or ambiguous. In any case, the issue is a fundamental one and deserves detailed study.

This issue is evident in the controversy regarding the determinants of the matrifocal or female-based household among the poor in general, and particularly among the American blacks.[21] It is argued that the experience of the particularly brutal form of American slavery established traditions that have persisted, and that this persistence has been ensured by the economic and social deprivations suffered by

21. E. Franklin Frazier, *The Negro Family in the United States* (Chicago: University of Chicago Press, 1939); Thomas F. Pettigrew, *A Profile of the Negro American* (Princeton, N. J.: D. Van Nostrand Co., 1964); and Jessie Bernard, *Marriage and Family Among Negroes* (Englewood Cliffs, N. J.: Prentice-Hall, 1966).

the Negro male. Consequently, blacks have developed attitudes and behavior patterns which are inimicable to a stable married life. On the other hand, it is argued that contemporary employment opportunities largely determine marital stability and the husband-wife interaction patterns. With the Negro male more limited in job opportunities than the Negro woman, little needs to be added to account for female-based households among poor Negroes. Thus, examining data over a decade's time, it has been shown that the proportion of nonwhite women who are separated from their husbands varies with the unemployment rate of nonwhite males.[22] And unemployment is high among nonwhites: in 1963, of the nonwhite men working or looking for work, 29 per cent were unemployed during the year.

A convincing explanation for the high incidence of female-based households among poor American Negroes requires extensive comparative analyses. The numerous studies on the family in the Caribbean and on poor whites in the United States are quite relevant. The findings indicating the high valuation upon a stable legal marriage and in the variations in separation rates associated with economic conditions indicate the limits of any explanation simply in terms of a cultural tradition. Moreover, it must be recognized, again, that we are discussing a difference in rates between whites and nonwhites, the poor and the affluent. Female-headed families are found in all strata and families with a husband and a wife are more frequent than are female-headed families in all strata in the United States, including the Negro poor.

There is some evidence directly relating particular beliefs and values to parental socioeconomic origins as well as to contemporary socioeconomic status. For example, Herbert Hyman, in his influential paper on the value systems of different classes, presents data on occupationally relevant values by the adult respondents' own occupational status and that of their parents.[23] The data reveal that not only the

22. See the "Moynihan Report": Office of-Policy Planning and Research, U. S. Department of Labor, *The Negro Family: The Case for National Action*, (Washington, D. C., U. S. Government Printing Office, 1965), pp. 19–25.

23. Herbert Hyman, "The Value Systems of Different Classes," in Bendix and Lipset, *op. cit.*, pp. 488–499.

respondents' contemporary status but also the status of the parental family affects certain values. Moreover, there is some additive effect. Thus, the percentage who said they regarded some college education as necessary for most young men to get along well in the world these days is highest among those of high current status *and* of high occupational origins, lowest among those who are low in both regards. It is also noteworthy that the effects of different socioeconomic origins varies for different values. For example, the effects are relatively small in regard to what respondents think important for a young man to consider in choosing his life's work.

Certainly, evidence can be cited that values, beliefs, and patterns of conduct learned in childhood are then maintained, and evidence can be cited to show that contemporary experiences affect adult values, beliefs, and conduct. Undoubtedly, too, traditions will not be maintained for long unless there is continuing support for them from contemporary experience. What is not so clear, however, is the relative importance of these different sources of influence for various values, beliefs, and practices. In addition the way in which current circumstances are experienced depends in part upon previous experiences; thus there may be an interaction between what has been acquired in the family-of-origin and contemporary influences. In other words, it cannot be said categorically that either previous experience or current situation is the sole determinant; but it is necessary to go beyond that and specify their relative importance and their possible interactions for particular values, beliefs, and patterns of conduct.

Influence Processes. The third major set of underlying issues is less clearly related to the differences between the cultural and situational approaches. Three interrelated subissues will be discussed here: (1) social versus nonsocial sources of influence, (2) relative emphasis upon subjective orientations or objective conditions, and (3) importance of persons learning through the inculcative efforts of others or by their own accommodations to circumstances.

In using the cultural approach to the study of persons in

poverty, analysts tend to emphasize how others in the same stratum are the major determinants of their way of life. We noted this in connection with the emphasis upon parents as a source of influence upon their children. In addition, people in each stratum tend to live, work, and play in settings which bring them into social relations with others of the same stratum. Thus, neighbors, friends, work colleagues, spouses and other relatives are all likely to be of the same stratum.[24] These persons will tend to induce each other to adhere to the orientations and patterns of conduct they themselves have. If these are important to the persons, they will support adherence through the social sanctions available to them. Insofar as a stratum has distinctive values, beliefs, and behavior patterns, each member will acquire and maintain the distinctive way of life.

Even writers emphasizing a cultural approach, however, do not consider such a way of life to be maintained merely by such socialization. After all, a way of life emerges as a collective response to a variety of social conditions including social relations with persons in other strata, and extending to nonsocial factors. With this in mind, writers emphasizing a situational approach are prone to give greater attention and weight to nonsocial conditions and to relations with persons in other strata.

Persons of other social ranks, and the organizations dominated by them, are undoubtedly a major determinant of the way in which poor persons live. Members of any stratum learn who they are and how they are supposed to act partly by the way they are treated by persons in other strata. This has particularly devastating effects upon persons who are at the bottom of a status hierarchy. They are subjected to humiliation, victimization, harassment, and manipulation even when ostensibly they are being assisted. Thus, police, social workers, and other functionaries of the agencies controlled

24. This has been studied most intensively in community studies in small cities, but the evidence for it in large metropolitan areas is also clear. See, for example, W. Lloyd Warner and Paul S. Lunt, *The Status System of a Modern Community,* Yankee City Series, II (New Haven: Yale University Press, 1942); and August B. Hollingshead, *Elmtown's Youth* (New York: John Wiley, 1949); and Gans, *op. cit.*

by the nonpoor attempt to maintain order, rehabilitate, and sustain their charges. In doing so, however, privacy is invaded and maturity and self-responsibility denied. As Lewis Coser writes,

> the very granting of relief, the very assignment of the person to the category of the poor, is forthcoming only at the price of a degradation of the person who is so assigned. To receive assistance means to be stigmatized and to be removed from the ordinary run of men.... In order to be socially recognized as poor, a person is obligated to make his life open to public inspection. The protective veil which is available to other members of society is explicitly denied to them.... When monies are allocated to them, they must account for their expenses and the donors decide whether the money is spent "wisely" or "foolishly." That is, the poor are treated in this respect much like children.... the poor are infantalized through such procedures.[25]

Even persons in no official relationship to the poor participate, to some extent, in the labeling of persons as poor and, consequently, treating them as somehow subordinate and inferior.

In addition, the services provided by public agencies are not equally allocated. For example, public schools in low-income neighborhoods have generally been inferior in physical facilities and in the number of regular, fully qualified teachers compared to schools in higher-income neighborhoods.[26] In the private sector, poor persons are confronted with even grosser inequalities, since their ability to obtain goods and services from the private sector is dependent upon money. Thus, in obtaining housing and in purchasing consumer goods, and in receiving professional services their ability to get the goods and services they want are circumscribed.[27]

Related to the social and nonsocial sources of influence on the self-conception of the poor is the relative importance we

25. Lewis A. Coser, "The Sociology of Poverty," *Social Problems*, 13 (Fall, 1965), pp. 144–145.

26. Patricia Cayo Sexton, "City Schools," in Ferman, Kornbluh, and Haber, eds., *op. cit.*, pp. 234–249; and Jonathan Kozol, *Death at an Early Age* (Boston: Houghton Mifflin, 1967).

27. For example, see: David Caplovitz, *The Poor Pay More* (New York: The Free Press of Glencoe, 1963); and Alvin L. Schorr, *Slums and Social Insecurity* (Washington, D. C.: U. S. Government Printing Office, 1963).

attribute to subjective orientations or to objective conditions. That is, we may emphasize the responses people make and how they define their situation, or we may emphasize the objective circumstances in which people exist. This distinction can be exemplified by different explanations of the smaller proportion of persons of low socioeconomic rank who belong to voluntary associations compared to persons of higher rank.[28] One might argue that the poor, or manual workers, are suspicious and hostile of others, have little commitment to impersonal or secondary relationships, and are fatalistic about controlling the alien world in which they must live. Or it may be argued that the occupations of higher socioeconomic ranks obligate participation, while in the lower ranks they drain the incumbents of energy, or that differences in income facilitate or inhibit participation. Furthermore, the claims of friends and relatives compete with such participation among persons of low socioeconomic rank; but persons of higher socioeconomic rank tend to move greater distances in relationship to employment, and—lacking more enduring primary relationships with extended families—are more prone to need and find attractive the secondary relationships of voluntary associations. Even residence in areas in which others participate in voluntary associations eases and obligates participation.

A third distinction related to how persons acquire particular orientations and habits is between accommodation and inculcation. To teach by example and imposition of rewards and punishments is largely inculcative. But people may not respond to the inculcation precisely as intended. A parent who tries to coerce obedience may find his children becoming more rebellious, and in resorting to more coercion find he has even less influence and control. Adults as well as children acquire habits and ideas by seeing what is really going on and accommodating to that reality, rather than to the stated values, beliefs, and preferred patterns of conduct. This

28. Alan F. Blum, "Social Structure, Social Class, and Participation in Primary Relationships," *in Blue-Collar World,* Arthur B. Shostak and William Gomberg, eds. (Englewood Cliffs, New Jersey: Prentice-Hall, 1964), pp. 195–207; Cohen and Hodges, *op. cit.;* Murray Hausknecht, "The Blue-Collar Joiner," in Shostak and Gomberg (eds.), *op. cit.*, pp. 207–215.

is most evident when one considers how nonsocial, objective conditions affect the way poor persons act and think. Writers emphasizing a cultural approach accord particular importance to subjective orientations, social relations, and the direct inculcation of a way of life; writers emphasizing a situational approach give particular attention to objective, nonsocial conditions and accommodation.

The differences between the situational and cultural approaches are especially evident when writers try to account for the persistance and change in adherence to the subculture or to particular values, beliefs, and patterns of conduct which might be considered typical of the poor. In attempting to account for variations among different strata, writers using a cultural approach emphasize childhood experiences (intergenerational processes) and also the direct and continuing inculcation by similarly situated others as well as the general subjective orientations through which all current experiences are filtered. Change is likely to be considered slow and require modifications of the poor people themselves. On the other hand, writers utilizing a situational approach emphasize the contemporary circumstances and the implicit accommodation people make to them, presuming that underlying general subjective orientations are widely shared by all strata or distributed with relatively little relationship to stratum position. Consequently, patterns of conduct among the poor can change quickly, if socioeconomic conditions are altered.

CONCLUSIONS

The discussion has indicated that there are methodological and conceptual problems that make it difficult to assess the accuracy of the various approaches. Both the cultural or situational approach can claim to be "correct," depending upon the question being asked, the way in which various terms are defined, and the kind of data used. Any assessment requires clear specification of the question and the particular setting within which the answer is being sought. Only by such specification can the issues be clarified and a more precise understanding of the poor (and other strata) be attained.

The assessment of the relative importance of various processes and conditions in accounting for particular aspects of the life style of the poor has important sociological and policy implications. The answers to many sociological questions regarding the nature of socioeconomic rank in American society depend upon the resolution of the issues discussed. For example, to what extent do persons in different social ranks have similar values and beliefs but act differently because they confront different circumstances? To what extent do persons in various strata possess an integrated cultural system which is intergenerationally transmitted? To what extent does the maintenance of the stratification system in the United States depend upon the intergenerational transmission of ways of life?[29] In addition, since the issues pertain to many aspects of social life, their resolution also has relevance for testing and specifying different theoretical approaches to the study of social conduct in general.

The resolution of issues also has great significance for social policy. Poverty in the United States can be eliminated by instituting a guaranteed annual income above the poverty line in every household in the nation, but would this change those aspects of the life of the poor which are distressing to the more affluent and perhaps to the poor themselves? Aside from such a step, there are already numerous programs to train youth and adults, to give a head start to preschoolers, to upgrade schools in low-income neighborhoods, to provide jobs, to facilitate husbandless mothers' employment by providing day-care centers for children, and to provide income, food, and housing for the poor. Each of these programs presume different causes for people remaining in poverty and different ways of remedying the causes. Without more knowledge of the issues raised, however, we cannot know which strategies are most effective. Presumably, some are more effective at certain stages of the life cycle, in particular problems, and for different segments of the poor. But we also want to know at which stages of the life cycle and in which areas of life style are the best leverage points to be found.

29. S. M. Lipset and R. Bendix, *Social Mobility in Industrial Society* (Berkeley: University of California Press, 1960), esp. pp. 227–259.

In this book, the significance of various processes in affecting particular values, beliefs, and patterns of conduct among low-income husbandless mothers will be examined. This will not resolve all of the issues raised, but it should contribute to their resolution. In the next chapter more specific ideas about the processes and conditions affecting the way of life of low-income fatherless families will be presented. In the following two chapters, the research design will be described; this will provide needed information about the basic characteristics of the people in the study and their general circumstances. In the remaining chapters, the main analysis will be presented to test some of the ideas about the factors that affect particular aspects of the life of the poor.

2. Conditions and Processes: Some Hypotheses

IN THIS chapter, we will examine in more detail the way in which particular conditions affect a variety of characteristics associated with life in poverty. The subcultural and situational explanations are broken down into explanations for different kinds of phenomena, for particular samples of persons, and with possibly varying interactions between elements of both kinds of explanations. The conditions of special interest here are: being responsible for raising children without a husband-father, living in low-income neighborhoods, having been reared in families of low socio-economic status, and alternative sources and amounts of income. We will consider how these conditions affect each other and a variety of values, beliefs, and behaviors associated with poverty.

IMPLICATIONS OF LACKING A HUSBAND

Despite the decline in the manifold functions of the family, even in urban America it is still a basic institution.[1] One consequence of the decline of functions has been a concentration of those that remain within the nuclear core of husband, wife, and children. This means an intensification of mutual dependence and influence. Furthermore, in a society in which the nuclear family is the ideal and statistical norm, other family types face special difficulties. In societies where death rates are so high that both parents are not likely to live until all their children are mature, or where illegitimacy or marital disruption is so high that many families are fatherless, extended family ties and other institutionalized relationships are available to help support the fragmented nuclear family. But in urban America many of the agents of organizations with which fatherless families interact are not prepared to make the necessary and appropriate departures from their usual patterns of conduct.

We are primarily concerned in this inquiry with the mothers in fatherless families, with certain consequences of being without a husband and the consequences of different ways of accommodating to the lack of a husband.[2] In order to understand what accommodations are necessary, it is useful to consider what contributions a husband ideally could make. What follows is a listing of areas of possible contributions.

A husband-father contributes to his family by his roles outside as well as inside the family. Among his extrafamilial roles, the husband's occupational role is of primary importance. Typically, his work is the only or major source of income for the family. Through his work role, he also generally has a wider range of social relations than his wife, and he is usually the family representative in dealing with governmental and other formal agencies. He serves as a link to many spheres of the external community, and he brings reports and concerns from these spheres into the home. This is

1. William F. Ogburn and F. Nimkoff, *Technology and the Changing Family* (Boston: Houghton Mifflin, 1955).

2. For analyses of some of the problems faced by mothers in accommodating the absence of a husband, see Peter Marris, *Widows and Their Families* (London: Routledge & Kegan Paul, 1958); William J. Goode, *After Divorce* (Glencoe, Ill.: Free Press, 1956); and Margaret Wynn, *Fatherless Families* (London: Michael Joseph, 1964).

not to deny that the wife may not have similar avenues and even additional ones for extensive relations. These relations can arise in the course of shopping, caring for the children, participation in voluntary associations, and maintaining interaction with relatives. To some extent, however, even in these activities, a husband contributes to the maintenance of such relations by acting as the socially required companion, helps provide a status identity, and is a resource to be exchanged with other mothers as well as to free the wife herself.

Within the family, the husband's role as father means that the children know another adult with skills, activities, attitudes, and feelings which can broaden their range of experience. His example, and distracting attention, may lessen the need for discipline. In the inevitable daily confrontations about control and direction of the children, the husband can provide many supports. He can provide a respite from the struggle, a strong voice and hand in what might otherwise seem an unequal struggle, and some solace when disappointments occur. Even the joys which the children provide are lessened if they cannot be shared with another adult who cares about the children.

In addition to the contributions a husband makes through his relations with the children and extrafamilial persons, he is an intellectual, emotional, and sexual partner for his wife. He is responsible for or shares responsibility for decisions about the management of the household and its physical maintenance.

In actuality, of course, husbands may make little or no contribution in many of these areas. From the point of view of the wife, some husbands may drain more than they add. A husband may not earn any money or he may be profligate in spending what there is. He may have few extrafamilial interests or activities or he may restrict his wife from engaging in them. He may be in conflict with his wife about raising the children or have nothing to do with his children. He may have little to do with his wife. On the other hand, a husbandless mother who is divorced or separated may find that her former husband still contributes some money to the household, sees her socially, and visits and helps with the children.

Nevertheless, in the aggregate, complete families tend to have such contributions from husbands, while fatherless families tend not to have them. Furthermore, the absence of each contribution compounds the difficulties caused by the absence of any other one. For example, the loss of income from the husband, unless fully compensated, means increased difficulties in maintaining the physical aspects of the household—fewer purchasable services and mechanical devices. This increases the need for aid in decision-making and in household maintenance. Fewer financial resources available for the children reduces the bases of direct and indirect control over the children. Again, this increases the need for the support of a husband-father in supervision and disciplining the children. In short, the loss of income caused by the absence of a husband-father increases the problems of maintaining a household and raising children. Beset by these problems, the weariness from the effort required in trying to deal with the compounded problems is further aggravated by the absence of a husband-father who would provide support in the problems and even on occasion, brief release from them.

But fatherless families survive; husbandless mothers endure and raise children. We must consider some aspects of the adaptations they may make; the adaptations utilized are what have consequences for the children and not simply the condition requiring some adaptation. Behaviorally, a husbandless mother may find substitutes for the contributions which a husband usually makes or she may reduce certain activities which cannot be maintained without a husband or without a compensating substitution. Substitution and reduction of activity vary in likelihood for different activities and for different husbandless mothers in varying circumstances. Attitudinally, the husbandless mother may reduce her subjective desires to match what she can realize. Her valuation of a clean household, of control of children, of a college education for her children, of participation in voluntary associations, or of many other activities may be reduced to match the level she actually attains. She may, on the other hand, maintain her desires or even raise them to compensate for the unsatisfactory present. In such cases, the husbandless mother may experience considerable distress, unhappiness, and anxiety.

The primary behavioral response is the attempt of the husbandless mother to substitute herself for the missing husband. She alone makes decisions which otherwise might be shared. For the husband's possible contributions arising from his relationship to the external world, the husbandless mother may substitute herself by going to work and by involving herself in community affairs. For the husband's contribution in caring for the children and the household, she may devote more time and energy herself than she would if her husband were living with her. But there are limits to the extent to which a mother can make all these substitutions. There are limits to her time and energy. Consequently, such substitutions are likely to be accompanied by cutting down on other activities that would otherwise be possible.

Other persons are also possible sources of substitutions. If her minor children are old enough, they too may substitute for a husband—in caring for younger children, as a source of some income, in household chores, and as companions. In addition, relatives, friends, and neighbors may be important substitutes. This may take the form of co-residence, sharing many of the household tasks, or simply occasional babysitting. In addition, formal organizations and the institutions which provide services may be used or purchased as substitutes. For example, participation in voluntary associations or the church may provide a link with the larger community and companionship which the missing husband might have provided. Finally, some government programs offer possible substitute contributions. Social security and welfare programs may be the source of at least a minimum income. Low-income public housing projects offer standard housing below regular market prices and provide an institutionalized way to have certain household maintenance tasks performed.

Obviously, all these possible substitutions are not equally available to all husbandless mothers. For example, a mother of a preschool child is less able to seek employment than is a mother of a child in school, and a woman without relatives living in the same city is not able to have her mother or sister substitute for the husband's contributions to child care or to companionship, nor can a relative free her for employment. Furthermore, each of these substitutions makes some other substitutions less likely to be realized while others are made more likely. If a mother is employed in order to substitute for the missing husband's income, she will be less able to maintain the necessary reciprocal requirements in neighborly relations; on the other hand, she may find herself exposed to more demands to participate in certain voluntary associations.

Aside from these limitations, complete substitution is not possible. Only certain contributions can be substituted for, and these only to varying degrees. The other alternative is to reduce activities.[3] A husbandless mother may reduce her housekeeping activities and maintain the home in a dirty and shabby condition. The children may be neglected. The mother without a husband may be socially isolated and have little companionship with anyone. But again, there are limits to the extent to which each and every activity can be reduced.

The primacy of the mother role, of the activities associated with rearing children, probably helps order the resolution of the various demands upon the husbandless mother. In one study, wives were asked, "What are the most important roles of a woman in order of importance?"[4] About 80 per cent of the respondents mentioned mother and more than a third listed mother first. Wife was mentioned by about 60 per

3. Consideration of reduced activities poses an analytic problem. Many of the activities mentioned are integrally related to possible substitutions. Thus, carrying on neighboring activities is the reciprocal of using neighbors as a substitute for a husband's contributions in caring for the home and children; being an active citizen is the other side of substituting political and associational activity for the missing husband's possible companionship and link to the extrafamilial world. Whether a particular activity is viewed as a substitution or as an activity whose maintenance or reduction is to be accounted for depends upon the context of the discussion and analysis. The distinction can be logically and analytically made, but it is often slippery. There are also substantive implications of the difficulties in making this distinction. Not only do the many possible substitutions affect each other but they are also mutually related to the whole set of activities under investigation.

4. Helena Znaniecki Lopata, "The Secondary Features of a Primary Relationship," *Human Organization,* 24 (Summer, 1965), pp. 116-123.

cent—the same percentage that mentioned the housewife or homemaker role. The homemaker role, it is true, was more frequently mentioned third than was the wife role. Evidence from the study reported in this book, also indicates the great importance of the mother role among the variety of possible demands a woman with children faces.

We should observe that many of the difficulties faced by the mothers and children in female-headed families are not inherent to that family structure. The difficulties, in part, stem from the expectations of others about what is a normal family, from the socially limited alternatives deemed appropriate for women, and the specificity of sex roles.

In terms of the general interest in studying poverty, it is worth noting that in many ways fatherless families are at an extreme end of the continuum of possible husband contributions. Husbands of low socioeconomic rank tend to make smaller contributions to their families than do husbands of higher rank. This is obviously so for income contributions. In addition, their extrafamilial activities are more restricted and they are less likely to share those activities with their wives. In general, social and emotional companionship is less prevalent among husbands of low socioeconomic status.[5] The accommodation which husbandless mothers make to the absence of a husband-father, then, may be indicative of the kinds of accommodations which are made more generally by married mothers living in poverty.

Social Origins

One of the basic issues in contention in explaining the life style of the poor is the extent to which elements of it are intergenerationally transmitted. In this section, I will discuss the factors which affect the likelihood that particular values, beliefs, and patterns of conduct are learned in the family of

5. For studies of the division of labor in the family and determinants of variations in role allocations, see Raymond T. Smith, *The Negro Family in British Guiana* (New York: Grove Press, 1956); Robert O. Blood and Donald M. Wolfe, *Husbands and Wives* (Glencoe, Ill.: Free Press, 1960); and Elizabeth Bott, *Family and Social Network* (London: Tavistock Publications, Ltd., 1957).

origin and maintained in adulthood and then expressed in ways which perpetuate them among their own offspring.

The processes by which attitudes and behaviors are acquired in infancy and childhood have been described in many psychological and social-psychological theories. It is sufficient for this study to recognize that such processes exist. The variety of processes, however, should be noted. Thus, children may acquire values, beliefs, and habits by direct inculcation from others, by identification with others, by generalizing from their own experiences, and by taking the role of others in interaction.

On the whole, it is reasonable to expect that predispositions acquired early in life would persist. They were acquired in a social and nonsocial set of circumstances which made them seem appropriate. Obviously, if the circumstances are not different, one should not expect alterations in ways of coping with the recurrent issues faced. But what if the person is in a new set of circumstances for which the previously acquired predispositions do not work well? To what extent are those values, beliefs, and patterns of conduct altered? It is reasonable that some characteristics are easier to maintain in changed circumstances than are others and that the variations in the circumstances affect the chances of persistence. I can state these possibilities more precisely.

Susceptibility to Contemporary Influences. Certain qualities of characteristics make them relatively susceptible to contemporary circumstances.[6] The qualities which presum-

6. I have discussed some of these points in greater detail, but formulated a little differently, elsewhere; see Louis Kriesberg, "The Relationship Between Socio-Economic Rank and Behavior," *Social Problems,* X (Spring 1963), pp. 334-353 and Louis Kriesberg, "Entrepreneurs in Latin America and the Role of Cultural and Situational Processes," *International Social Science Journal,* XV (1963), pp. 581-594. See also Benjamin S. Bloom, *Stability and Change in Human Characteristics* (New York: John Wiley, 1964). Studies of the relative acceptance of various innovations also provide insights into this matter. See, for example, Elihu Katz, "The Social Itinerary of Technical Change: Two Studies of the Diffusion of Innovation," *Human Organization,* 20 (Summer, 1961), pp. 70-82; F. C. Fliegel and J. E. Kivlin, "Farm Practice Attributes and Adoption Rates," *Social Forces,* 40 (May, 1962), pp. 364-370; and Steven Polgar, Howard Dunphy, and Bruce Cox, "Diffusion and Farming Advice: A Test of Some Current Notions," *Social Forces,* 42 (October, 1963), pp. 104-111.

ably contribute to the malleability of individual characteristics are: serial independence, noncentrality to the person, lack of feedback, and dependence upon circumstances for expression. By serial independence, I mean the extent to which the level of a characteristic does not depend upon its previous state or fixed prerequisites. Obviously, this is a matter of degree. At one extreme we find characteristics which are so cumulative and irreversible that very good predictions of the future level of a characteristic can be made by knowing what it was at some previous time. Thus, the height of a person is largely determined by his previous height. Social characteristics cannot be so completely determined and serially dependent; on the other hand, no human characteristic is completely independent of its previous state. Our knowledge of the variation in serial independence of different characteristics is small; we can only suggest gross comparisons. Thus, the level of intellectual skills is almost certainly more dependent upon previous intellectual skills than are aspirations for specific goals dependent upon earlier aspirations.

Consequently, we would expect that intellectual skills acquired in the family-of-origin would be more likely to be predictive of later intellectual skills than would be the case for educational aspirations. Even if some characteristic is more likely to be affected by family-of-origin experiences than is another, however, this does not necessarily mean that the socioeconomic level of the family-of-origin is more likely to be related to the former than to the latter characteristic. The likelihood that attributes associated with socioeconomic status are intergenerationally transmitted is also affected by the extent to which the relevant experiences are associated with the socioeconomic status of the families-of-origin. Thus, if the circumstances affecting intellectual skills are not highly associated with the rank of the family-of-orientation but are highly associated with aspirations, then it is still possible that the socioeconomic rank of the family-of-origin is more predictive os aspirations than of intellectual skills.

The second quality of characteristics which affect the likelihood that they will be subject to contemporary sources of influence is distance from the core of the person's self or personality. Presumably, attributes are more or less central to a person's self-conception or the organization of his character. Certainly characteristics may vary in this regard by societies, categories of persons, and even among individuals; but again, gross comparisons can be suggested. Characteristics related to one's sexual identification are probably more persistent than characteristics related to more secondary identifications, for example as a citizen. Evidence for this assertion may be found in the findings of a study in value orientations made by Caudill and Scarr.[7] Using items developed by Kluckhohn and Strodtbeck,[8] they compared the orientations of Japanese children and their parents for a variety of values. One of the areas in which they found the greatest similarity between parents and children pertained to the way a man should work—as his own boss, as a member of a collectivity, or as a subordinate in a hierarchy. They found much less intergenerational similarity about how one should select a delegate to represent a group.

I also hypothesize that general orientations—such as about the proper amount of autonomy and independence children should have in relationship to their parents—are more central to the person's self than are specific aspirations for the children or the way one actually supervises the way children spend their time. The former are probably more crucially part of one's sense of parenthood than the latter. Aspirations or patterns of control are less central to one's self-conception, being particular ways of expressing general orientations. Consequently, a person can choose one or another way of expression, depending upon the contemporary conditions in which he finds himself.

The third basic quality which affects the lack of persistence of a characteristic from earlier circumstances is the possibility of feedback. Characteristics vary in the extent to which their consequences can be monitored by persons possessing

7. William Caudill and Harry A. Scarr, "Japanese Value Orientations and Culture Change," *Ethnology*, I (January, 1962), pp. 53-91.

8. Florence Rockwood Kluckhohn and Fred L. Strodtbeck, *Variations in Value Orientations* (Evanston, Ill.: Row, Peterson, 1961).

the characteristics. The greater the opportunities for such monitoring, the greater the possibility for altering the characteristic in response to contemporary circumstances. The possibility of feedback is affected by the frequency with which an attribute is expressed, the clarity of the consequences, and the length of time needed to express or execute the characteristic. Thus, activities which are frequently carried out, require relatively little time to perform, and whose consequences can be readily observed are particularly subject to contemporary circumstances. One implication of this is that general orientations are more likely to persist intergenerationally than are specific patterns of conduct or specific beliefs.[9]

Evidence for these ideas can be found in a study of the persistence of values and patterns of conduct over three generations, as reported by Aldous and Hill.[10] They found that religious affiliation was much more likely to remain the same over three generations than the way in which husband-wife roles are divided. Presumably, the division of roles in the household must be worked out and tested day-by-day in interaction with someone else.[11] The consequences of different divisions of labor are manifested in the strains of interaction. Alternative religious affiliations, on the other hand, cannot be easily tested out, and the consequences of maintaining a particular religious affiliation are difficult to assess.

Finally, the extent to which a characteristic is dependent upon circumstances external to the individual affects the likelihood that it will be perpetuated intergenerationally. Some activities can be carried out with little regard to the enabling or constraining social and nonsocial environment, while other activities are very dependent upon the conduct of other

9. Thus, Caudill and Scarr *op. cit.*, found that responses to an item regarding how one should get help if his crop failed showed more variation between generations than responses to an item about the best way to think about the past, present, and future.

10. Joan Aldous and Reuben Hill, "Social Cohesion, Lineage Type, and Intergenerational Transmission," *Social Forces*, 43 (May, 1965), pp. 471-482.

11. Joan T. Werner, "A Family Typology and Some of Its Determinants," Unpublished D.S.Sc. dissertation, Syracuse University, 1968.

persons or the availability of the appropriate resources. For example, the attainment of a particular occupational role depends in large part upon other persons providing access to that role. On the other hand, expressing a desire to attain a particular occupational role is less subject to the direct control of others.

On the whole, then, values, norms, and general orientations are much more likely to be maintained between generations and not be altered by contemporary circumstances than are specific patterns of conduct.[12] By this reasoning, we would expect that the values and orientations of poor families tend to be passed on from generation to generation more than are actions and specific beliefs and aspirations. Actually, however, persons in different income strata vary less in their values than in their actual conduct. This suggests a circumscribed role for intergenerational processes in the perpetuation of the life style of the poor. Aspects of the way of life most subject to intergenerational processes are not as distinctive between strata as are those aspects which are relatively subject to contemporary influences. To the extent to which there are distinctive general orientations among the poor, they may partly have persisted from childhood. Explanations of differences in conduct, however, should be sought in the contemporary circumstances of the poor. This assumes some independence between general value orientations and specific patterns of conduct.

One other possible interpretation of the greater differences in conduct than in values among income strata should be noted. Values are not immune to contemporary experiences and sources of influence. The poor are probably more aware of the values and beliefs of the nonpoor than of their actual

12. As Bernard Berleson and Gary A. Steiner write in *Human Behavior: An Inventory of Scientific Findings* (New York: Harcourt, Brace & World, 1964), p. 576: "Behavior, being visible, is more responsive to extreme pressures and accommodations. [Opinions, attitudes, and beliefs], being private until expressed, can be maintained without being subject to question or argument. And there is no reason for [opinions, attitudes, and beliefs] and behavior to be in harmony; we are polite to acquaintances we really don't like, we go along with the majority in a committee action rather than make a fuss, we go to the polls even though we really don't care about the outcome."

conduct. The mass media and even interpersonal interaction between people of different income strata reveal what people think is right and desirable more than how they actually behave. The nonpoor can control the visibility of their conduct more successfully than the poor can. Consequently, the poor are more subject to influence about the values and beliefs of the higher income strata than about their behavior.

In addition to variations in the characteristics being considered, the relative role of intergenerational and of contemporary processes cannot be assessed without specifying the population being studied. It should be obvious that if one is studying a population whose contemporary circumstances vary little, then intergenerational processes will appear important in accounting for whatever variation in conduct and attitudes exists. Similarly, if there is little variation in relevant aspects of their parental generation, contemporary circumstances will appear to be relatively significant determinants. Furthermore, if there are general changes between the generations, those will appear as important factors in accounting for shifts in individuals'conduct, values, or beliefs. Thus, if there has been a marked change in the general material circumstances between two generations, contemporary circumstances will be especially significant in accounting for conduct and attitudes. Or suppose there is a general shift over time in some particular value; then intergenerational processes would not appear important in accounting for the present variations in that value. For example, if a high school education becomes almost a universal minimal value in the society, intergenerational processes are not likely to appear important in accounting for that particular evaluation. Consequently, one must be aware of the peculiarities of the sample studied and the historic social changes in which that sample has lived.

Relative Susceptibility of Fatherless and Complete Families. Given the concerns of the present study, we must consider the possible differential role of intergenerational and contemporary processes in affecting husbandless as compared to married mothers. In general, married mothers should be less affected by either their family-of-origin or their contemporary circumstances than husbandless mothers. The husband is another source of influence for many attitudes and behaviors. Such a competing influence would tend to lessen the direct impact of other factors for married mothers, compared to husbandless mothers. A husbandless mother, shorn of this competing influence, is likely to maintain attitudes and patterns of behavior acquired earlier and is also more likely to respond directly to her immediate circumstances.

One other consideration is important. Attributes are more or less dependent upon having a husband. If one is studying behavior that depends upon having a husband, there will be little variation among husbandless mothers in the behavior. Furthermore, neither intergenerational nor contemporary circumstances could appear to be as powerful determinants as among married mothers. Thus, certain kinds of partying and visiting patterns are restricted for husbandless mothers and the effects of background and current circumstances would be muted, compared to married mothers. On the other hand, kinds of behavior that are not dependent upon having a husband could be the subject of a husband's facilitation or constraint. In that case, it is the husbandless mothers' conduct which will be accounted for by their background and personal interests or circumstances to a greater extent than among married mothers. For example, whether or not husbandless mothers vote in an election is more likely to be related to their own interest in voting than would be the case among married mothers.

Area of Residence

Another major variable possibly affecting the life style of the poor is their area of residence. Pople live in neighborhoods segregated by income. Characteristics of the areas where the poor live—for example, their density, schools, and commercial services—confront everyone in the area with similar problems. As each individual and family tries to cope with the problem, they may develop similar solutions. Moreover, the persons in the same area may support each other in the solution reached, develop collective solutions, and define for each other what the problems are and how they are to be handled. The possible role of neighborhoods occupied largely by poor people in the development and maintenance of certain aspects of the life of the poor, then, deserves attention.

Sociological research provides ample documentation that the rates of many kinds of behavior vary widely in different residential areas.[13] Behavior variation among areas, as among other collectivities, may be accounted for by two kinds of explanations. On the one hand, selective processes may result in the concentration of persons with particular past or current experiences in each residential area. For example, people may originate from different size communities, may be at different stages in the family life cycle, or may have different kinds of work experiences. On the other hand, there may be "structural" or "compositional" effects. That is, the residential areas may present distinctive social and nonsocial experiences which influence those who live there. For example, neighbors may influence each other so that particular patterns of behavior develop and are maintained. In addition, a neighborhood may have physical characteristics and institutional facilities which ease or inhibit certain kinds of behavior.

Obviously, these two types of explanations, selectivity and structural effects, are not mutually exclusive. They interact, and the degree to which one explanation rather than another accounts for a particular finding will vary for different kinds of behavior, neighborhoods, and people. The basic issue is

13. See, for example, Otis Dudley Duncan, "Residential Areas and Differential Fertility," *Eugenics Quarterly*, 11 (June, 1954), pp. 82-89; Charles V. Willie, "The Relative Contribution of Family Status and Economic Status to Juvenile Delinquency," *Social Problems*, 14 (Winter, 1967), pp. 326-335; Eshref Shevsky and Wendell Bell, *Social Area Analysis* (Stanford: Stanford University Press, 1955); Morris Axelrod, "Urban Structure and Social Participation," *American Sociological Review*, XXI (February, 1956), pp. 13-18; Wendell Bell and M. Boat, "Urban Neighborhoods and Informal Social Relations," *American Journal of Sociology*, XLIII (January, 1957), pp. 391-98; Walter T. Martin, "The Structuring of Social Relationships Engendered by Suburban Residence," *American Sociological Review*, XXI (August, 1956), pp. 446-453; and Peter Willmott and Michael Young, *Family and Social Class in a London Suburb* (London: Routledge & Kegan Paul, 1960).

not to decide which explanation is correct. It is not even enough to determine if there is a structural effect for a given kind of behavior for a certain category of persons in a particular collectivity; it is also necessary to specify the processes by which the structural effects occur.

Several techniques for measuring structural or compositional effects have been developed.[14] These techniques can help in assessing the relative importance of the two kinds of explanations for area variations in the rate of a given kind of behavior. As with any analytic technique, however, interpretation requires some substantive propositions, hypotheses, or theory. None of the techniques is completely adequate to disentangle selective factors from structural effects; the results have to make sense according to some ideas about how the effects occurred. Without such ideas, formulated as premises or hypotheses, the chances of making incorrect inferences are increased.

We must, therefore, at least outline the processes by which residential areas may affect various attitudes and behaviors and the conditions which affect the outcomes of those processes. This discussion has relevance to the study of structural effects in general as well as to the specific analysis of the effects of residence in different kinds of public housing projects. Conversely, we can draw upon the findings and theory from a wide range of studies to understand our findings.

Processes. Three major processes by which residential areas may affect residents' attitudes and behaviors may be distinguished: (1) normative control by others, (2) response to the examples which others present, and (3) accommodation to the circumstances which the neighborhood social and nonsocial world presents.

14. In particular, see Peter M. Blau, "Structural Effects," *American Sociological Review*, XXV (April, 1960), pp. 178-193; James S. Coleman, *The Adolescent Society*, (New York: The Free Press of Glencoe, 1961); James S. Davis, Joe L. Spaeth, and Carolyn Huson, "A Technique for Analyzing the Effects of Group Composition," *American Sociological Review*, XXVI (April, 1961), pp. 215-225; and Arnold S. Tannenbaum and Jerald G. Bachman, "Structural Versus Individual Effects," *American Journal of Sociology*, LXIX (May, 1964), pp. 585-595.

Co-residents may make normative judgments about behaviors or attitudes and try to use sanctions to induce compliance. The object of the social control may be a person's values or his conduct. Considerable emphasis is placed upon normative control in the sociological literature, but the role of normative control in explaining residential-area effects is likely to be limited. For such control to be effective, neighborhood residents must have high consensus about a particular value or conduct. They must feel that it is proper to exercise sanctions regarding the attitude or behavior, and they must have effective sanctions which they can use to enforce the norms. In contemporary American urban neighborhoods, these conditions do not exist for a wide spectrum of attitudes and behaviors.

In the second process, people observe others and respond to what they see. Co-residents provide examples of holding certain values and beliefs, of exhibiting certain conduct, and of the consequences of doing so. Each person may modify his own values, beliefs, and conduct as he evaluates those of his neighbors in terms of his own set of experiences and his relationship to the neighbors. In short, the values, beliefs, and behaviors which exist in a neighborhood present stimuli to which one may react positively, negatively, calculatingly, or indifferently. Of course some of the patterns in the neighborhood are not known and no response is made.

With the exception of reference group phenomena, this process has been relatively little studied.[15] Nevertheless, it may have considerable significance for residential area effects since it does not depend upon affective relations nor upon any coercive elements of social control, characteristics generally lacking in urban neighborhoods.

Even values may be acquired by observing the behavior of others. Seeing what other people do, a person may infer the values and beliefs that underlie the action. Of course the

15. See, for example, Herbert Hyman, *The Psychology of Status,* Archives of Psychology No. 269 (New York: Columbia University, 1942), and Robert K. Merton and Alice S. Kitt, "Contributions to the Theory of Reference Group Behavior," in *Continuties in Social Reserach: Studies in the Scope and Methods of "The American Soldier."* Robert K. Merton and Paul F. Lazarsfeld, eds. (Glencoe, Ill.: Free Press, 1950), pp. 40-105.

person may make incorrect inferences and these, in turn, may result in widespread pluralistic ignorance. For example, persons may observe well-kept flower beds and infer that people value gardening; in actuality, the values involved may be propriety and a decent respect for the opinions of others. Or persons may observe children running around without parental supervision and infer that the parents are not interested in exercising parental control. This may in turn affect their own neighborly interaction and control over their children.

A person may not only learn values, beliefs, and behaviors by observing others and generalizing from their experience with such attitudes and conduct. He may also add the other persons' characteristics to his repertory as he interacts with them, since he must know their attitudes and patterns of conduct in order to effectively and successfully communicate with them.

Finally, we turn to the process which may be of greatest significance in explaining residential area effects—the accommodation process.[16] This process is least dependent upon affective relations or even interaction among neighbors. Neighbors and neighborhood conditions may facilitate or inhibit the realization of a particular kind of behavior. The population density in a neighborhood, the physical arrangements of housing, and the existence of certain kinds of institutions each permit certain kinds of conduct and inhibit others. Consequently, behavior will be affected without first modifying any values.

In addition to such conditions directly affecting the conduct being investigated, the effects may result from a chain of adaptations to situations. Thus, accommodating to one set of conditions may set up circumstances which affect another kind of behavior. For example, a high proportion of families with small children in a neighborhood may facilitate pooled

16. This same process seems to be of major significance even within collectivities in which socialization might be expected to be of major significance—colleges and universities. See, for example, Louis Kriesberg and Lathrop V. Beale, "Career Specification Among Medical Students," *Journal of Health and Human Behavior*, 3 (Fall, 1962), pp. 204-212; and James A. Davis, "Locals and Cosmopolitans in American Graduate Schools," *International Journal of Comparative Sociology*, II (September, 1961), pp. 212-223.

child-care and exchanged babysitting, and this social pattern in turn facilitates part-time employment or organizational involvement by some mothers. Or, high neighborhood density and many crowded households could encourage teenagers to congregate on the street corners, and the parents, lacking the opportunity for casual and indirect control of their children, may attempt stringent direct control over them.

Relative Susceptibility of Fatherless and Complete Families. In the present study, the residential areas of special concern are low-income public housing projects. Public housing projects, limited as they are to families of low income might be expected to be relatively homogenous—within each project and among various projects. Actually, considerable variability exists within and among projects. They vary in the proportion of various ethnic groups, sources of income, and family composition. In addition to such variations in social composition, projects vary in size, neighborhood setting, and physical design. The popular imagery of low-income public housing projects is dominated by the immense projects of New York City, Chicago, and other metropolises. The projects, however, can be small and located outside of slum neighborhoods. This is the case for some of the projects in this study. All of the projects are relatively small and are located in a medium-sized city, but they differ in composition, physical structure, and neighborhood setting. If huge projects in other cities were included in the analysis, we would expect to find greater differences attributable to areas of residence than is likely in the present study.

Residence in public housing is not necessarily cheaper than residence in private housing, particularly for fatherless families. It is likely to mean, however, better housing for the same price. Fatherless families are more highly concentrated in public housing projects than in most urban neighborhoods.[17] The complete families living in public housing are

17. For a discussion of reasons for this and some consequences of residence in public housing, see Kurt Back, *Slums, Projects and People: Social Psychological Problems of Relocation in Puerto Rico* (Durham, N. C.: Duke University Press, 1962); Helen Icken Safa, "From Shanty Town to Public

not much better off financially than the fatherless families and frequently may have less socially clear and legitimate reasons for their straits. All this may mean that husbandless mothers who live in housing projects experience a significantly different condition than those outside. Husbandless mothers living in public housing projects, compared to those who do not, may find it easier to belong to informal neighboring and mutual aid networks. They may also be more likely to have a sense of propriety and self-respect than they would have living elsewhere—given equally poor incomes. On the other hand, public housing tenancy may induce apathy and despair and a withdrawal from the larger community.

A person's relationship to his neighborhood obviously affects the degree to which he is subject to the influences of the neighborhood. In general, we can expect that women, more than men, will be affected by their neighborhood. If a man is employed, he is subject to a whole set of other influences independent of the neighborhood, and he spends less time in the neighborhood than does a woman. This is particularly true if the woman is responsible for raising minor children. Furthermore, a husbandless mother, shorn of the competing influence of a husband, and more house- and neighborhood-bound than a married mother, would be particularly subject to the effects of the areas in which she lives. This would be true especially of attitudes and behaviors that tend to be affected through accommodative or imitative processes.

If normative processes are particularly important for a given characteristic under study, then married mothers might be more affected by their residential areas than husbandless mothers. My reasoning is as follows. For normative control to be effective, a person must be included in the community: attempts at control are made upon those who belong. Furthermore, feeling that one is a member makes one subject to

Housing: A Comparison of Family Structure in Two Urban Neighborhoods in Puerto Rico," *Caribbean Studies*, IV (April, 1964), pp. 3-12; and Helen Icken Safa, "The Female Based Household in Puerto Rico: A Case Study," *Human Organization* XXIV (Spring, 1965), pp. 135-139.

sanctions that otherwise would be trivial. It is likely that in many neighborhoods, married mothers are more integrally a part of the social community than are husbandless mothers.

Of course, in the analysis reported here we will not be examining the relative importance of all the possible processes for different categories of persons in each residential area. Rather, our concern is to discover whether or not living in public housing and different kinds of public housing projects have particular effects, and what those effects are. This discussion should alert us to the kinds of area attributes which may have an effect and how the effects can occur. If we examined persons who were more or less integrated in a residential area, we might find the neighborhoods affects only the integrated persons.[18] This could be interpreted as an indication that the normative process was the important one for the attitude or behavior under study. But that would take us afield from our primary purpose. We want to know what the impact of different neighborhood areas is on attitudes and behavior relevant to continuing poverty and dependence, given the distribution of personal integration for the population under study.

Susceptibility to Residential Area Effects. Areas of residence can affect some social characteristics more than others. Characteristics relatively susceptible to contemporary rather than intergenerational processes would clearly also be more susceptible to neighborhood influences. We can suggest even more specific qualities of characteristics which make them subject to residential area effects: (1) visibility, (2) the extent to which other contemporary sources of influence can affect the expression of the attitude and behavior, and (3) the dependence of the characteristics upon residentially-related circumstances for expression.

The visibility of a particular behavior and of its consequences has relevance in several ways. First of all, visibil-

18. The same point can be made in regard to the intergenerational transmission of attitudes and behavior. If we examined such transmission for persons who differed in their relationship with their parents, we would find that such transmission is more important than if we ignore the relationship. Yet, for our analysis, this would not be appropriate. We wish to look at the degree of intergenerational transmission, given the distribution of highly identified and estranged parent-child relationships that exist in the study population.

ity means being observable to the actor and to the neighbors. Behaviors which are public and evident to the eye can be taken as examples to be imitated or avoided; if they are not evident, they cannot be directly effective in altering other persons' conduct. From the perspective of the neighborhood as a collectivity, behaviors that are public and evident to the eye can be subjected to effective neighborhood observation and control.

The visibility of behavior is determined by normative as well as non-normative factors. Strong norms enjoin privacy in conjugal sexual relations in our society. The low visibility of household-task allocation, however, does not have the same explanation since there is little deliberate effort to hide such facts from outsiders who have a minimal relation with family members.

The frequency with which a characteristic is expressed or exhibited also affects its susceptibility to neighborhood influence, if it is visible. The more often a characteristic is exhibited and can be seen, the greater its potency as a stimulus. For example, neighborly interaction should be more subject to residential area effects than voting or not voting, since neighborly interaction can be more frequently performed than voting in political elections.[19]

The second quality to be considered is the extent to which the attitude or behavior can be subject to non-neighborhood influences. The relative influence of the neighborhood depends in part on the number and intensity of other contemporary social relationships and affiliations of the individual relevant to the behavior. Some characteristics are usually displayed and frequently performed only in the neighborhood and therefore are relatively impervious to influence from elsewhere. For example, maintaining a well-kept lawn, sitting outside with little children, or neighborly exchange of help are more subject to neighborhood influence than are leisure-time activities conducted outside of the neighborhood or work-related attitudes and behaviors.

Finally, characteristics vary in the degree to which they are

19. This comparative analysis is reported in Louis Kriesberg and Seymour S. Bellin, "Fatherless Families and Housing: A study of Dependency" (Syracuse University Youth Development Center, November, 1965; offset).

dependent upon residentially-related circumstances for expression. This quality, obviously, is most closely related to the process of accommodation. Some behaviors and most attitudes are not dependent upon neighborhood conditions to be expressed. Whether or not a husband does the dinner dishes is not dependent upon neighborhood circumstances. But the kind of child supervision a mother exercises *is* likely to depend upon neighborhood conditions such as the distribution of children of similar ages and the kind of control other mothers exercise. Similarly, the nature and level of parental involvement in the schools is likely to be affected by the interests and efforts of the principal and teachers of the neighborhood school.

Amount and Sources of Income

The final major set of conditions which are of primary interest in this study is the amount and source of income. Poverty is defined in terms of income and it is necessary to examine the way in which money *per se* may affect particular attitudes and behavior patterns. If the amount of money a family has is directly related to particular aspects of the life of poverty, independently of social origins or residence, then this would tell us much about the permanence of a culture of poverty and of the means of altering the way of life of the poor. The *source* of income has additional implications. We would like to know not only what affects the choice between welfare dependence and employment, but also the consequences of the choice for the development and maintenance of values, beliefs, and patterns of conduct associated with poverty.

Fatherless families who receive public assistance usually do so through the Aid to Families with Dependent Children program. Under this program, as with other public assistance programs, a family whose income from all sources is below the minimum public welfare standards is eligible to receive money sufficient to bring the family income up to the minimum. We will examine two implications of a husbandless mother's reliance on welfare support. One is income. A family dependent partly or entirely on welfare support is poor.

Analyses by income, then, can reveal some of the consequences of this aspect of current welfare programs. The second implication of welfare support is usually nonemployment by the husbandless mother. If she is employed full time, her family income is likely to be above the minimum welfare standards. By studying the effects of maternal employment, then, we will be assessing another important aspect of current welfare programs. The results of such analyses may indicate whether or not welfare programs should be devised to encourage employment.

Of course all poor fatherless families are not entirely dependent upon public welfare. Some husbandless mothers may work part time or work full time irregularly and the welfare benefits supplement such income. Even some nonworking husbandless mothers may not be wholly or partly dependent upon welfare benefits—they may have adequate income from insurance or alimony. In short, we are studying certain conditions related to welfare dependence but not identical with it. This mode of analysis highlights policy issues in regard to the level and conditions of welfare benefits. It also makes it possible to relate the findings to other research concerning social stratification and working mothers.

Income and employment vary among the families in this study. Such variations can be expected to have different effects for different attitudes and behaviors. Freedom from employment may permit more control of children but less participation in extrafamilial activities. Reliance on welfare may free persons to engage in activities which prepare themselves and their children to become independent, or it may result in attitudes and conduct which would perpetuate poverty and dependency.

Although work and income are highly related, we will discuss separately the ways in which each can affect attitudes and behaviors. As in the discussions of social origins and residential area, we will outline the processes by which each condition can affect the characteristics under study and then review the qualities of characteristics which make them particularly subject to effects from each condition.

Working for pay involves social relationships; therefore.

the processes by which employment can affect attitudes and behaviors may be classified into the same categories as those outlined in the case of residential areas. A person may be subject to normative control from his co-workers as well as co-residents. A person can learn attitudes and behavior from the example of others and by reference to people at work as well as in the neighborhood. A person must accommodate to the conditions related to being employed at one or another job.

Obviously the outcomes of these processes will vary greatly, depending upon the particular job. In this study, however, we are not studying the impact of different jobs. Basically, we are interested in whether or not the mother is employed. This masks a great variety of possible effects. Perhaps one reason for the generally negative findings in the search for effects of maternal employment is that the variety of jobs and therefore different directions of influence are ignored.[20]

Nevertheless, we will argue that there are some common possible effects resulting from employment *per se*. At the least, employment entails some social interaction with other persons, usually outside of the family and neighborhood. This means that there are additional sources of influence competing, for example, with the neighborhood influences. It is also likely to mean extrafamilial relations and the possibility of increased interests and knowledge about spheres of life outside of the home. Employment is also likely to mean time away from home and competition for time to be spent in recreational, community, and family activities. Of course, to some extent the money earned can be used to purchase goods and services which compensate for the time at gainful employment. For some jobs some of the conditions may be practically nonexistent. For example, consider the mother who regularly takes care of her neighbors' children. She may be earning some money, but her time limitations and the extent of her social relations are hardly different from another mother who is not working.

Money, of course is another aspect of employment. But

20. See, for example, the studies in F. Ivan Nye and Lois W. Hoffman eds., *The Employed Mother in America* (Chicago: Rand McNally, 1963).

income is of special and separate interest in this study. Income levels can affect the behavior and attitudes under study through processes different than the ones we have considered. We will discuss two ways. First, the amount of income one has affects one's position in the economic market for all commercial goods and services. Second, other persons expect people to act according to their income and will treat them differently according to their income.

The measurement of income levels is deceptively simple. Usually we simply consider the gross dollar income in the preceding twelve months. For many purposes of analysis, income should be considered in relationship to assets, obligations, future income expectations, and services and goods which are received without expenditure of money. In this study we usually do not consider these related economic conditions. I do, however, use two different income measures. One measure is of the gross household income of the preceding twelve months; the other is the per capita disposable household income. Per capita disposable income is a relatively pure indicator of a household's place in the economic marketplace. Gross annual income is more likely to indicate the social as well as economic meaning of income levels.

Husbandless Mothers' Susceptibility to Income and Employment Effects. In general, we expect to find that employment affects the attitudes and behaviors of husbandless mothers more than of married ones. First, because the time demands involved in employment bear more heavily upon a husbandless than upon a married mother. A married mother may be able to have some aid from her husband in the regular, or at least crisis, demands of the household.

In addition, a husbandless mother's work experiences cannot compete with a husband's influences. Whatever influence there may be from co-workers or employers is not filtered by or competitive with the influences from a husband. Finally, some of the possible extrafamilial experiences which come from employment can be provided vicariously to a married woman by her husband, but a husbandless mother who is not working is more isolated from the work world than a nonworking married mother.

Furthermore, even in we find more relationship between employment and various ways of thinking and acting among married than among husbandless mothers, the finding might be spurious. As we shall see in Chapter 6, married mothers are more likely to work out of choice than are husbandless mothers. This may mean that the married mothers who work have values, beliefs, and patterns of behavior which differ from married mothers who do not work. Such differences may precede employment and not be a consequence of it.

On the whole, the impersonality of the economic market is such that one would expect to find husbandless and married mothers equally affected by differences in income. But access to the commercial market is not simply determined by income. For some commodities or services, additional resources are needed to use the money. Husbandless mothers lacking such resources may be more restricted in their use of money. Income, then, would not be as highly related to their choices as is true of married mothers. For example (as discussed in Chapter 5), husbandless mothers may have particular difficulties in the housing market. Landlords may be chary of renting to a mother without a husband, fearing the children will be less controlled than if a father were present. Owning a house is likely to be more difficult without a husband to take care of activities traditionally considered a male's. In addition, a husband may provide some services to the maintenance of a household that a husbandless mother may have to pay for in the commercial market. These considerations suggest that income differences would have more marked effects among husbandless than among married mothers, but we expect such differences to be small even for those behaviors for which these considerations are relevant.

Money as an indicator of social status position, however, is likely to differ in significance for husbandless and married mothers. For this condition, it is the married mothers who are likely to be more affected than husbandless mothers. A family's social status position is judged in large measure by the husband's occupation and income. A female family head cannot be as readily placed in the social status hierarchy. She stands, in a sense, outside of the hierarchy. Without a husband, the criteria of occupation and income cannot be easily used in ranking a fatherless family. The status hierarchy does not encourage making evaluations in terms of reasons for breakup of marriage, the occupational status of the former husband, or the husbandless mother's own education, socioeconomic origins, occupation, and style of life. Yet all these criteria must have a larger role in the prestige ranking of a female-headed family than of a male-headed one.

There is another reason for expecting that gross annual income will be more highly related to attitudes and behaviors among married than among husbandless mothers. Gross income of a complete family is an indicator of the husband's occupational and social-status rank. He, too, is subject to all the experiences of his rank and these experiences and the husband's accomodation to them become part of the wife's experiences.

Qualities of Attributes. The general qualities which make values, beliefs, and behaviors vulnerable to contemporary influences also make them vulnerable to work and income conditions. Furthermore, there are some qualities which make attitudes and behaviors particularly likely to be affected by these two conditions.

On the whole, activities which require large expenditures of time are more likely to be affected by employment than activities which require little time expenditure. Activities and attitudes which are related to knowledge, interest, and opportunities unrelated to family and neighborhood are more likely to be affected by work status than are those which are expressed only in the neighborhood. On the other hand, activities related to employment are obviously affected by work status, for example, membership in certain voluntary associations.

Attitudes and behaviors that require goods and services that must be paid for in money obviously are more likely to be affected by income than are ones which do not. Per capita disposable income should be particularly relevant in this context. Attitudes and behaviors which are indicators of social status may also be affected by income level, particularly by gross annual income. Thus, certain kinds of behaviors, values, and beliefs may be expected by others of persons with a given income level. Such status-related characteristics, then, are particularly likely to be subject to income effects.

Conclusions

The fundamental issues in the controversies regarding explanations of the life style of the poor cannot be resolved without specifying the relevant processes and conditions and then examining data to see how well they fit alternative formulations. In this chapter, I have outlined specific ideas relevant to the major issues presented in the preceding chapter. We have considered some possible determinants of the way of life: family structure, social origins, area of residence, and sources and amount of income. In discussing these conditions, we have also considered the processes by which they could affect different aspects of the life of the poor. We have also tried to point out what qualities of various characteristics make one or another condition particularly important in affecting different characteristics. We have also pointed out some of the ways these conditions and processes would affect husbandless mothers differently than married mothers.

This kind of specification suggests that various characteristics associated with poverty will change at different rates for different sets of people. This means that a tightly integrated culture of poverty is unlikely to be found in this society. The poor, if defined in terms of income, are heterogeneous in too many ways. Even taking a segment of the poor—families with minor children—the backgrounds and current circumstances are probably varied enough to result in considerable variations in specific characteristics believed to be associated with poverty.

Another important implication follows: If conduct is more likely to be affected by current circumstances than are values and general orientations, we can expect to find discrepancies between values and conduct which an observer might presume to be related. Furthermore, if we assume people tend to develop some consistency between their values and conduct, then values are more likely to change after conduct alters than is conduct likely to change following a value change.

In the remainder of this book, we will examine a set of data from one particular study to test some of the ideas developed in this chapter. In the next chapter, the design of the study, the nature of the samples, and the characteristics of the families studied will be described. In the following chapters we will examine various aspects of the life of the families: the areas in which they live, the move into low-income public housing, the decision to work or accept public assistance, the extent of intergenerational perpetuation of poverty and broken families, the way in which children are reared for independence, and the rearing of children for educational achievement.

3. Research Design and Characteristics of Families in the Study

IN ORDER to test the ideas presented in the preceding chapter, we need to examine a wide variety of data. Most of the analysis in this study is based upon interviews with husbandless and married mothers. All the relevant ideas cannot be the subject of any single inquiry. In the present work, most of the data are drawn from a single, if complex, study. Findings from other studies are also utilized, but the bulk of the analysis is based upon data about female- and male-headed families from one city in the United States. The research design of the study and the nature of the resulting samples must be kept in mind in interpreting and generalizing the findings. In this chapter, then, I will describe the research design of the study and in doing so will discuss some of the distinctions that will be utilized throughout the work. I will also describe some of the basic circumstances of the fatherless and intact families studied.

RESEARCH DESIGN

The Samples and the Sources of Data. The design of this study consists of three major sets of data: (1) interviews with a cross-section of families in low-income public housing projects and the neighborhoods surrounding them, (2) interviews with a panel of applicants for public housing who were reinterviewed about a year after the initial interview, and (3) observations by participant observers living in the housing projects. Most of the analysis reported upon is based upon the cross-sectional sample and, unless otherwise indicated, that sample is used as the source of data.

The cross-sectional survey consists of personally conducted interviews with a cross-section of persons living in four public housing projects and in the neighborhoods surrounding each project. Varying sampling ratios were used in the residential areas in order to yield approximately one hundred families from each area.[1] Whenever it was possible, the husband and wife were both interviewed. Details of the sampling and interviewing procedures are set forth in Appendix A.

1. When using all of the cases together for analysis, we have not weighted those drawn from areas with lower sampling ratios, because we are not using the sample to represent the universe of people in public housing projects or of neighborhoods surrounding housing projects. One set of respondents is weighted in the analysis. In one of the housing projects, Grant, about half of the dwelling units are set aside for elderly tenants. We wanted to insure a minimum number of cases of the proper age and family structure from each area, and in order to achieve this without gathering a large number of interviews in Grant project, we used a much lower sampling ratio for the people in the elderly units than in the non-elderly units. However, in order to characterize Grant project, it is necessary to weight-up thrree-fold the respondents from the units reserved for the elderly. In order to be consistent in handling the data and in interpretation, the analysis has been carried out with the weighted cases, except when using certain statistical techniques. Because elderly persons may live in units other than those set aside for the elderly, and non-elderly may live in units reserved for the elderly, it happens that at least one original case has been weighted-up three times for women in each family type. There are 135 husbandless mothers who were interviewed; this is the unweighted number. Two cases are weighted three times, so that the total sample, including weighted cases, is 141. The original number of married families is 411; with one case weighted three times, the total becomes 414.

The sample has definite advantages, but also disadvantages, for the purposes of our present analysis. By selecting public housing projects as the primary focus for the samples, we were certain to obtain interviews with married and husbandless mothers living in public housing projects. By interviewing a sample of all tenants, we could obtain information to characterize the areas of residence by a wide variety of phenomena. In addition, the housing projects are located in neighborhoods of widely varying socioeconomic levels. Consequently, by interviewing in the surrounding neighborhoods, we obtained interviews with high- as well as low-income married and husbandless mothers. The interviews with the neighbors outside of public housing projects also provide information to characterize the settings of the projects. This design yielded a sample of complete and fatherless families of different income levels, varying degrees of dependence upon welfare benefits, and of residence outside of public housing and in different kinds of public housing projects.

The major disadvantage to this design is that there are separate sub-samples of eight areas, and adding them together does not constitute a sample of any clearly definable universe. Given the size of our samples, this is a severe limitation. For certain kinds of analysis we must aggregate all the subsamples. But much of the analysis makes comparisons by residential areas. Consequently, we have a regular check upon the propriety of making generalizations.

All four public housing projects are located in Syracuse, New York.[2] Syracuse was not selected because it is representative or typical of any universe of cities. Rather, social scientists working in Syracuse saw the opportunity to study the effects of living in public housing projects located in different kinds of neighborhoods. The research was designed to exploit this opportunity. There is no reason, however, to consider Syracuse to be completely unrepresentative of other similar-size American cities. Syracuse has a population of

2. Actually, one of the low-income public housing projects was on the city boundary line. Therefore its surrounding neighborhood extended, on one side, outside of Syracuse proper.

approximately 215,000. It is in Onondaga County, the core of the metropolitan area; Onondaga County has a population of almost a half a million. Syracuse has a diversified economy and is relatively thriving.[3]

The panel survey consists of personally conducted interviews with applicants to public housing over a two-year period. The respondents were reinterviewed about one year later, whether or not they entered one of the projects. The names of the applicants were supplied by the Housing Authority and the sample was limited to eligible families with a minor child. Husbands and wives were both interviewed whenever it was possible. A detailed description of the sample and data collection procedures is provided in Appendix B. One observation about the period during which the first wave of panel interviews were conducted must be made here. The neighborhood around one of the public housing projects, Park, was scheduled for urban renewal when the study began. This area was largely occupied by low-income Negro families. Families dislocated by the urban renewal program were given high priority for public housing. This, coupled with the fact that they had to move, meant that during the period of the first-wave interviews, applicants for public housing and those accepted as tenants were more likely to have come from this area than was true in the past. This accounts for some of the differences between the panel and cross-sectional samples reported in this chapter.

In the course of one year, some applicants moved into one of the housing projects and left in less than six months and the marital status of some respondents changed. For pur-

3. There are several studies of Syracuse that provide useful information about the city. See Alan K. Campbell, and others, *The Negro in Syracuse* (Syracuse, N.Y.: University College of Syracuse University, 1964); Linton C. Freeman, and others, *Local Community Leadership* (Syracuse, N.Y.: University College of Syracuse University, 1960); Linton C. Freeman, and others, *Metropolitan Decision-Making* (Syracuse, N.Y.: University College of Syracuse University, 1962); Charles V. Willie and Morton O. Wagenfeld, *Socio-Economic and Ethnic Areas, Syracuse and Onondaga County, N.Y., 1960* (Syracuse, N.Y.: Syracuse University Youth Development Center, 1962); Roscoe C. Martin and Frank J. Munger, eds., *Decisions in Syracuse* (Bloomington: Indiana University Press, 1961); and C.E.A. Winslow, *A City Set On a Hill* (New York: Doubleday, Doran, 1934).

poses of comparison between Wave I and Wave II of the panel, we will not include those cases in the core sample. Characteristics of the husbandless and married mothers presented in this chapter will only occasionally be based upon the total panel sample.

The participant observer data comes from information provided by observers who lived in each of the four public housing projects. In addition, extended life-history interviews were conducted with some families, a participant observer spent a summer with a group of youths in and around one project, and another spent a summer as a maintenance worker in one of the projects. These sources of information are used to help interpret and illustrate the survey analysis; they are reported more fully elsewhere.[4]

The Distinction Between Fatherless and Complete Families. The kinds of persons included in the category "fatherless families" vary depending upon the population studied and the definition of fatherless families utilized. The ambiguities in any definition of fatherless families suggests the heterogeneity of the category and suggests too that they do not constitute a separate, self-perpetuating subculture. Let us begin with what is a deceptively straight-forward definition. A fatherless family consists of a husbandless mother and her minor children. The terms "husbandless" and "her children" each have ambiguities which require specification. As we specify these terms, the possible heterogeneity among fatherless families and complete families will become clear. Then we will examine the actual distribution of different kinds of mothers within both family types.

4. See Helen Icken Safa, "Profiles in Poverty," (Syracuse University Youth Development Center, Syracuse, N.Y., 1966; mimeo); Helen Icken Safa, "An Analysis of Upward Mobility in Low Income Families" (Syracuse University Youth Development Center, 1967; mimeo); George A. Freskos, "The Role of the Maintenance Man in Public Housing," unpublished Master's thesis, Department of Sociology and Anthropology, Syracuse University, 1962; David Cumming and Elaine Cumming, "The Everyday Life of Delinquent Boys," in Irwin Deutscher and Elizabeth J. Thompson, eds., *Among The People: Encounters With The Poor* (New York: Basic Books, 1968), pp. 146–160; Irwin Deutscher, "The Bureaucratic Gatekeeper in Public Housing" in Deutscher and Thompson, *ibid.*, pp. 38–52.

"Husbandless" is a crucial term in the definition.[5] We consider a woman married if a man regularly occupies the husband role in relationship to her. If a man does, the woman is married whether or not the marriage is legally confirmed. Thus, a man and woman living together are considered married to each other even if one or both are legally married to someone else. A woman is considered married if she says she is, even if her husband is absent from the household, as in the cases in which the husband is in the armed forces. On the other hand, a woman is husbandless if she says she is not married and she does not give the interviewer consistent indications that she is living with a man. She may be husbandless because she is separated, divorced, widowed, or has never been married.

The other crucial term is "her minor children."[6] Minor children are defined as persons eighteen or younger who are neither married nor the parent of any children. The children are "hers" if she has the primary maternal responsibility for raising them. Thus, natural mothers, women with adopted children, or grandmothers or aunts raising children who are not living with their own mothers are all possible components of fatherless families as defined for this study. For editorial purposes, mothers and mother surrogates will be referred to as mothers, unless the distinction needs to be made.

Given the formal distinction between fatherless and complete families and given the samples used in this study, we can now examine the variety of ways in which families meet the criteria of a fatherless or a complete family. The ambi-

5. Our marital status distinctions differ from those of the U.S. Bureau of the Census in two minor respects: (1) In the census reports, separated persons are classified as "married, spouse absent." (2) Our category "married, spouse absent" is "other married, spouse absent" in the census reports. Paul C. Glick has an extended discussion of census family concepts in his monograph *American Families* (New York: John Wiley, 1957), Appendix A.

6. Our definition of "minor child under the responsibility of a woman" differs from the U.S. Bureau of the Census definition of children in two important respects: (1) "Our Children" in the census reports does not include a grandchild, niece, or nephew. They are categorized as "other members [of the household] under 18 years old," (2) We include an unmarried eighteen-year-old child as a minor, and the Bureau of the Census does not.

guities in the distinction between complete and fatherless families are further revealed when we see the kinds of families included in each category.

As already noted, the term "husbandless" is crucial to the definition of fatherless families. The definition of "married" presented earlier includes a wide variety of relationships; so does "husbandless." Some of the husbandless mothers may be separated and still maintain close relations with their former husbands, others may have adult male friends who are participants in the family more than are husbands of legally married women. The data shown in Table 3.1 provide a base to begin consideration of this issue. In the cross-sectional sample about one-fifth of the husbandless mothers of minors are widowed while one-half are separated; in the panel sample, the proportion separated is much higher.

Table 3.1. Marital Status of Husbandless and Married Mothers in the Cross-Sectional and Total Panel Samples

Marital Status	*Cross-Sectional Sample* *Husbandless Mothers*	*Cross-Sectional Sample* *Married Mothers*	*Total Panel Sample* *Husbandless Mothers*	*Total Panel Sample* *Married Mothers*
Married	—	97.3	—	98.5
Married, spouse absent	—	2.7	—	1.5
Separated	50.4	—	71.3	—
Divorced	25.5	—	12.0	—
Widowed	19.2	—	9.3	—
Unmarried, with child	5.0	—	7.4	—
Totals %	100.1	100.0	100.0	100.0
(N)	(141)	(414)	(108)	(203)

Each husbandless mother in the cross-sectional sample was asked if her former husband was still alive; 77 per cent reported that he was. Many of the women in this sample of fatherless families, then, can maintain a relationship with their former husbands. This is limited by changes in residence, as when the woman migrates from a southern state to Syracuse. Among the women whose husbands are still alive,

37 per cent report that their former husbands help support them. Asked how frequently the former husband keeps in touch with the children, 19 per cent report that he does so at least once a week, 31 per cent report less frequent association, and 50 per cent report that this never occurs. Finally, each woman was asked how frequently she herself gets together socially with her former husband; only 7 per cent report doing so at least once a week and three-fourths of the women report never doing so. Former husbands are more likely to maintain social relations with their children than with their former wives.

The information which we have about a husband whose presence in the household was not acknowledged to the interviewer is obviously limited. In about 5 per cent of the cross-sectional and 10 per cent of the panel sample, the interviewer reported evidence of this situation. In a few cases the presence of a husband was acknowledged in the course of the interview. Unless the respondent herself gave some clear indication that she was living with a man in the role of a husband, she was not classified as married. On the other hand, some of the marriages of the women who said they had husbands may be quite transitory. Finally, a few of the married women with minor children have husbands who are absent from the household.

All this clearly indicates that wherever one draws the line between being married and not being married some persons will be misclassified by one criterion or another. In a sense, marriage is a continuum; for purposes of analysis a cutting point must be established, but that does not alter the reality. One might look at finer gradations along the marriage continuum by considering the number of years a married woman has been married to her husband, or by his presence in the household, and by considering the extent of a husbandless mother's continuing relationship with the former or estranged husband or the number of years she has been husbandless. The size of the sample in this study and the nature of the analysis generally does not make worthwhile such fine distinctions.

The distribution of kinds of maternal surrogate relationships with minor children can be described briefly. Among the fatherless families in the cross-sectional sample, 6 per cent are grandmothers raising minor grandchildren. There are no cases of husbandless mothers raising other minor relatives or nonkin. Among the married women with minor children under their care, less than 1 per cent are responsible for raising grandchildren or other minors. These differences between fatherless and complete families are small.

The formal distinction between fatherless and complete families obviously is an arbitrary one. If we consider families over a number of years, the distinction is even more arbitrary. After all, except for the few women with minor children who have never been married, marriage precedes separation, divorce, or widowhood.

In a sense, for many women, being a husbandless mother is a stage in the life cycle. We are talking about women at a given moment in their lives and it is important to keep in mind that being a husbandless mother is not a fixed status. Nearly all the husbandless mothers were once married, and many will be again; on the other hand, many of the women in complete families will be in fatherless families or already have been. Some of our data indicate the magnitude of the transitory status of being in a complete or a fatherless family. Among the women in fatherless families, 6 per cent have been separated, divorced, or widowed for less than a year; 15 per cent, for one year; 19 per cent, for two or three years; 22 per cent, for four or five years; 18 per cent, for six to nine years, and 20 per cent, for ten or more years.

The respondents were also asked, "Would you like to get married again?" Among the mothers without husbands, 40 per cent answered yes, 52 per cent said no, and 8 per cent did not know. What is even more revealing, when they were then asked, "Do you think you will ever get married again?" only one-third said no, 29 per cent expected to remarry, and 37 per cent did not know. Undoubtedly, most of these husbandless mothers will not remain so. In the panel sample of this study, 13 per cent of the husbandless mothers remarried between the Wave I and Wave II interviews. About 8 per cent of the mothers married at the time of the first interview were husbandless at the time of the second interview. One mother managed to become divorced and remarry during that period. Evidence about divorcees also supports the expectation that these mothers will remarry. Of all women divorced at age 30, about 94 per cent *ultimately* remarry.[7] In Goode's study of divorced mothers, more than half of the mothers remarried within 26 months after the divorce.[8] He found that younger divorcees were much more likely to remarry in that time period than were older mothers. Despite the association between age and number of children, mothers with more children were somewhat more likely to remarry than those with fewer children.

On the basis of the discussion thus far, it is clear that husbandless mothers will tend to be older than the married mothers. In the cross-sectional sample, for example, 43 per cent of the women with minor children who are married are under 30 years old; but only 22 per cent of the mothers without husbands are under 30 and 53 per cent of them are between 30 and 44 years old. Similarly, husbandless mothers are more likely to have older children than are married mothers. Thus, in 31 per cent of the families in which the mother is married, all her children are five years of age or younger; among the fatherless families, only in 11 per cent of the cases are all the children five or younger. The same point is evident if we consider whether or not the mother has *any* children five or younger: among the complete families, 71 per cent include at least one child under six, but in the fatherless families only 40 per cent include at least one child under six. In the panel sample, too, husbandless mothers are less likely to have preschoolers at home than are the married mothers.

7. *Statistical Bulletin*, XXVI:5 (1945), pp. 1–3, cited in William J. Goode, *After Divorce* (Glencoe, Ill.: Free Press, 1956), p. 207.

8. Goode, *op. cit.*, pp. 278 ff. On the basis of computations from U.S. census data, widows appear to be less likely to remarry than divorcees. But the remarriage rates are still substantial. The chance of a widow aged 25 to 29 remarrying within one year is 182 out of 1,000; for a divorced woman of the same age range, it is 264 out of 1,000. Of course widows are likely to wait longer before remarriage than are divorcees. Remarriage rates are higher for younger than for older women, for white than for nonwhite women, and for women not in the labor force than for those employed. See Glick, *op. cit.*, pp. 130–140.

But on the whole, the mothers in the panel sample have younger children than do those in the cross-sectional sample; thus, in the panel sample, 93 per cent of the complete families and 68 per cent of the fatherless families include at least one child under six. This reflects the fact that applicants to public housing tend to be at an earlier stage in the life cycle than a cross-section of public housing tenants or of the neighborhood populations.

Complete Families as a Standard of Comparison. In order to examine the consequences of not having a husband-father in the family and the mother's adaptation to this circumstance, it is necessary to have some standard of comparison. One might argue that the most useful comparison is with the husbandless family prior to the loss of the husband-father. Occasionally in the analysis we will note some characteristics of the former spouses of the husbandless mothers in the sample. But there are disadvantages to comparing husbandless mothers only with their former married state. Basically, the difficulty is that marriages which dissolve may be of a special variety. In many ways the postmarried stage may appear better or more satisfactory than the married stage, at least in many of the divorced or separated cases. This problem would be less if one compared husbandless mothers to the full complement of married mothers. I think the latter comparison is more useful than even a comparison with some selected category of married mothers—such as those who are as impoverished as the husbandless mothers. Since impoverishment is highly associated with not having a husband-father in the family, a comparison of impoverished married and husbandless mothers would obscure a basic consequence of being husbandless and utilize a sample of married mothers that would have many special characteristics.

We are interested in examining the husbandless mother's adaptation; our standard of comparison is our sample of married mothers. The sample, of course, is not a random one of the universe of married mothers. Persons in public housing and low-income families in general are overrepresented. In this sense married mothers are not as dissimilar from the husbandless mothers as would be the case if a random sample of Syracuse were used.

The difficulties in finding a suitable comparison group exist in every research design and are especially troublesome in cross-sectional surveys, regardless of the sample utilized. Whatever comparison categories are chosen, many characteristics are related to members of each category in ways which are not known and which may be undesirable for purposes of the analysis. For example, if we compare old and young persons, we are probably comparing many other characteristics at the same time—the extent of formal education, stage of the life cycle, income, and energy level. Having a random sample of any particular universe, a nation or a city, does not change this. The only solution is to know what the important correlates of the categories being compared are and to compare the members of the categories within many subcategories. In this chapter we will simply describe the fatherless families in comparison to complete families in our sample for characteristics of particular relevance. The fatherless families might appear different if we used another comparison group. For most of the analysis in the report we will look at husbandless mothers under varying conditions and compare them with married mothers under the same conditions.

A Semantic Note. The very words we use to denote the family types betray the expectations and evaluations of members of the society. The words "husbandless," "fatherless," "incomplete," "broken," or "disrupted" all suggest that the woman and her children suffer from some lack. They do not have what they should have: a husband-father. Even if we use a more neutral phrase such as "female-headed family," then we must contrast that to a "male-headed family" and that term obviously is another kind of misnomer. So I will generally use the relatively colloquial terms of "fatherless" and "complete families" and of "husbandless" and "married" mothers. But I do not wish to convey any evaluative connotations. After all, one of the purposes of this study is to examine some of the consequences of living in a female-headed family.

Characteristics of the Families in the Sample

Sources of Income. The husband is normally the main earner of the family's income, while a mother of minor children has conflicting claims upon her possible employment. Therefore, the husbandless mother is likely to face financial hardship. If the mother is widowed and her former husband had adequate life insurance or was covered by Social Security, at least a minimal family income is provided. If the mother is separated or divorced and the former husband's income is sufficient to maintain two households, he may provide part or all of the fatherless family's income. In other cases, the fatherless family is dependent upon relatives, the mother's employment, or public welfare. Various combinations of all these sources are also possible.

As part of the husbandless mother's adaptation, she and her children may live together in a household with other adults. In addition to companionship and aid in child rearing, such an arrangement can have important economic benefits. Savings by sharing expenses may be possible. More importantly, the other adult may be the earner or may free the mother for employment. In the cross-sectional sample, practically no fatherless families share a household with an adult man, but 13 per cent live in a household with one or more other adult women. These other women are usually mothers or, in a few cases, sisters of the husbandless mothers. In comparison, 6 per cent of the complete families share a household with an adult woman.

The fact that so few female-headed families are in households with other adults is not explained by the fact that most of the fatherless families in this sample are living in public housing projects and most of the public housing dwelling units are two-bedroom units. There is no significant difference in household composition among households with fatherless families living in public housing projects and those living outside. It may be that the desire to have a separate household is sufficiently great and the financial aid is sufficiently high that most female-headed families maintain an independent household. In the panel sample, at the time of the first interview, 25 per cent of the husbandless mothers were living in households with one or more other adult females; this was also true of 21 per cent of the married mothers. The higher proportion of very poor families in the panel sample, compared to the cross-sectional sample, probably accounts for the greater frequency of families doubling-up.

In many ways, the household, rather than the family, is the basic economic unit. Therefore, in the discussion of the fatherless families' economic situation and in later analyses, we will consider both household and family income. First of all, we will review the sources of income for the families in the samples. As can be seen in Table 3.2, about half of the fatherless families in the cross-sectional and panel samples lived in households with no earned income within the preceding 12 months. Fifty-three per cent of the fatherless families in the cross-sectional sample and 62 per cent in the panel sample were completely or partially dependent upon public assistance. The amounts could be small—aid for one or two

Table 3.2. Sources of Household Income by Family Type in Cross-Sectional and Core Panel (Wave I) Samples

Sources of Household Income	*Cross-Sectional Sample*		*Core Panel Sample*	
	Fatherless Family	*Complete Family*	*Fatherless Family*	*Complete Family*
No earnings, but:				
Only or partly welfare sources	42.1	2.7	45.5	3.3
Nonwelfare sources	7.1	1.0	5.1	.5
Earnings, and:				
Only or partly welfare sources	12.9	15.8	19.2	12.5
Nonwelfare sources	17.1	26.9	13.1	8.2
Earnings only:	20.7	53.6	17.2	75.5
Totals %	99.9	100.0	100.1	100.0
(N)	(140)	(412)	(99)	(184)

months or payments for medical care—but, receiving any assistance means that the members of the household are living in poverty. The nonwelfare, nonearned income includes support from the former spouse, insurance benefits, or aid from relatives. Again, the fatherless families in the panel sample are even less likely to have such sources than are those in the cross-sectional sample. Twenty-one per cent of the cross-sectional fatherless families and 17 per cent of the panel fatherless families derive all their income from earnings. As noted earlier, the applicants for public housing who constitute the Wave I panel sample, are largely from the low-income neighborhood surrounding Park project which was being cleared under an urban renewal program. They apparently are somewhat more destitute than the usual public housing applicants and tenants who remain in public housing.

The complete families are much less frequently dependent upon public assistance than are the fatherless families. This is true in the cross-sectional sample in part because the sample also includes families outside of public housing in middle-income neighborhoods. Even in the panel sample, however, only 16 per cent of the complete families receive any public assistance. The households whose earnings are supplemented by welfare benefits indicate the low earnings and unsteady employment of the earners in the complete families. Three-fourths of the complete families in the panel sample received all their income from earnings; the figure for the cross-sectional sample is lower because some households have nonwelfare additions to their income from stocks, rental property, or other sources.

The earnings reported for the households with fatherless families are nearly always those of the husbandless mother herself. About 30 per cent of the husbandless mothers were full-time employees at the time of the interview; about a fifth of them had been employed in the course of the preceding 12 months or were employed part time. Though employment was not as extensive among the married mothers in the sample, it still was high and was an important addition to the income of many households. Fourteen per cent of the married mothers were working full time when interviewed, and more than a quarter of them worked part time or had been employed in the preceding 12 months. In the panel sample, at the time of the first wave interviews, 35 per cent of the husbandless mothers were employed full time and 15 per cent were employed in the course of the year or were employed part time when interviewed. Among the married mothers, 10 per cent were employed full time and 49 per cent were employed in the preceding year or were part-time employees when interviewed. In the nation as a whole, among married mothers of children age 17 or younger, 30 per cent were in the labor force in 1962; that is, they were working or looking for work. Among widowed, divorced, or separated mothers with children 17 or younger, 55 per cent were in the labor force.[9]

Amount of Income. Given the samples in the study, and as the sources of income already indicate, many of the families in the study are very poor. Just how many are poor is shown in Table 3.3. In the cross-sectional sample, half of the fatherless families have annual family incomes under $3,000. The

Table 3.3. Family Income for Last 12 Months Among Fatherless and Complete Families in Cross-Sectional and Core Panel (Wave I) Samples

	Cross-Sectional Sample		*Core Panel Sample*	
Family Income	*Fatherless Family*	*Complete Family*	*Fatherless Family*	*Complete Family*
Less than $2,000	17.4	4.4	23.6	7.5
$2,000 to $2,999	31.8	5.9	45.3	20.6
$3,000 to $3,999	23.5	13.2	17.9	38.2
$4,000 to $4,999	19.7	24.6	8.5	24.1
$5,000 or more	7.6	52.0	4.7	9.5
Total %	100.0	100.1	100.0	99.9
(N)	(132)	(387)	(106)	(199)

complete families in the sample are relatively better off: only 10 per cent have such low incomes. Of course this is largely

9. Computed from Jacob Schiffman, "Marital and Family Characteristics of Workers, March, 1962," *Monthly Labor Review* (January, 1963), Table G, as cited in Herman P. Miller, *Rich Man, Poor Man* (New York: New American Library, Signet Book edition, 1964), p. 201.

because many of these families live outside of public housing and in middle-income neighborhoods. Even in the panel sample, however, the male-headed families are relatively better off than ones headed by females. Note, too, that the panel sample includes a higher proportion of the very poor than does the cross-sectional sample. Among the fatherless families at the time of first interview, 69 per cent had incomes under $3,000 and 28 per cent of the complete families had such low incomes. As noted earlier, the applicants for public housing were drawn form the Negro low-income neighborhood surrounding Park project to a greater extent than were previous applicants.

We calculated a variety of other income figures for the cross-sectional sample, all highly related, and in the analysis we will use per capita disposable income and annual household income most frequently. These and other measures can be briefly described. In household income, the income of other persons living with the family under study is included.

Table 3.4. Per Cent of Fatherless and Complete Families in Cross-Sectional Sample with Given Income, Variously Measured

Income Measure and Level of Income	*Family Type*	
	Fatherless	*Complete*
Gross household income less than $3,000	48.0	10.5
	(129)	(382)
Disposable household income less than $3,000	69.8	22.0
	(129)	(368)
Per capita disposable household income less than $500	53.6	18.7
	(129)	(368)
Welfare ratio less than 90%	48.6	33.9
	(128)	(378)
Welfare ratio excluding rent less than 90%	52.8	19.4
	(129)	(366)

As can be seen in Table 3.4, the proportion with incomes under $3,000 is barely affected.

The next income measure is a little more complex. The money paid in the preceding twelve months for housing (utilities and rent or mortgage payments) was subtracted from household income to yield disposable income of the household. One significant implication can be drawn by comparing complete and fatherless families by this income measure relative to gross household income. The difference in income between complete and fatherless families is not reduced and perhaps increased when housing expenses are subtracted. This suggests that fatherless families are economically disadvantaged in the housing market, even when we consider a sample of families largely drawn from public housing. The number of rooms for a fatherless family is not less than that of a complete family with the same number of children, but their income tends to be less and rent is partly related to size of units even in low-income public housing.

The next two income measures are based upon a budget of minimum standards, taking into account number of persons in the household and their ages, sex, and employment status. The budget is adapted from a schedule developed by the Community Council of Greater New York to be used by private agencies in New York City as a standard in determining eligibility for assistance and free medical care.[10] Following Morgan, David, Cohen, and Brazer, a welfare ratio was constructed by dividing the household's budget requirements by the gross household income. A household with income less than 90 per cent of its budget requirements is considered to be living in poverty. On the basis of this measure, about half of the sample of fatherless families are poor and a third of the complete families are living in poverty. In a

10. The budget was adapted to make it possible to allocate costs according to characteristics of the household as they were coded. This budget is an adapted version of Table 16-1 in James N. Morgan, Martin H. David, Wilbur J. Cohen, and Harvey E. Brazer, *Income and Welfare in the United States* (New York: McGraw-Hill Book Company, 1962), p. 189. Morgan *et a.*, adapted the budget from *Budget Standard Service, Annual Price Survey and Family Budget Costs* (New York: Community Council of Greater New York, 1959).

national survey, on the basis of this measure, 45 per cent of families in which the head is single and has children are poor and 20 per cent of all families are poor.[11]

Since a large proportion of the sample is living in public housing, we calculated a special welfare ratio—subtracting rent and utilities from the budget requirements and the payments for them from the income. On the basis of this measure, about half of the fatherless families are still below the poverty line, but only about one-fifth of the complete families are poor.

Despite the elegance of an income measure based upon budget requirements, in most of the later analysis we will be using a simpler approximation: per capita disposable household income. This measure is obtained by dividing the disposable household income by the number of persons in the household. The measure is almost perfectly correlated with the welfare ratio—excluding housing costs—and the distribution is almost identical with the welfare ratio—excluding housing costs. The simpler measure has the advantages of easier comprehension and comparability.

In short, whatever measure of income is used, about half of the fatherless families in the sample live in households that are poor. From 10 per cent to a third of the complete families are poor, depending upon the measure used; probably about one-fifth is the most reasonable estimate. This is consistent with the sources of income as shown in Table 3.2. More than half of the fatherless families lived in households in which welfare benefits were at least one source of income, and this is true of about one-fifth of the complete families.

These findings are what one would expect, given the eligibility standards for welfare benefits. The Onondaga County Welfare Department's allowance schedule for food, clothing, personal incidentals, and household supplies was calculated for two families at the time of the study. A husbandless mother with an 8-year-old and an 11-year-old child would have an allowance of about $1,200 a year, excluding housing costs; this comes to a per capita figure of about $400. A

11. Morgan, and others, p. 194.

complete family with an employed man and his wife and children of the same ages would have an allowance of about $1,600, or $400 per capita. These figures include estimates of the cash value of food packages distributed through the federal government's surplus commodity program and were included in the income for the families and households.

In summary, about half of the fatherless families in this sample are poor. This is true also for the nation as a whole.[12] A majority of the families are dependent, at least partly, upon public assistance. Nationally, almost 40 per cent of the single-headed families with children receive public assistance.[13] Without a husband, but responsible for raising minor children, these mothers appear to face intractable financial hardship. Yet, when asked, "Five years from now, do you expect that your family income will be much more than it is now, a little more, about the same, or less?" the responses of the husbandless mothers do not differ from those of the married mothers. About one-third of both replied, "much more," 40 per cent, "a little more," 16 per cent, "about the same," and only 3 per cent said less; 6 per cent did not know. In part, wishes are probably distorting the expectations of both married and husbandless mothers. Husbandless mothers may also be looking forward to remarriage or to employment when the children are a little older. As we observed earlier in this chapter, being a husbandless mother is not a permanent condition.

Social Background. Before concluding this comparison of fatherless and complete families and turning to their residential areas, I wish to note a few other characteristics which may be thought to characterize these family types. The differences between the fatherless and complete families in social background are not as marked as the differences in

12. Mollie Orshansky, "Counting the Poor: Another Look at the Poverty Profile," *Social Security Bulletin*, XXVII (January, 1965), Table 11, as reprinted in *Poverty in America*, Louis A. Ferman, Joyce L. Kornbluh, and Alan Haber, eds. (Ann Arbor: The University of Michigan Press, 1965), pp. 42–82, and Charles E. Goodell and Albert H. Quie, "Poverty in America," in *Republican Papers*, Melvin R. Laird, ed. (Garden City: Anchor Books, 1968), p. 168.

13. Morgan, and others, *op. cit.*, Table 16–24.

economic status. As can be seen in Table 3.5, in the cross-sectional sample, half of the married mothers and almost half of the husbandless mothers grew up in Syracuse;

Table 3.5. Per Cent of Husbandless and Married Mothers in Cross-Sectional and Total Panel Samples with Selected Characteristics

	Cross-Sectional Sample		*Total Panel Sample*	
Characteristics	*Husbandless Mothers*	*Married Mothers*	*Husbandless Mothers*	*Married Mothers*
Grew up in Syracuse metropolitan area	43.3 (141)	50.4 (413)	31.5 (108)	44.3 (203)
Completed 12 or more years of formal education	39.0 (136)	48.3 (404)	27.8 (108)	36.7 (202)
Father's occupational socioeconomic index 18 or lower	56.5 (122)	54.0 (354)	75.5 (102)	64.3 (190)
Negro	45.4 (141)	26.8 (414)	66.4 (104)	57.9 (190)

the proportions are much lower in the panel sample. This is related to the mothers' race and migration from the South. In the cross-sectional sample, 30 per cent of the husbandless mothers were raised in the South, compared to 19 per cent of the married mothers; in the panel sample, the percentages are 38 and 22 respectively.

Most of the mothers did not complete high school and the husbandless mothers are less likely to have done so than the married mothers. As we would expect from what we have already noted about the panel sample, even fewer of these mothers have completed high school.

As an indication of social status origins, we are using the father's occupation. Duncan's occupational socioeconomic index is used to measure occupational status.[14] The index is highly correlated with the prestige rating of the occupations as measured in occupational prestige studies. The index ranges from 0 to 96; for purposes of tabular presentation, we have grouped the index scores into six categories. The grouping is based upon: (1) the occupational status distribution of the total sample, (2) the occupational status distribution of the national labor force (as reported by Duncan) and, (3) to a very limited degree, congruence with the Bureau of the Census major occupational categories.

The reader is referred to Duncan's discussion of the socioeconomic index for a complete description of the scoring procedure and for the listing of the index scores for specific occupations. I will simply list the six categories used here and indicate the kinds of occupations which may be found in each category.

1. Index: 0-13: nearly all laborers, service workers such as elevator operators, a few craftsmen such as metal molders
2. Index: 14-18: operatives such as smeltermen and truck drivers, service workers such as waiters and barbers, some craftsmen such as painters, farm owners and tenants
3. Index: 19-30: operatives such as metal grinders and welders, service workers such as bartenders and ushers, craftsmen such as plasterers and auto mechanics, clerical workers such as shipping clerks

14. See Chapters VI and VII by Otis Dudley Duncan and Appendix B in Albert J. Reiss, Jr., *Occupations and Social Status* (New York: Free Press of Glencoe, 1961). The Index was based upon the 1947 National Opinion Research Center Survey of Occupational Prestige. A 1963 replication shows no appreciable change; see R.W. Hodge, P.M. Siegel, and P.H. Rossi, "Occupational Prestige in the United States, 1925-63," *American Journal of Sociology*, LXX (November, 1964), pp. 286–302.

4. Index: 31-49:	operatives such as carpenters, craftsmen such as machinists, service workers such as firemen and policemen, clerical workers such as dispatchers, sales workers such as sales clerks in retail stores
5. Index: 50-65:	clerical workers such as mail carriers and ticket agents, sales workers such as real estate agents, foremen in some manufacturing industries, craftsmen such as toolmakers, some managers and self-employed proprietors such as those in the wholesale trade
6. Index: 66-96:	All the professions, technical and kindred workers, most managers, sales workers such as insurance agents

Occupations with indices of between 66–96 constitute the highest decile of the national population; those with indices of 50–65, the second highest decile; those with indices of 0–13 and 14–18, the lowest two deciles.

The socioeconomic index was discussed in detail because it will be used throughout the book. Frequently, as in Table 3.5, the index will be dichotomized: 18 or lower versus over 18. As can be seen in Table 3.5, a majority of both the married and husbandless mothers in the cross-sectional sample had fathers with occupations of low socioeconomic status. No difference appears when an analysis is made using a more detailed breakdown of the socioeconomic index. The mothers in the panel sample are somewhat more likely to have had low socioeconomic origins than the mothers in the cross-sectional sample and this is most marked among the husbandless mothers.

The racial composition of the two samples is considerably different. Two-thirds of the husbandless mothers and almost 60 per cent of the married mothers in the panel sample are

Negro. In the cross-sectional sample, less than half of the husbandless mothers and about one-fourth of the married mothers are Negro. Of course, many of the married mothers live outside of the housing projects and three of the neighborhoods surrounding the four projects studied are occupied predominantly by white families.

Summary

The distinction between complete and fatherless families is ambiguous. Complete families vary in the degree and extent to which the husband-father is part of the family. Fatherless families vary in the time the former husband-father has been absent and the degree to which he is still a member of the family. Fatherless families also differ in the degree to which another man fills the role of a husband-father. Nevertheless, we are making a sharp distinction between fatherless and complete families. Only occasionally will we note some of the possible consequences of varying degrees of complete or fatherless families.

The sharp distinction between husbandless and married mothers is not made only for ease of analysis. The two categories do tend to have different sets of characteristics—even if the characteristics overlap the line between the categories. The largest differences we have noted in this chapter are those inherently associated with the absence of a husband-father: those related to the stage of the life cycle and to economic circumstances. Thus, compared to married mothers, husbandless mothers are older, have older children, are more likely to receive public welfare benefits, to work full time, and to be poor.

On the whole, there are few marked differences between husbandless and married mothers in characteristics that are not inherently associated with marital status. The husbandless and married mothers in this sample do not differ markedly in social background except that in the cross-sectional sample the husbandless mothers are much more likely to be Negro than are the married mothers.

These similarities and differences have implications for the analytic strategy to be followed in this book. We will be using complete families as the standard of comparison for the fatherless families. Using a full range of complete families makes it possible to examine all the consequences of being a husbandless mother. Given some of the inherent differences, however, certain controls must sometimes be employed.

The similarities between the two categories of mothers in other characteristics facilitate analysis by reducing the necessity of controlling for those factors. In the case of race, we must consider it a possible control variable for certain portions of the analysis. Since race is not a central concern of this book, however, such analyses will usually be referred to only in notes.

In this chapter we have not discussed the distribution of husbandless and married mothers by residential area. Since place of residence is of such primary concern in the book, this is discussed in a separate chapter. In the next chapter we will present the distribution of the husbandless and married mothers in the housing projects and surrounding neighborhoods and then analyze each area, as well as the relationship between each project and its surrounding neighborhood.

4. Enclaves of Poverty

FOR THE development and maintenance of a subculture of poverty, the poor must live in areas that provide an opportunity for frequent interaction with each other and constrain them from interaction with the nonpoor. People in such enclaves of poverty can then develop and perpetuate their own collective solutions to the problems they have in common. One of the purposes of this chapter is to examine, for the population studied, the extent to which the poor live in homogenous communities with clearly demarked social boundaries. Obviously the housing market generally segregates people by income.[1] People live in communities within metropolitan areas which are similar in income, race, and ethnicity. Field studies of the poor also reveal that they live in circumscribed social worlds of intimates with similar socioeconomic status.

1. An abridged version of this chapter was previously published in Louis Kriesberg, "Neighborhood Setting and the Isolation of Public Housing Tenants," *Journal of the American Institute of Planners*, XXXIV (January, 1968), pp. 43–49. The maps were prepared by Douglas Grant.

Although we know this is true in general, we know little about the actual and potential variation in social isolation of the poor. A poor family may have some friends, relatives, and acquaintances who are not poor; it may live in neighborhoods which have considerable heterogeneity, even within the low-income range; and it may live in neighborhoods with higher incomes in which interaction with the nonpoor can occur. In this chapter, we will consider some of these possibilities. The analysis is focused upon four low-income public housing projects. This should reveal particularly high social isolation of the poor; the projects are formally restricted by income and their physical differences from the surrounding area can readily symbolize barriers to social interaction. Insofar as we find, even here, evidence of heterogeneity and easily crossed boundaries, the idea of restricted enclaves of poverty must be qualified.

This analysis serves another purpose. A description of the housing projects and surrounding neighborhoods is a necessary introduction to the analysis of possible area effects in later chapters. For this purpose, too, we are interested in the variation in the housing projects in the study. All low-income projects might seem to be alike. They are all restricted by income and consequently the residents are likely to share many other social characteristics. Even low incomes, however, can vary—from direst poverty to a minimally adequate level. Low income, moreover, may be due to a wide variety of causes—the retirement of the wage earner from the labor force, the absence a husband-father in the family, or low wages of the family's main earner. Projects are likely to vary in the proportions of people who have low income for these different reasons and the family structure, age composition, and other social characteristics of the tenants will then also vary. Furthermore, projects differ in physical structure, size, racial composition, and even the tenants' social origins. As a result of these and other variations, projects are also likely to differ in the degree of neighboring and social cohesion. Finally, housing projects may vary significantly in their neighborhood settings. This brings us to the final purpose of this chapter: a consideration of the possible consequences of locating low-income public housing projects in middle-income neighborhoods.

The neighborhood within which low-income public housing projects are constructed is properly a matter of social concern. Locating such projects in middle-income neighborhoods would seem to offer tenants of the projects an opportunity to learn, develop, and express the life style of middle-income families. This can occur through several processes. Members of low-income families may participate in churches, schools, and other institutions serving middle-income persons. Such participation can provide new models, new opportunities for action, and better services than those available in low-income neighborhoods. Residence in a middle-income neighborhood can make possible the observation of models of behavior rarely seen in low-income neighborhoods and less exposure to models of conduct low-income families think disreputable. The very circumstances of a different neighborhood style of life can facilitate new forms of conduct. For example, in low-income urban neighborhoods, mothers may believe that their children are subject to undesired influences from other children and their children are highly involved in peer relations; in the face of these circumstances the mother may fight a losing battle to exercise parental authority. In a middle-income neighborhood, the peer life may be less intense and the children's conduct more supervised by parents; a low-income mother may not be thrust into conflict with her children and yet exercise indirect supervision successfully. Finally, through personal acquaintanceship and friendship, new desires, knowledge, and skills may be acquired. Such personal relationships would make more effective each of the other processes.

Placing low-income public housing in middle-income neighborhoods, however, may have other consequences. The differences between tenants and the neighborhood residents may be so great that the project tenants are socially isolated. They may be barred from participating in the neighborhood life and thrust upon themselves to such an extent that the processes listed above would not be operative. They may become more resigned, discouraged, and frustrated than before. Social isolation also may indicate that the neighborhood residents are fearful or antagonistic to the project tenants and feel that their interests are threatened by the location of a housing project in the area.

The extent of social interaction between project tenants and the residents in the neighborhood surrounding a project is not determined solely by the socioeconomic differences between them. As neighbors, wives, husbands, mothers, and fathers, interests are shared, and propinquity can provide opportunities to discover a basis for continuing social interaction. Therefore, factors which affect the chances to interact also affect the social isolation of project tenants. Thus, the physical arrangement of the project apartments, the size of the project, and facilities which encourage meetings are all relevant. In this chapter, I will examine the extent of social isolation between project tenants and residents in the surrounding area as affected by the socioeconomic differences between them as well as by other factors.

The Public Housing Projects and Surrounding Areas

The Four Low-income Public Housing Projects. All of the projects in Syracuse are small and have low density, compared to the immense low-income public housing projects of America's largest cities. Even within Syracuse, however, the public housing projects differ in significant ways. The social composition of a housing project is affected by the rules defining eligibility, by who applies from among eligible families, by housing authority rules and practices which select from the applicants those who will be offered an apartment, and by the length of time different kinds of families remain in public housing. These processes and factors affect the social composition of low-income projects in general, as well as that among housing projects.

Of the four housing projects in Syracuse, two are federally subsidized projects and two are state subsidized. The federal projects, Evans and Stern, have slightly higher maximum income limits for eligibility and continued residence than do

Park and Grant, the two state projects. Among the eligible families, those who are particularly disadvantaged in the private housing market because of inadequate income, social discrimination, or the lack of housing suitable to their family needs are most likely to apply.[2] Some of these same families, however, may also have difficulty in being accepted for public housing. This is true, for example, of families with a history of rent delinquency, persons who have a criminal record, and unwed mothers.[3] In the past, the local housing authority has permitted accepted applicants some choice among apartments, within limits set by its efforts to minimize vacancies. An applicant could refuse a vacancy for the next available one if he wished. This probably has resulted in more homogeneity within projects and between a project and its surrounding neighborhood than would otherwise be the case.

Physically, Evans housing project is the smallest and most attractive of the four. It consists of 200 dwellings grouped into four courts, as shown in Map 1. Small porches frame the main entranceways, which, unlike those in the other projects, face outward into the street rather than into the courtyards. The density is the lowest of all the projects.

Park, with 677 units, and Grant, with 528, are the largest projects in Syracuse. Both have units reserved for elderly persons: more than half in the case of Grant and about one-third in Park. The units reserved for the elderly are in high-rise buildings, a fact which accounts for Grant having the highest density of all the projects. Aside from these high-rise buildings, the units in Park and Grant are in at-

2. As part of the study of public housing and social mobility, a survey was made of families eligible for low-income public housing who were living in an area about to undergo urban renewal and who, therefore, faced relocation. Some of the findings from the survey are reported in Seymour S. Bellin and Louis Kriesberg, "Relations among Attitudes, Circumstances and Behavior: The Case of Applying for Public Housing," *Sociology and Social Research*, 51 (July, 1967), pp. 453–469; and in Irwin Deutscher and Laurence T. Cagle, "Housing Aspirations of Fatherless Families" (Syracuse University Youth Development Center, 1964; mimeographed).

3. Irwin Deutscher, "The Bureaucratic Gatekeeper in Public Housing," Irwin Deutscher and Elizabeth Thompson, eds., *Among the People: Encounters With the Poor* (New York: Basic Books, 1968), pp. 38–52.

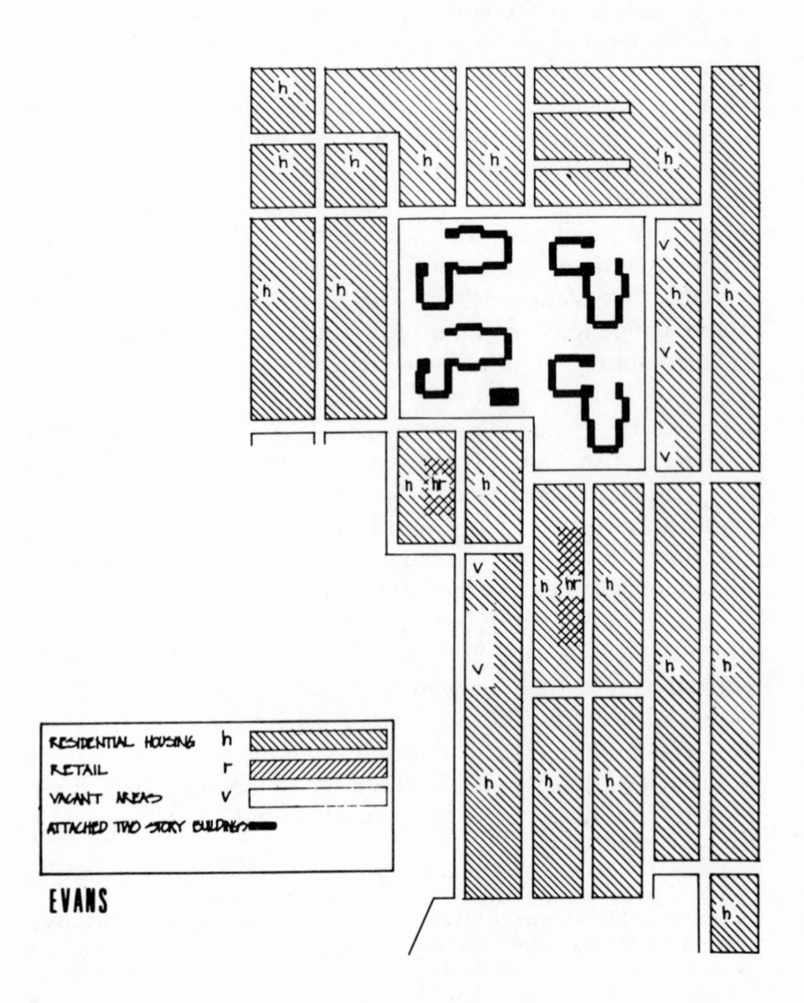
h
h
h
h
h
h
h
v
h
h
h
v
v
h
h
hr
h
v
h
hr
h
v
h
h
RESIDENTIAL HOUSING h
RETAIL r
VACANT AREAS v
ATTACHED TWO STORY BUILDINGS
h
h
h
h
EVANS

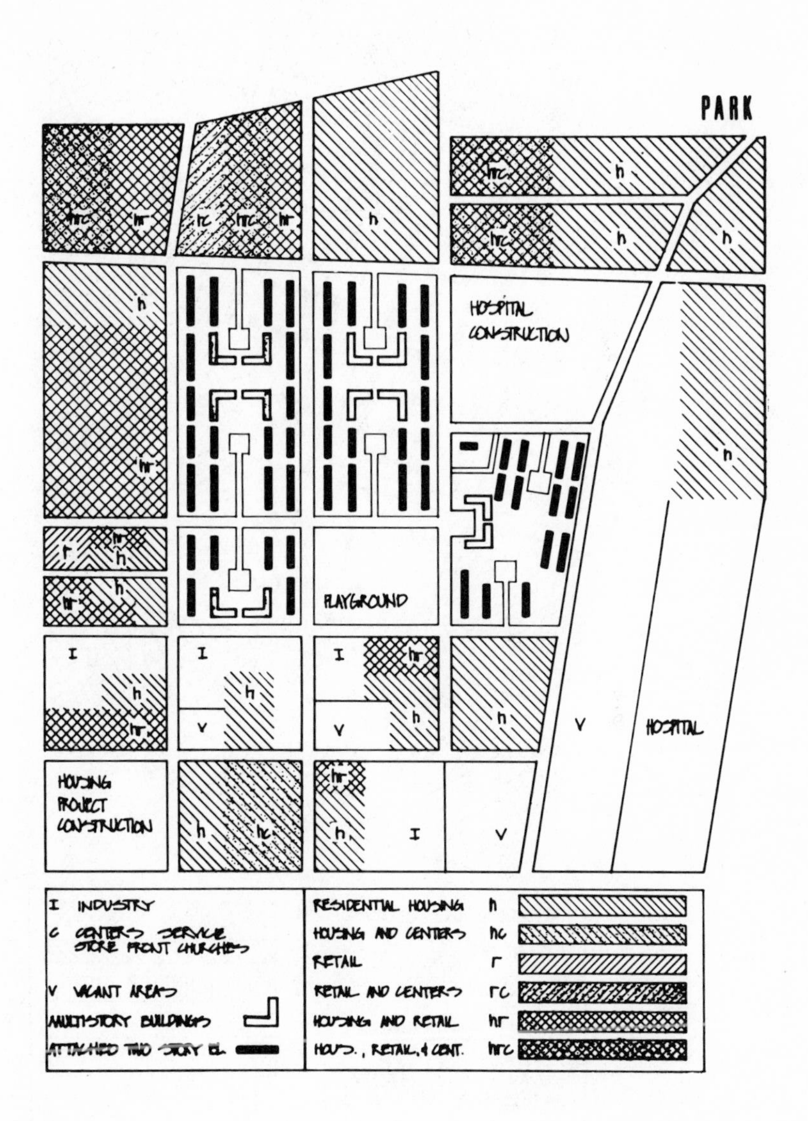
PARK
HOSPITAL CONSTRUCTION
PLAYGROUND
HOSPITAL
HOUSING PROJECT CONSTRUCTION
I INDUSTRY
C CENTERS SERVICE STORE FRONT CHURCHES
V VACANT AREAS
MULTISTORY BUILDINGS
ATTACHED TWO STORY BL.
RESIDENTIAL HOUSING h
HOUSING AND CENTERS hc
RETAIL r
RETAIL AND CENTERS rc
HOUSING AND RETAIL hr
HOUS., RETAIL, & CENT. hrc

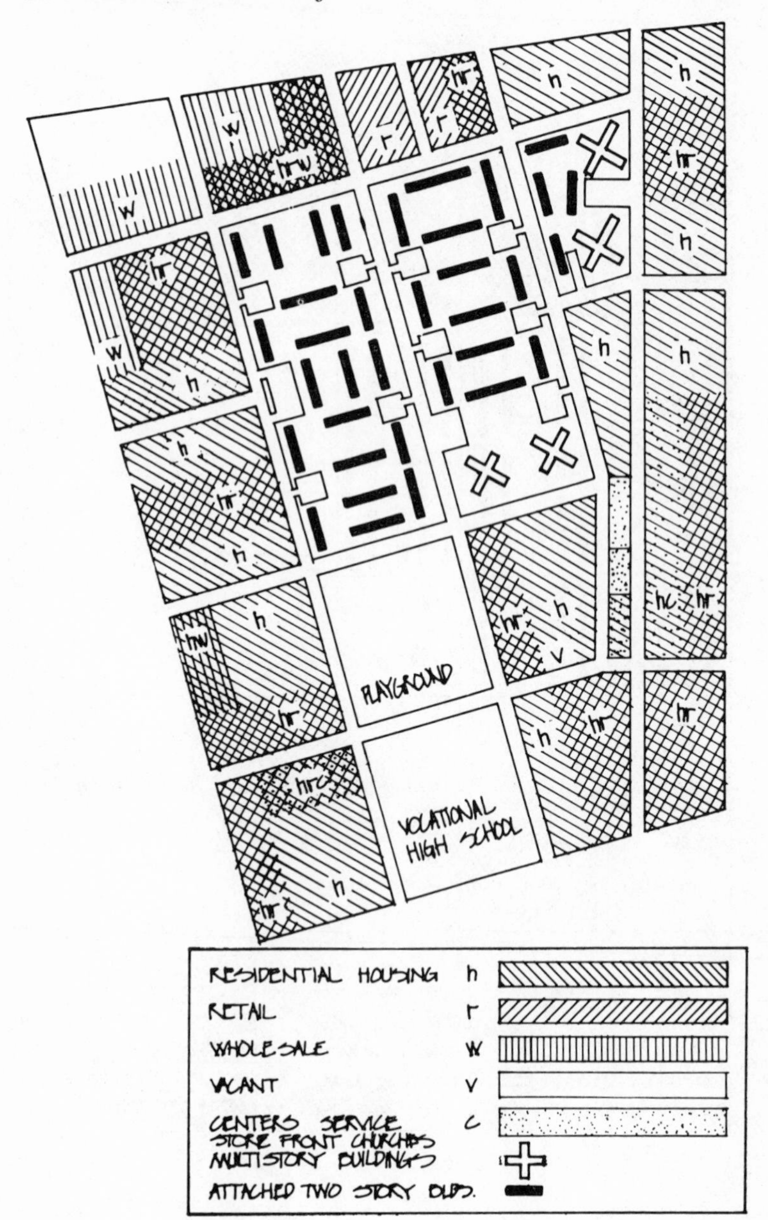
PLAYGROUND
VOCATIONAL HIGH SCHOOL
RESIDENTIAL HOUSING h
RETAIL r
WHOLESALE w
VACANT v
CENTERS SERVICE
STORE FRONT CHURCHES c
MULTISTORY BUILDINGS
ATTACHED TWO STORY BLDS.

GRANT

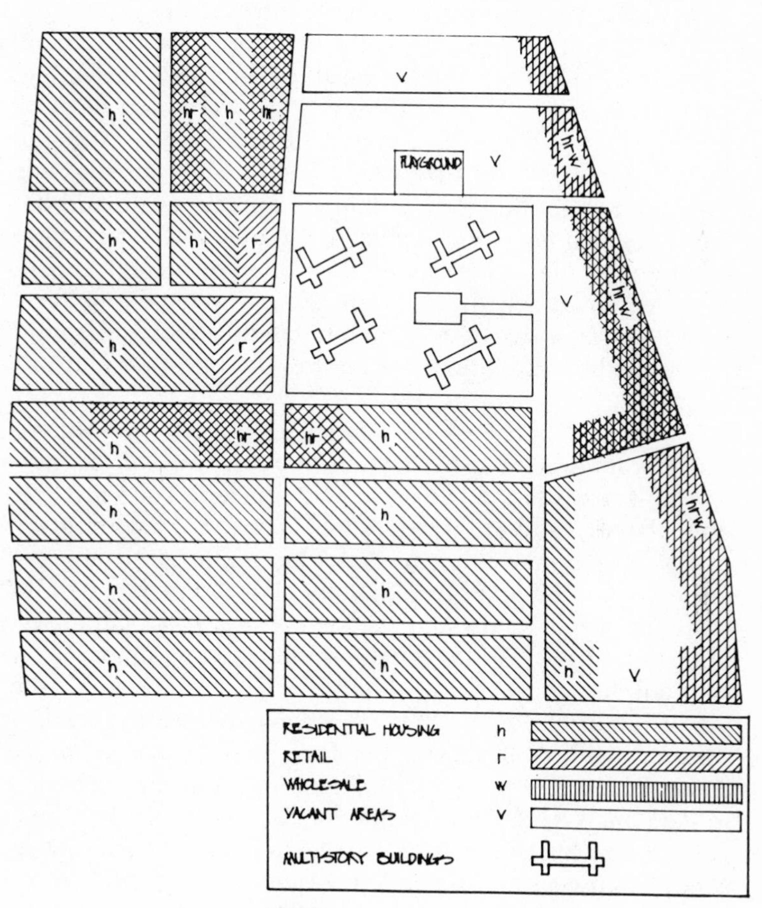
PLAYGROUND
RESIDENTIAL HOUSING h
RETAIL r
WHOLESALE w
VACANT AREAS v
MULTISTORY BUILDINGS

STERN

tached two-story, single-family houses grouped around courtyards. Individual lawn areas provide space where children play and adults gather. Each dwelling unit has one entrance facing the court and another on the street or parking lots. The courtyards may facilitate neighborly interaction.

Stern is quite different from the other projects. Its 213 units are in four buildings which are three-and four-stories high, without elevators. The buildings face inward onto black-top courts where children can play. The high-rise construction, however, makes child supervision difficult: courtyard play cannot be controlled from within the apartment. In addition, the living quarters are cramped, and the lack of a yard where children can play under supervision often results in using the dark, windowless hallways as play areas—to the discomfort of neighbors. In a survey of complete families that had applied for public housing, Stern was least preferred of all four projects.[4]

Since Grant and Park have units set aside for the elderly, the distribution of family types in these projects is quite different from that in the other two projects. Thus in Grant, only about a third of the households consist of a couple with at least one minor child; in Park, the proportion is about 40 per cent. On the other hand, 59 per cent of the Stern and 67 per cent of the Evans households consists of a couple with minor children. These variations, however, cannot be accounted for simply by the elderly. If we consider only mothers of minor children, the proportion who are husbandless varies considerably among the four projects and helps account for the low proportion of couples with minor children in Park and Grant. Thus 42 per cent of the mothers of minor children are husbandless in Park, 33 per cent in Stern, 30 per cent in Grant, and 23 per cent in Evans.

Evans is the most homogeneous project; it is predominantly a project of small complete families. Stern is

4. Stern is unpopular among both Negroes and whites, unlike the other projects which differ in appeal or acceptance for Negroes and whites. Among white applicants, Park has the lowest rank preference; among Negroes, Evans ranks lowest. See Ronald Ley, "An Analysis of Project Preferences of Applicants for Public Housing" (Syracuse University Youth Development Center, 1961).

more varied; a majority of the households consist of a couple with a few minor children, but it also contains fragmented nuclear families without minor children, plus a somewhat larger percentage of fatherless families than Evans. Park is composed of about one-third elderly-couple or single-person households, one-third complete, and one-third fatherless; the families are relatively large and in some cases include adults outside of the immediate nuclear family. In Grant, about one-half of the households consist of elderly couples or single persons, about one-third consist of complete families, and slightly more than one out of ten households consist of fragmented nuclear families with minor children; the number of minor children in these households is relatively large.

Table 4.1. Sources of Household Income by Project

Sources of Household Income	*Projects*			
	Evans	*Grant*	*Park*	*Stern*
No earnings, but:				
Only or partly welfare sources	7.7	16.0	35.8	10.6
Nonwelfare sources	11.5	31.1	8.1	10.6
Earnings, and:				
Only or partly Welfare sources	8.7	10.7	15.5	14.2
Nonwelfare sources	29.8	15.5	16.3	16.8
Earnings only	42.3	26.7	24.4	47.8
Totals %	100.0	100.0	100.1	100.0
(N)	(104)	(206)	(123)	(113)

The variations in the distribution of household types among the four projects is necessarily reflected in the economic characteristics of the households. Since Evans predominantly consists of complete families, employment is the major source of income (see Table 4.1). Park and Grant have a high proportion of households with income from nonearned sources, but in Park the proportion drawing upon welfare sources is particularly high. Stern project resembles Evans, except for a slightly higher proportion of the households utilizing public assistance.

The differences in sources of income are reflected in the

household incomes. Evans has the highest average income, as can be seen in Table 4.2, but even in this project the average welfare ratio is at the poverty line. On the whole, families in Evans are relatively homogeneous in income no matter which income measure is considered. The measure of heterogeneity or dispersion which we have used is the standard deviation. Evans has the smallest dispersion in household incomes, but Park is even less varied than Evans in per capita disposable household income, welfare ratios, and occupational socioeconomic index of family.

Grant and Park, with their high proportion of elderly and therefore low percentage of earners, have the lowest average income. Park, however, is particularly low. The figures for Park may seem puzzling considering that it has fewer elderly families than does Grant. The explanation is indicated by the occupational socioeconomic index of the family. This index refers to the occupation of the husband in the family, whether he is working, unemployed, or retired. If there is no man in the respondent family, the woman's occupation is taken; if she has no occupation, her former husband's occupation is used. The low socioeconomic index of Park tenants indicates that the elderly couple or woman, as well as the husbandless mother, may be in particularly strained financial conditions. This follows from the fact that a man with a low-status job is usually not able to provide adequate income for his family when he retires, dies, or leaves the family. The family is therefore likely to be dependent upon public welfare. On the other hand, Grant project, despite its high proportion of elderly families, has families with a relatively high occupational socioeconomic index.

On the whole, Park has the poorest households and lowest occupational index scores among the four projects and is relatively homogeneous. Grant is the next poorest and has relatively high variability in occupation and in occupational status. Stern and Evans have somewhat higher average incomes than do Park and Grant. Evans has the highest income and is relatively homogeneous; the average occupational socioeconomic index is also higher in Evans than in Stern.

Given the demographic and economic characteristics of the

Table 4.2. Means and Standard Deviations of Selected Income and Occupational Measures by Housing Project

Measures		*Evans*	*Grant*	*Park*	*Stern*
Annual household income in dollars	Means	4,195	3,072	3,023	3,791
	Standard Deviations	1,408	1,757	1,584	1,498
Annual per-capita disposable household income in dollars[a]	Means	855	813	653	894
	Standard Deviations	372	487	369	493
Welfare ratio (.90=poverty line)[b]	Means	1.02	.86	.75	.95
	Standard Deviations	.29	.32	.26	.35
Welfare ratio – excluding rent[c]	Means	1.33	1.18	1.00	1.31
	Standard Deviations	.52	.56	.44	.57
Occupational socioeconomic index of family[d]	Means	29.82	31.89	18.20	25.16
	Standard Deviations	16.12	22.32	12.25	16.74

[a] Income from all sources for all persons in the household was summed and then the annual payment for rent was subtracted and difference divided by the number of persons in the household.

[b] Welfare ratio calculated based upon a budget of minimum standards, taking into account the number of persons in the household, and their ages, sex, and employment status. The welfare ratio was constructed by dividing the household's budget requirements by the gross household income. A household with income less than 90 per cent of its budget requirement is considered to be living in poverty. See James N. Morgan and others, *Income and Welfare in the United States* (New York: McGraw-Hill, 1962), p. 189.

[c] Welfare ratio calculated as above except that budget allotment for rent was excluded and payments for rent were subtracted from gross household income.

[d] The occupational socioeconomic index is the measure developed by Otis Dudley Duncan. See Chapters VI and VII by Otis Dudley Duncan and Appendix B in Albert J. Reiss, Jr., *Occupations and Social Status* (New York: Free Press of Glencoe, 1961).

people living in the four public housing projects, we would expect a similar variation in other status criteria. Considering ethnicity, class origins, education and subjective class position of the tenants of the four projects, the parallels, however, are not uniform.

Park housing project is predominantly Negro (75 per cent), and the whites are largely the elderly. Grant, the other relatively poor project, has few Negroes (10 per cent); as already noted, the poverty there is attributable to the high proportion of elderly. Stern is almost one-third Negro, and Evans is almost entirely white (96 per cent). Negroes constitute about 6 per cent of the Syracuse population; aside from Evans, the projects have a disproportionate percentage of Negroes.

Syracuse is heavily Catholic, perhaps up to 50 per cent, and this is reflected in the housing projects: Evans, Grant, and Stern have between 40 to 55 per cent Catholics. Park, largely Negro, is predominantly Protestant. In Evans and Grant, about two-thirds of the tenants have national origins from northern, western, and central Europe. A relatively small percentage in any of the projects have eastern European or Mediterranean area ancestry.

When we turn to the occupational status of the tenants' fathers, we find a parallel variation among the projects. About 30 per cent of the tenants in Evans had fathers who had white collar occupations (professional, managerial, clerical, or sales). In Stern the percentage is about 24; in Grant, 13; and in Park, only 7. More than one-third of the Park tenants had fathers who were farmers or farm laborers, and in Grant, almost one-fourth of the fathers were farmers. Furthermore, among the Park tenants, 9 per cent report they had no father or father surrogate while they were growing up, or that the father was disabled; in Grant, the percentage is 6, and in Evans and Stern, 4 per cent.

Table 4.3 presents the distribution among the projects of the fathers' occupational socioeconomic index. The Park tenants generally are of low occupational status origins; Grant residents are next, followed by Stern. Evans residents are most likely to have relatively high social status origins. Indeed, some Evans families have lower social status positions themselves than did their families-of-origin. The same pattern exists if one examines the fathers' educational attainment. Over 40 per cent of the fathers of Evans residents had at least completed high school, compared with almost 30 per cent of the Stern tenants and about 15 per cent of the Grant and Park residents. These differences are affected by the age distributions in the various projects, but that cannot account for all the differences.

Table 4.3. Father's Occupational Socioeconomic Index by Housing Project

Father's Occupational Socioeconomic Index	*Evans*	*Grant*	*Park*	*Stern*
66-96	7.4	1.6	0.7	2.2
50-65	13.4	10.2	3.7	13.7
31-49	22.2	16.5	8.8	24.5
19-30	20.1	11.8	11.0	13.7
14-18	24.8	43.7	53.3	23.0
0-13	12.1	16.1	22.6	23.0
Totals %	100.0	99.9	100.1	100.1
(N)*	(149)	(254)	(137)	(139)

* Respondents without fathers or paternal surrogates are not included.

It should come as no surprise that the tenants' own educational attainment follows the pattern of their fathers' occupational status. The absolute level of the educational attainment, however, may be surprising. Over half of the respondents in Evans have at least completed high school, as have about 40 per cent of the tenants in Stern; in Grant, the percentage is 28 and in Park, only 16.

Given these marked variations in objective class measures, one would expect similar variations in subjective class position. This, however, is not the case. The respondents were all asked, "Some people say there are four classes in the U.S.: upper, middle, working and lower class. Which of these four do you belong to?" There is little variation between Evans, Grant, and Park: almost 40 per cent in each project say upper or middle class. In Stern, however, about 30 per cent say upper or middle class. It may be that the Stern residents are somewhat less likely to identify themselves as middle class because of the neighborhood setting. As we shall see, the neighborhood surrounding Stern is the most prosperous and 77 per cent consider themselves middle or upper class. Apparently, the comparison with the people around them is one of the bases of class identification.

The Adjacent Neighborhoods. Without the homogeneity imposed by income limits and size of apartments, the neighborhoods around the public housing projects naturally are more varied among themselves and each is more heterogeneous than are the public housing projects. The "neighborhoods" around each project refer to the four or five blocks extending out from each side of each project. In some cases, barriers such as a river, a railroad, or a main thoroughfare established a neighborhood boundary rather than the arbitrary five-block limit.

Table 4.4. Sources of Household Income by Neighborhood

Sources of Household Income	*Evans*	*Grant*	*Park*	*Stern*
No earnings, but:				
Only or partly welfare sources	0.0	9.9	7.0	0.0
Nonwelfare sources	9.9	14.3	11.0	9.1
Earnings, and:				
Only or partly welfare sources	1.1	8.8	16.0	3.0
Nonwelfare sources	35.2	33.0	20.0	49.5
Earnings only	53.9	34.1	46.0	38.4
Totals %	100.1	100.1	100.0	100.0
(N)	(91)	(91)	(100)	(99)

Evans housing project lies on the northern border of the city. The neighborhood around it is middle income, and the family heads are engaged in upper blue-collar and lower white-collar occupations (see Tables 4.4 and 4.5). Many of the people in the area have risen from lower socioeconomic statuses. Fewer than a fourth of their fathers had white-collar jobs. Almost 40 per cent of the fathers had occupations with

Table 4.5. Means and Standard Deviations of Selected Income and Occupational Measures by Neighborhoods

Measures		*Evans*	*Grant*	*Park*	*Stern*
Household income in dollars	Means	7,562	4,887	5,369	9,492
	Standard Deviations	3,150	2,819	3,796	5,486
Per capita disposable household income in dollars	Means	1,957	1,653	1,474	3,096
	Standard Deviations	1,243	1,670	1,413	3,038
Welfare ratio	Means	1.84	1.41	1.37	2.56
	Standard Deviations	.75	.82	.99	1.86
Welfare ratio—excluding rent	Means	2.45	1.85	1.76	3.47
	Standard Deviations	1.30	1.46	1.65	3.12
Occupational socioeconomic index of family	Means	40.21	24.78	20.21	54.35
	Standard Deviations	19.64	18.60	16.80	25.01

socioeconomic indices of 18 or lower (see Table 4.6). Only a little over half of the persons in the Evans neighborhood sample had 12 or more years of formal education, and 25 per cent of the fathers had had at least 12 years of education.

Most of the families in Evans neighborhood, then, have experienced some upward class mobility from their parental generation. They have achieved a respectable position in the American status system. But fewer than half of them identify themselves as middle class.

The area surrounding Evans housing project consists almost entirely of households with married couples: 61 per cent consist of a couple with minor children and a quarter consist of a couple with no minor children. There are almost no fatherless families. The households, moreover, are not

Table 4.6. Father's Occupational Socioeconomic Index by Neighborhood

Father's Occupational Socioeconomic Index	*Evans*	*Grant*	*Park*	*Stern*
66-96	5.8	1.8	2.9	16.8
50-65	6.5	7.1	7.3	16.8
31-49	26.8	18.6	11.0	32.9
19-30	12.3	14.2	8.8	10.1
14-18	26.1	44.3	46.0	16.8
0-13	22.5	14.2	24.1	6.7
Totals %	100.0	100.2	100.1	100.1
(N)*	(138)	(113)	(137)	(149)

*Respondents without fathers or paternal surrogates are not included.

particularly large. For example, only 11 per cent of the households are composed of six or more persons. This is partly due to the relatively small number of children in the families: 39 per cent have no minor children in the households, 18 per cent have only one and 23 per cent have two. The social homogeneity of the neighborhood surrounding Evans housing project is matched by the physical homogeneity. The area consists predominantly of single-family, owner-occupied homes (85 per cent of the households in the Evans neighborhood sample own their homes). The homes are modest frame houses arranged in a simple gridiron of tree-lined streets. Evans project nestles in the midst of the neighborhood and is not obviously distinct from the surrounding neighborhood.

Certain characteristics of the Evans neighborhood and of Evans project affect housing applicants' preferences for residence there. Negroes do not choose Evans as a project in which they would like to live—it is located far from the Negro area of the central city in a neighborhood that is almost completely white.

The neighborhood around Stern housing project is more varied and of a higher income, occupational, and educational level than is Evans neighborhood. The average household income in the few blocks around Stern is about $9,500 (see Table 4.5). The per capita disposable household income is even higher, compared to the other neighborhoods, than is the gross income. The standard deviations are also high, indicating the variety of income levels found here. The neighborhood lies between the central business district and Syracuse University. Some faculty members as well as managers, proprietors, and upper white-collar workers live in the area.

The socioeconomic origins of the residents of Stern neighborhood are also relatively high. Over half of the residents in the Stern neighborhood sample had fathers who had white-collar occupations. Fewer than one in four had fathers with occupations with a socioeconomic index of 18 or lower (see Table 4.6). Over a half of the respondents had fathers with 12 or more years of education; 25 per cent had 13 or more years. Over half of the respondents had at least some college education and another 25 per cent had completed high school. By self-identification as well as objective measures, this is a predominantly middle-class neighborhood: three-fourths of the respondents say they are in the middle or upper class.

Almost all of the Stern neighborhood residents are white (98 per cent). Jews are the largest religious category in the area; Protestants and Catholics are about equally represented, each constituting between a third to a fourth of the sample. More than 40 per cent of the respondents in the area trace their national origins to Russia or Poland.

The households have a greater variety of family types than in Evans neighborhood. Fewer than half of the households consist of a couple with minor children; almost a third consist of a couple without minor children, and almost a fourth are made up of a household headed by an unmarried, widowed, or divorced person. The households are smaller than in Evans, with fewer adults and children.

The housing around Stern project is relatively expensive. Adding charges for utilities to rent or, if owner-occupied, mortgage payments, 53 per cent of the households have monthly housing costs of $125 or more; 25 per cent pay $150 or more. In Evans neighborhood, the comparable percentages are 40 and 15.

Physically, the neighborhood around Stern housing project is quite varied. There are some two-family homes, but typically the residents live in their own single-family houses (60 per cent of the households in the sample own their own homes). The homes, however, do not surround the project. To the north of Stern are a few wholesale establishments, a few poorly maintained houses, and then a major high-speed boulevard. To the east is a playground and undeveloped land. To the south are some supermarkets and specialty bakery and delicatessen stores. Only to the west do the homes face the project directly. The fact that Stern housing project consists of three and four story buildings further sets it off from the surrounding neighborhood.

The neighborhoods around Park and Grant are predominantly working class. Park housing project is close to the central business district. The neighborhood surrounding the project had been the area of the first Jewish settlement in Syracuse. As the Jews left the area, moving to the neighborhood near Stern and then further east away from the central business district, the area near Park project became a Negro ghetto. Some whites remained and the neighborhood's proximity to Syracuse University has meant that a few students and faculty members live in the area. In the few blocks that constitute the sample area, 80 per cent of the residents are Negroes.

The change in neighborhood racial composition and the increase in the number of Negroes has transformed Park housing project into a predominantly Negro project. Even as recently as 1960, 50 per cent of the units in Park were occupied by whites; in 1963, it was three-fourths Negro. In a 1961 survey of public housing applicants, few whites would accept Park tenancy.[5] Negroes are only about 6 per cent of the Syracuse population; between 1950 and 1960, however, they increased by 144 per cent.[6] The sudden influx of people into the previous Negro area was accompanied by deterioration of the buildings. Old frame houses were converted into apart-

5. *Ibid.*

6. Alan K. Campbell, and others, *The Negro In Syracuse* (Syracuse, N.Y.: University College of Syracuse University, 1964), p. 3.

ments housing more than one family. At the time of the survey, the area was undergoing urban renewal; many houses were already vacant, awaiting the bulldozers. Institutions, middle-income housing, and a new thruway were to displace most of the population. As in other cities, the urban renewal program and the increase of Negroes in Syracuse has led to an increased proportion of Negroes who entered public housing.[7] Between 1961 and 1962 the proportion of Negroes in Stern changed from about 12 per cent to 30 per cent, and in Grant, from 6 to 10 per cent. Only in Evans has the increase been minute, from 3 to 4 per cent.

Most of the households in the Park neighborhood have low incomes, but the average income is above the poverty line as measured by the welfare ratio (see Table 4.5). The occupational status of the family heads is generally low, as are the respondents' class origins (see Table 4.6). Only 10 per cent of the fathers of the residents' fathers were in white-collar occupations, 25 per cent had a high school education or more, and over one-half had completed fewer than eight grades. Among the respondents themselves, three-fourths had completed eight years or more of school, and one-fourth had completed high school or more. Generally of low current socioeconomic status and of low socioeconomic origins, only 28 per cent of the respondents in the Park area consider themselves middle class.

Households are more likely to consist of broken families in this area than in any of the other neighborhoods. Almost 40 per cent of the households consist of couples with minor children and about 20 per cent contain a couple without minor children. The households in Park neighborhood are generally large: 22 per cent have six or more persons, in part because extended families share the household quarters and many families have several children.

The neighborhood around Grant housing project is similar in a number of ways to the Park neighborhood. There are many multi-family houses; about 70 per cent of the house-

7. For example, see Elizabeth Brenner Drew, "The Long Trial of Public Housing," *The Reporter*, July 17, 1965, pp. 15–18.

holds in the sample rent their apartments (compared to 88 per cent in Park neighborhood). The rents are relatively low. Considering the monthly costs for utilities and rent or mortgage payments, only 10 per cent of the households pay $125 or more (in Park, the comparable figure is 14 per cent). Almost 20 per cent of the households pay under $50 a month in Grant neighborhood, compared to 8 per cent in Park, 6 in Stern, and 4 in Evans neighborhood. The neighborhood is also near the central business district, but on the west side of the city. Warehouses, factories, trucking firms, and a railroad depot are located nearby.

The income, occupational, and educational levels in Grant neighborhood are similar to those in Park neighborhood, though a small proportion of Grant residents rank higher on measures of socioeconomic status. In terms of social origins, the Grant neighborhood residents are as unlikely to have had fathers in white-collar occupations as Park area residents, but they are more likely to have had fathers who were craftsmen, foremen, or kindred workers (24 compared to 17 per cent) or operatives (27 compared to 19 per cent) and less likely to have had fathers who were farmers or farm laborers (19 compared to 33 per cent). In short, Grant neighborhood is predominantly working class and of working-class origins; only one-third of the residents identify themselves as middle or upper class.

The population is overwhelmingly white (91 per cent), and more than half of the adult respondents in the sample area are Catholic. A large Catholic church and school faces Grant project. No particular nationality category is dominant in the area; the entire gamut of European nationalities is represented.

In terms of family organization, only one-third of the households contain couples with minor children. The household organization which sets this neighborhood apart from the others is the relatively high proportion of households consisting of elderly single persons and elderly couples without children. Considering only the female respondents in the sample, almost one in four is at least 65 years old; more than half do not have minor children; one-third have no minor children and no husband.

The Isolation of the Public Housing Projects from the Neighborhoods

Isolation means several things: that housing project tenants know few people in the adjoining neighborhoods and interact infrequently with those they know; that few persons in the surrounding area know any tenants and rarely interact with those they know; and that a high proportion of the tennants' neighboring and friendship interactions are with persons living in the project rather than with persons in the adjoining neighborhood. Of course, isolation also may mean lack of visibility and opportunity to observe the life of the people in the surrounding neighborhood. For some kinds of influence, visibility is sufficient. Here, however, I will restrict the discussion to the social-interactional isolation of the projects from the surrounding neighborhoods.

Conditions Affecting Project Isolation. Four major conditions may affect the degree of housing tenant isolation from the surrounding neighborhood. First, the socioeconomic distance between project tenants and neighborhood residents may vary; presumably, the greater the socioeconomic distance, the less likely is interaction to occur. Second, there may be varying physical barriers separating the project from the neighborhood. Third, projects and neighborhoods can have varying levels of social interaction; presumably, the higher the level of interaction within the project relative to the level outside, the greater the tenants' isolation. Finally, tenants may have moved from the surrounding neighborhood into the project; in that case they can easily maintain old ties to the neighborhood.

In terms of socioeconomic distance, Stern tenants are most dissimilar from the neighborhood residents. For example, the average gross income of Stern households is only 25 per cent of the average income of Stern neighborhood households. At the other extreme, the average income of Grant project households is more than 60 per cent that of Grant neighborhood households. For Evans and Park projects, the household incomes are a little over 50 per cent of the average income of the households in the adjacent neighborhoods. Similarly, for every social status characteristic—education, father's occupation, race, and religion—Stern project tenants are more often unlike residents in the surrounding neighborhood than are the tenants of any other project. Even the difference in the distribution of types of families is greater between Stern project and neighborhood than between the other projects and their adjacent neighborhoods. The relative dissimilarity of the other projects and their respective neighborhoods is difficult to rank. On the whole, the tenants are similar to the residents in the surrounding neighborhoods. In terms of the distribution of family types and household composition, Grant project and its neighborhood are most similar. In terms of the various social status measures, one or another project-neighborhood pair is most similar. Interestingly, Evans tenants are somewhat more likely to have high socioeconomic origins than Evans neighborhood residents, although their current status is lower.

These objective similarities and differences between the projects and their adjacent neighborhoods are reflected in the perception of the neighborhood residents. The respondents in each neighborhood were asked about the nearby housing project, "Do you think you have a lot in common, quite a bit in common, little in common, or nothing in common with the people living in (name of project)?" It is clear that simply living in public housing constitutes a barrier. A substantial minority in each neighborhood replied that they did not know how much they had in common with the people in the nearby project: 30 per cent in Park, 25 per cent in Stern, 24 per cent in Evans, and 21 per cent in Grant neighborhoods. When asked about persons in their own neighborhoods outside of public housing, the percentage who said they did not know how much they had in common with their neighbors was much lower, varying from 12 to 7 per cent. Furthermore, considering only those persons who could say how much they had in common with persons in the adjacent projects, only a small minority said they had a lot or quite a bit in common with the project tenants: 28 per cent of the Park neighborhood residents, 19 per cent of those in Grant neighborhood, 18 per cent in Evans neighborhood, and only 9 per cent in the Stern neighborhood. More felt they have quite a bit or a lot in common with people living in their neighborhood outside of public housing. In terms of the relative isolation of the four projects, clearly Stern is seen as most different by the neighbors outside, as we would expect from the data already considered.

Physically, residents of Stern housing project have the greatest barriers to interaction. The neighborhood homes face only one side of the project. The project itself faces inward, and most of the tenants do not live on the street level. The other three projects are more difficult to rank. The units of Evans face out towards neighborhood housing of similar style. This is less true for Park and Grant, but the streets and the stores of Park and Grant neighborhoods are more active centers of neighborhood life than is true in Evans neighborhood.

In the neighborhood surrounding Park and Grant housing projects, the small owner-operated stores serve only the local market, unlike the supermarkets and specialty stores in the areas near Stern and Evans. Bars and pool halls provide hangouts for adult men. Moreover, streets run through Park so that neighborhood residents walk or drive through this project to use neighborhood facilities. Grant project, on the other hand, has several nonresidential areas on its perimeter: a Catholic school, a city high school, and a playground.

The third condition to be considered is the degree to which the projects and neighborhoods provide opportunities for desirable associations. Presumably, in large, homogeneous projects where physical arrangements of the housing units are conductive to neighboring, the opportunities for interaction within the project would be great.[8] Evans project is small, but it is most homogeneous. Grant and Park projects are heterogeneous, but the major categories within each are large. Stern is small and heterogeneous. As a subjective measure of the opportunities for interaction, we can look at the responses to the question about how much the tenants in each project feel they have in common with others in the

8. For the classic demonstration of the effects of physical design of a housing complex upon neighborhood interaction, see Leon S. Festinger and Kurt Back, *Social Pressures in Informal Groups* (New York: Harper, 1950).

same project. A large proportion in Evans and Grant feel they have a lot or quite a bit in common with others in the same project (40 per cent and 50 per cent respectively). The proportion in Stern is expectedly lower than in Evans or Grant (27 per cent of the tenants feel they have a lot or quite a bit in common with others). Park is surprising; the same proportion as in Stern feel they have a lot or quite a bit in common with others in Park housing project. This is lower than one would expect, given the objective characteristics of the population in Park housing project. One reason for this peculiarity is that Park tenants and neighborhood residents are highly involved in kinship relations and in friendship networks of limited scope. In this privatized network there is less room for extensive identification. Another explanation is the lack of distinction between Park and the surrounding neighborhood. As noted previously, Park neighborhood residents are most likely to feel they have something in common with Park housing tenants. Park housing project does not have as great a separate identity as do the other projects. Consideration of the last factor affecting project isolation will help explain these findings.

If project tenants are drawn from the neighborhood immediately surrounding the project, they are able to maintain associations with their old friends in the neighborhood. The project tenants are less likely to form close relations with their new neighbors and develop a sense of commonness with others in the project. Most of the Park tenants previously lived in the neighborhood around Park. Only a small minority of the Evans and Stern tenants previously lived in the immediate vicinity of their respective projects. A majority of the Grant tenants previously lived in the immediate surrounding area. We should also note that it takes time to get to know people and Park is the oldest project in Syracuse, having been opened in 1939. Stern was opened in 1949, Evans in 1952, and Grant in 1954. A higher proportion of Park tenants than those in the other projects have lived at their present address for several years.

The Degree of Project Isolation. The ranking of the projects' isolation may be different, depending upon the indicators of isolation used. An analysis of the differences in relative isolation of the projects should indicate the relative importance of the factors determining project isolation. We will examine several measures of project isolation separately. All the tenants in each project were asked, "Do you know anyone in the neighborhood around (name of project) well enough to talk to?" As can be seen in Table 4.7, more than half of the respondents in every project knew at least one person in the immediate neighborhood well enough to talk to. In Park project, three-fourths so reported. Furthermore, half of the Park respondents said they knew seven or more persons in the neighborhood; about one-fifth to one-fourth of the tenants in the other projects reported knowing as many. The other three projects are very similar, there is only a slight tendency for Grant tenants to report knowing twenty or more persons in the surrounding area.

When we consider the number of persons in the neighborhood who reported their acquaintanceship with persons in the adjacent project, also shown in Table 4.7, the pattern is slightly different. Only in Park neighborhood does more than

Table 4.7. Number of Neighbors Known Across Project Lines by Area

	Areas							
	Project Tenants Knowing Neighbors Outside				*Neighborhood Residents Knowing Project Tenants*			
Number of Neighbors Known	*Evans*	*Grant*	*Park*	*Stern*	*Evans*	*Grant*	*Park*	*Stern*
None	41.0	46.4	22.7	42.9	73.9	58.9	44.9	72.6
1-6 persons	39.8	30.6	25.3	33.3	21.6	34.9	33.3	25.5
7-19	11.8	9.4	20.0	15.7	3.9	4.7	11.6	1.3
20 or more persons	7.5	13.7	32.0	8.2	0.7	1.6	10.2	0.7
Totals %	100.1	100.1	100.0	100.1	100.1	100.1	100.0	100.1
(N)	(161)	(278)	(150)	(147)	(153)	(129)	(147)	(153)

a majority claim to know someone in the project. Park neighborhood residents are more likely to know someone and to know many persons in the adjacent project than are the residents in any other neighborhood. Grant neighborhood residents are more likely than Evans or Stern residents to know persons in the adjacent project. One difficulty in interpreting these results is that Park and Grant projects are much larger than Evans and Stern; the chance of knowing someone in one of those projects is considerably greater than in the smaller projects of Stern and Evans. Computing the percentages in terms of the relative sizes of the projects reveals no differences among the four neighborhoods in the proportion knowing someone in the adjacent project.

Project tenants who said they knew at least one person in the surrounding neighborhood and neighborhood residents who said they knew at least one person in the adjacent project were asked a series of questions about the one person with whom they had most to do. One question was, "How often do you usually get together with (him) (her)?" The area variation in response to the question is presented in Table 4.8. The patterns are the same. Park tenants are most likely to

Table 4.8. Frequency of Getting Together with Person Across Project Line by Area

	Areas							
	Project Tenant and Person Outside				*Neighborhood Resident and Project Tenant*			
Frequency of Getting Together	*Evans*	*Grant*	*Park*	*Stern*	*Evans*	*Grant*	*Park*	*Stern*
Never get together or do not know anyone	46.9	51.9	26.0	45.6	81.6	62.5	50.7	80.2
Less often than once/ week	18.1	15.2	10.0	21.5	10.9	18.0	17.1	12.5
once/week	14.4	7.8	20.7	14.1	4.1	7.8	15.8	2.0
More often than once/ week	20.6	25.1	43.3	18.8	3.4	11.7	16.4	5.3
Totals %	100.0	100.0	100.0	100.0	100.0	100.0	100.0	100.0
(N)	(160)	(283)	(150)	(149)	(147)	(128)	(146)	(152)

get together more often than once a week with the neighborhood resident with whom they have most to do; the other projects do not differ from each other. Looking at the proportion of the neighborhood residents who get together often with the most frequently seen person in the adjacent neighborhood, we find again that Park is highest, followed by Grant, and followed by Stern and Evans, which are alike. Again, taking into account the relative size of the projects, there is no real difference among the neighborhoods.

Racial characteristics are relatively visible and therefore may be of particular importance in effecting interaction between project tenants and the residents in the surrounding areas. Among Park tenants, it is true that white men and women are less likely to know someone, to know many persons, or to interact frequently with someone they know in the surrounding area, compared to Negroes. This may be due to the fact, however, that whites in Park are generally elderly persons. In Grant and Stern projects, where the number of Negroes makes a comparison possible, there is no clear evidence that race is an isolation barrier. Indeed, Negro men are more likely than white men to know someone and interact often with someone in the surrounding area; they are just as likely to know many persons in the neighborhood. Among the women, there are no consistent differences between Negroes and whites. A somewhat higher proportion of white women in Stern frequently see someone in the surrounding area, compared to Negro women; but Negro women in Grant are more likely than white women to know many persons in the surrounding area. Otherwise, there are no differences between Negro and white women in Stern and Grant in terms of these measures.

The respondents were asked about friends as well as neighbors. They reported how many friends they had. Then they were asked a series of questions about the two friends with whom they felt closest; in this series they were asked if each friend lived in the housing project, the adjacent neighborhood, or elsewhere. Among the Park tenants, 39 per cent have at least one of their two closest friends in the neighborhood around Park project; the corresponding percentages for Evans, Grant, and Stern are 15, 16 and 13 respectively.[9] Conversely, 13 per cent of the Park neighborhood residents have at least one friend in the Park project; among the Grant and Evans neighborhood residents, only 2 per cent have at least one of their two closest friends living in the adjacent project; none of the Stern neighborhood residents in the sample had either of their two closest friends in Stern project. By every measure, there is more interaction between the Park tenants and their neighbors in the adjacent area than is the case for the other three projects and their adjacent areas.

Does this mean that Park tenants are *least* likely to have their closest friends in the housing project? Actually we find that almost two-thirds of the Park tenants have at least one of their two closest friends living in Park project (one-third have both of their closest friends in the project). In Evans, Grant, and Stern, only one-third of the tenants have even one of their closest friends in the project. Interestingly, the pattern in the adjacent neighborhoods is similar, if less marked; the proportion in each neighborhood who have at least one close friend in the neighborhood is 57 per cent in Park neighborhood, 41 per cent in Evans and Grant neighborhoods, and 36 per cent in Stern neighborhood.

What accounts for this apparent discrepancy is the proportion of persons in each area who have close friends *elsewhere than in the project or the neighborhood.* Among the Park tenants, only 37 per cent have one of their two closest friends living elsewhere; the percentages are 71, 70 and 74 for Evans, Grant, and Stern respectively. Again, the pattern is the same for the adjacent neighborhoods; the proportion of neighborhood residents with friends elsewhere is 53 per cent for Park neighborhood, but 82 per cent for Evans and Grant, and 87 per cent for Stern residents.

In short, it appears that most of the Park tenants and neigh-

9. Respondents who said they had no friends are excluded from the analysis. Persons who said they had only one friend were classified by the location of that one friend. That is, when we say both friends are located in a particular place, we mean both of the two friends mentioned or, in the few cases in which only one friend was mentioned, where his or her one friend lives.

borhood residents live in a social world with relatively narrow physical boundaries, but the project itself is not an important barrier to social interaction. Neighbors and friends are likely to be the same people. Racial segregation in housing tends to restrict friends and relatives to the same section of the city.[10] In the other three projects and adjacent neighborhoods, most persons have their closest friends outside their immediate areas of residence. As a matter of fact, more than 50 per cent in each of the three projects and each of the three adjacent neighborhoods have *both* their closest two friends living elsewhere. Apparently, persons whose friends live elsewhere are likely to engage in casual neighborly interaction but the project boundary is a barrier to such interaction for most of them—the neighborly interaction is confined to immediate neighbors.

CONCLUSIONS

The kinds of people living in a low-income housing project vary a great deal—even comparing four projects in one medium-sized city. The physical characteristics of the projects and the surrounding areas, and the processes of self-selection by tenants and of admission by the housing authorities all affect the social composition of each project.

Given such variability, it is possible to study how certain conditions affect the social isolation of project tenants from residents in the surrounding area. Of course studying only four cases does not permit assessing the relative importance of each condition. The results of the analysis, nevertheless, yield some clear findings. First of all, residence in public housing does constitute a barrier to social interaction. This seems to be the case unless the project tenants are largely drawn from the surrounding neighborhood and no marked physical impediments to interaction exist, no major social differences exist (which is likely to be true if the tenants are drawn from the surrounding area), and the project tenants do not develop a strong community.

Considerable overall differences in socioeconomic status

10. Campbell, *op. cit.*, pp. 25–30.

between project tenants and residents in the surrounding area is not, however, an important impediment to social interaction. Thus, although socioeconomic differences were most marked in the case of Stern, the social isolation of project tenants was not higher than in the case of Evans or even Grant. This is true despite the fact that the physical conditions conducive to interaction are also the least between Stern tenants and the residents in the surrounding areas. Apparently the reservoir of possible associations in the neighborhood outside Stern was sufficiently large that interaction could occur at the same low level as for the Evans and Grant tenants. Perhaps if the socioeconomic differences were much greater they would have a noticeable effect despite the importance of so many other factors affecting the level of interaction. On the basis of the evidence from this analysis, however, it seems that the heterogeneity within a project and within the area surrounding a project is often large enough to provide the basis for establishing neighborly relations and even friendships. After all, people are not alike only because they have similar incomes or levels of education. They are also alike and share interests because they have other qualities as men, women, mothers, fathers, shoppers, husbands, renters, residents in a general area of a city, and consumers of popular culture.

The findings of this chapter cannot be simply generalized to large metropolitan areas with huge public housing projects. Vaster areas of poverty must restrict the opportunities for interaction across community lines. The findings do indicate, however, that if low-income housing were located in middle-income areas, the social barriers to interaction are not insurmountable. The findings regarding heterogeneity of persons living in low-income areas are probably more readily generalizable even to larger tracts of low-income residential areas.

5. The Selection of Housing

Living in low-income public housing projects might be viewed as an expression of welfare dependency. Poor people who lack the values and capacities of the dominant middle-class way of life find a sanctuary in public housing. Congregated together, they can reinforce each other in developing their own subculture. In this chapter, we will consider to what extent self-selection determines tenancy and which characteristics are most determining of the self-selection. We want to know to what extent intergenerational processes affect the choice of residence. If residential choice is not solely or largely a result of subcultural processes, the maintenance and perpetuation of a subculture of poverty is limited.

Who lives in low-income public housing is not merely an expression of desire on the part of the tenants. It is not even simply a matter of persons eligible for public housing choosing among housing alternatives. The other side of the interaction also affects the outcome: the number and kinds of vacancies in public housing, the rules of eligibility, and the informal selective process of the housing authorities. The interplay between possible tenants and the housing authority occurs at several stages: applying for public housing, entering, and remaining as a tenant. In this chapter, we will examine the interplay and outcomes, particularly for fatherless families compared to complete families.

Such an examination will help account for the social composition of public housing projects described in the previous chapter. It will also elucidate some of the difficulties fatherless families have in obtaining housing. In particular, the place of public housing in meeting some of their difficulties will be discussed. This analysis is also a necessary step before studying the possible consequences of residence in low-income public housing projects.

Female-headed families are handicapped in many ways in trying to find housing in the private market. The widespread poverty among them is of course the fundamental handicap. Adequate rentals are difficult to find with very low incomes. Low income and no prospects of improvement make it difficult to obtain a mortgage with which to purchase a home. Not having a husband compounds these difficulties. A husband may have greater familiarity and be better able to deal with bankers, realtors, or landlords—who are usually males. A husband can also be expected to take care of some of the necessary physical maintenance of an apartment and more especially of a house.[1] In addition, husbandless mothers may face discrimination in searching for housing, only partly justified in terms of the above considerations. Discrimination may be rationalized too, by arguing that fatherless children are less likely to be supervised and more likely to damage property. On the other hand, public housing would seem relatively attractive. Since rent is geared to income, those who are extremely poor would be relatively better off in public housing. Maintenance at least at a minimal level, is

1. In a study of working-class London widows, it was noted that many of the widows missed their husbands especially in taking care of tasks about the house such as wallpapering and painting. See Peter Marris, *Widows and Their Families* (London: Routledge & Kegan Paul, 1958), p. 47.

assured. Finally, the possibility of living with similarly situated families may be attractive to husbandless mothers [2]

Housing authorities, however, may also discriminate against fatherless families—on the same grounds as do private landlords. Depending upon the formal and informal procedures followed, they may be more or less able to do so. The possible reasons for discrimination should be recognized however. Housing authorities may be concerned about the racial balance of projects; they may want to maintain a high proportion of tenants paying rents at the higher end of the project's range, rather than at the lower end; they prefer tenants who pay their rent on time and otherwise cause no trouble; and they may even be concerned about not having all or any particular project become largely occupied by broken families. The housing authorities must also be concerned about keeping their vacancy rates low. As long as there are long waiting lists, vacancies will be of little concern, but the possibility of a project becoming unattractive to potential tenants can exist. Indeed, some potential tenants may refuse to move into public housing if the available project is not acceptable to them.

Who moves into and remains in public housing, then, is the result of a complex interplay of many processes and conditions. In examining how this works out in the projects reported upon here, we will utilize several sets of data. The two major sources of data described in Chapter 3 will be utilized: (1) the cross-sectional survey of residents in each project and each surrounding area and (2) the panel survey of applicants for public housing. In addition, I will use the data from a sample of residents in a relocation area.[3] Since this

2. Several studies of public housing in Puerto Rico document the appeal of public housing for fatherless families. See Kurt W. Back, *Slums, Projects, and People: Social Psychological Problems of Relocation in Puerto Rico* (Durham, N. C.: Duke University Press, 1962); Chester Hartman, *Family Turnover in Public Housing* (San Juan, Puerto Rico: Urban Renewal and Housing Administration, n.d.); and Helen Icken Safa, "The Female-Based Household in Public Housing: A Case Study in Puerto Rico," *Human Organization*, 24 (Summer, 1965), pp. 135-139.

3. This study is reported in more detail along with analyses of particular issues in: Laurence T. Cagle and Irwin Deutscher, "Housing Aspirations of

sample has not been described earlier, and will be used to begin the analysis in this chapter, a brief description of the sample is necessary.

In the summer of 1961, a sample of families eligible for public housing and living in the Near East Side Urban Renewal Area of Syracuse were interviewed. All of them had been informed in writing and in person by a relocation assistant that they would have to move within a specified period of time and that certain kinds of assistance were available to them under the law. More than two years later, the respondents were interviewed again and Housing Authority records were examined to see who had applied for public housing and who had entered.

Mothers in 24 fatherless and 44 complete families constituted the sample. A fatherless family was defined as a mother and her child or children, the youngest of whom was under 21 years of age. A complete family includes a father as well as a mother. Seventy-five per cent of the fatherless families and 64 per cent of the complete families in the sample were Negro. Complete families had a median annual income of $4,071 and fatherless families, a median annual income of only $2,056. Two-thirds of the fatherless families were receiving AFDC benefits.

The several sets of data used in this chapter provide complementary information. The relocation sample can reveal something about who is interested in applying for public housing and who enters—within an eligible population facing the need to find new housing. During the relocation period, observations of the intake procedure at the Housing Authority provide information about the other side of the interactional system. The panel sample can tell us, in more detail, among those who apply, who actually enters. Furthermore, the panel sample was studied at a little later time period—when changes in Housing Authority policies were

---

Low Income Fatherless Families" (Syracuse University Youth Development Center, 1964, mimeo); and Seymour S. Bellin and Louis Kriesberg, "Relationship among Attitudes, Circumstances, and Behavior: The Case of Applying for Public Housing," *Sociology and Social Research*, 51 (July, 1967), pp. 453-469. The results reported upon here from the relocation sample are drawn largely from Cagle and Deutscher, *op. cit.*

made. Fianlly, the cross-sectional sample provides us with information about who remains and expects to remain in public housing projects.

Interest in Public Housing

In each of the surveys, the respondents were asked whether or not they thought it was a good idea for the government to build public housing. Support for the idea seemed about universal.[4] Asked this question in the first wave of the panel survey, a young unwed mother of two little children replied:

> Yes, it's the best thing they can do. You take me, I don't want to be on welfare, Honey. I prefer to get me a good job. Some people ain't able to get them an apartment and got to go into housing. They tearing all these places down and, Honey, pretty soon they gonna be building lots of housing projects because people *got* to have a place to live.

Support for the idea of public housing is based upon the recognition that some people cannot find adequate housing on the private market as presently constituted. This husbandless mother feels she is one of those kind of people. Public housing need not be desired in an absolute way in order to be preferred to any likely alternative.

The relocation sample provides clear evidence of the husbandless mothers' difficulties in finding adequate housing and their interest in living in public housing. Although both complete and fatherless families lived in the same area, the husbandless mothers seemed less able to be critical of it: 29 per cent said it was a very bad place to live in, compared to 39 per cent of the married mothers. Thirteen per cent of the husbandless and 34 per cent of the married mothers could find *nothing* they *liked* about the neighborhood. This probably reflects, in part, their estimation of what their alternatives are.

4. Similarly, in a study of families which had moved out of public housing projects, 95 per cent of the respondents thought that low-income public housing was a good idea. The study was conducted in nine localities throughout the United States. See Public Housing Administration, *Mobility and Motivations. . .Survey of Families Moving from Low-Rent Housing,* Washington, D.C.: Public Housing Administration, 1958), p.8.

Public housing, however, seemed relatively attractive to the husbandless mothers. Asked what they thought of public housing as a place to live, what is good about it and what is bad about it, the husbandless mothers mentioned more advantages and fewer disadvantages than did the married mothers. Among the advantages cited, better facilities in the apartments was most frequently mentioned (by 63 per cent of the husbandless and 50 per cent of the married mothers). Low rent or more for your money was also somewhat more frequently mentioned by the husbandless mothers than by the married mothers (46 and 36 per cent respectively) and, similarly, the belief that the public housing was nice and/or clean (46 per cent compared to 20 per cent). On the other hand, 46 per cent of the husbandless mothers and only 18 per cent of the married mothers said they could think of no disadvantages. Among the disadvantages lack of privacy and too many rules were most frequently mentioned. Again, the husbandless mothers were less likely to mention these disadvantages than were the married mothers (25 per cent of the husbandless mentioned no privacy compared to 41 per cent of the married, and 17 per cent of the husbandless compared to 25 per cent of the married mentioned too many rules).

On the basis of such findings, it should be no surprise that husbandless mothers are much more likely than married mothers to express an interest in living in public housing. Among the relocation sample, about 80 per cent of the husbandless and 50 per cent of married mothers said they were interested in doing so. Negroes, as well as fatherless families, are handicapped in the housing market.[5] Since, in this sample, fatherless families are somewhat more likely to be Negro than are the complete families, it may be that race rather than family structure affects interest in public housing. As a matter of fact, race is highly related to interest in public housing, but this does not explain away the difference be-

5. See, for example, Nathan Glazer and David McEntire, eds., *Studies in Housing and Minority Groups* (Berkeley and Los Angeles: University of California Press, 1960); Commission on Race and Housing, *Where Shall We Live?* (Berkeley and Los Angeles: University of California Press, 1960); and Alan K. Campbell, and others, *The Negro in Syracuse*, (Syracuse, N. Y.: University College of Syracuse University, 1964).

tween fatherless and complete families. Thus, among the Negroes, about 90 per cent of the husbandless mothers compared to 65 per cent of the married mothers expressed an interest in public housing. Among the whites, about half of the husbandless and one-fifth of the married mothers said they were interested.

The panel survey provides additional information about the relative interest and reasons for interest in public housing between married and husbandless mothers. Since the respondents in the panel survey were all applicants to public housing, they were asked, at the time of the first interview, "What made you decide to apply for public housing?" Most respondents mentioned advantages of public housing, but 22 per cent of husbandless mothers and 7 per cent of the married mothers explained that they were forced to move from where they were—because of urban renewal or other reasons such as eviction by the landlord or insistence of the welfare department that the family obtain cheaper housing. Negroes were slightly more likely than whites to say they applied for public housing because they were forced to move.

The respondents, asked what the advantages were of living in public housing, stressed the financial advantages. About two-thirds of the respondents made statements such as: "It's cheaper," "It's cheaper for the lower income bracket," or "I heard the rent comes from how much you're making; I figured it wouldn't be too steep." The other major kind of advantage, mentioned by almost 20 per cent of the applicants, pertained to the physical condition, maintenance, and facilities of the apartments and projects. Husbandless mothers, particularly the nonwhite husbandless mothers, were only slightly more likely to mention the physical condition of the apartment and project, compared to the married mothers. Interestingly, nearly 10 per cent of the *married* mothers mentioned friends or relatives living nearby as an advantage of public housing, but this was not one of the first mentioned advantages among the husbandless mothers.

Earlier in the first interview, the respondents had been asked whether or not they were looking for a place to live and then asked whether or not they had had any luck in finding a place to live. Only about 15 per cent of the respondents said that they had had luck and found a satisfactory place to live. The percentage among whites was higher than among Negroes (24 per cent and 12 per cent respectively). The respondents who had not had luck (aside from applying for public housing), were asked what the trouble was. About 15 per cent of the Negroes mentioned race discrimination and 23 per cent of the husbandless mothers mentioned discrimination having to do with their household composition.

The evidence from the relocation and panel surveys indicates that husbandless mothers find public housing residence more attractive than do married mothers, but this attractiveness is relative to the alternatives available in the private sector. Furthermore, the economic advantage of public housing residence is the dominant attractive feature. We have found little or no evidence that public housing tenancy is attractive as a way of life and appeals to applicants on that ground.[6]

Getting Into Public Housing

As already suggested, the desire of husbandless mothers to live in public housing does not necessarily mean that they will do so. As a matter of fact, when the respondents in the relocation survey were reinterviewed and the Housing Authority records examined more than two years after the initial interviews, it was found that only about one-half of the fatherless families as compared to about three-fourths of the complete families actually had entered a public housing project. Recall, this compares with about 80 per cent and 50 per cent of the husbandless and married mothers respectively who had expressed an interest in living in public housing. Apparently some of the complete families encountered enough difficulties in obtaining adequate private housing that public housing seemed more attractive than initially.[7] On the other hand, some fatherless families were unable to gain admittance to public housing. The failure of husband-

6. Bellin and Kriesberg, *op. cit.*
7. *Ibid.*

less mothers to enter any housing projects cannot be attributed to interest not followed up with actual application: the fatherless families were more likely to apply and to apply soon after being notified about the urban renewal plans than were the complete families.

Fortunately for our research purposes, an observer was in the Housing Authority offices and he helps explain what happened.[8] He observed the application officer as she processed all the applicants for public housing. Although there are formal rules determining eligibility and priority, the assessment of priority involves subjective elements. Furthermore, as long as the risk of vacancies is not high, informal policies could be followed which led to the admission of some applicants and the exclusion of others or to the selective placement of tenants in particular projects. Of special relevance in the present context is the observation that the gatekeeper tried and nearly always succeeded in excluding unwed mothers. She considered even "legitimate" fatherless families undesirable and gave them very low priority. In part, this expressed her own preferences, but her policy was not countered by others in the administration. There was a widespread belief that husbandless mothers might be the source of trouble in the projects, being objects of possible temptation to fathers in other families and the maintenance crews in the projects.

The panel survey of applicants to public housing was begun one year after the relocation survey and extended for two years. By then, the Housing Authority office had been reorganized and the gatekeeper was no longer the same person. Morever, as described in Appendix B, the Housing Authority had agreed to randomly assign applicants, within limits set by the applicants' willingness to move into particular projects. The chances of a fatherless family entering public housing had increased. Among the applicants for public housing interviewed in the first wave of the panel survey, 74 per cent of the fatherless families had signed a lease with the Housing

8. Irwin Deutscher, "The Bureaucratic Gatekeeper in Public Housing," in Irwin Deutscher and Elizabeth Thompson, eds., *Among the People: Encounters with the Poor,* (New York: Basic Books, 1968), pp. 38-52.

Authority within about a a year, while 69 per cent of the complete families had done so.

This does not tell the whole story. We need to examine which fatherless and complete families entered public housing and which projects they entered. First of all, which projects can be entered is limited by the vacancies in each. During the period of the panel survey, for the families in the study, 215 leases were signed: 75 in Park, 57 in Grant, 48 in Stern, and 35 in Evans. The number of vacancies reflects the size of the project and the turnover rate of tenants. Park has by far the largest number of units available for non-elderly households, but the turnover rate is lower than for Grant and Stern. Evans has the fewest number of units and also has as low a turnover rate as Park.

The relative proportion of fatherless and complete families moving into each project, nevertheless, differs. Fatherless families disproportionally entered Park and complete families were somewhat more likely to enter Stern than were fatherless families. Such summary findings obscure rather than enlighten the crucial determinants of applicants' admission to public housing and to particular projects. It should already be clear that in regard to marital status, no overall discriminatory admission policies were being practiced by the Housing Authority during the period of the panel phase of the study. The race of the applicants, however, was still an important factor in the admission process, largely because of the applicants' feelings about the various projects.

The respondents in the panel survey were asked whether or not they would accept a vacancy in any of the projects. Interestingly, about two-thirds of the respondents said they would *not* take any vacancy. Although they had applied for public housing, not every project would be acceptable. The whites were much more likely than the Negroes to assert that they would reject some projects: 87 per cent of the white mothers compared to 58 per cent of the Negro mothers so stated at the time of the first wave interview.

Presumably, unwillingness to accept tenancy in any project reflects a balance between the unattractiveness of some projects and the attractiveness of possible alternatives. On both counts, the whites would be expected to be less willing to move into any project. A predominantly Negro project was more unattractive to them than was a predominantly white project for Negroes and the housing available to whites was less restricted than that for Negroes. There was no difference between married and husbandless mothers among the Negroes in their willingness to accept any project. Among the whites, the husbandless mothers were slightly more willing to accept any project.

In order to examine the selective and self-selective processes, it is necessary to see what percentage of families moved into public housing and into which projects, taking into account race and willingness to accept any project. This is presented in Table 5.1. First looking at those who did not enter public housing after having applied, it is clear that the complete families were less likely to get into public housing than were the fatherless families. The only exception is among Negroes not willing to accept any project. Among them, the husbandless mothers most frequently entered Park—not the project most of them would insist was unacceptable; the married Negro mothers entered Stern, Park, and, to a smaller extent, Grant.

It is difficult to understand variations in which applicants do and do not enter public housing without taking into account which projects are entered. Yet it is fair to say that complete families have better alternatives outside of public housing but they are also offered preferred projects among those available, compared to fatherless families. These conditions counteract each other so that the proportion of fatherless and complete families entering public housing as a totality does not differ very much.

This has implications for the variation in project assignment between married and husbandless mothers. On the whole, there is practically no difference in such assignments among white applicants. Among the Negroes, however, the fatherless families are especially likely to enter Stern. This does not reflect any difference between married and husbandless mothers in their preferences for different projects. Their preferences are almost identical: more than one-third of each prefer Park, about 15 per cent prefer Grant, a few per cent prefer Stern and Evans, and more than one-third of each have no preference. One must surmise that the Housing Authority channels applicants, presumably taking into account the already existing social composition of each project and what would be acceptable to the applicant family.

Such channeling is much more evident by race than by marital status. Hardly any white families entered Park during the period of the panel survey and hardly any Negroes entered Evans. Moreover, among those who would be willing to accept any project, none entered Evans. Evans is the most preferred project among white applicants and the white applicants who would not accept any project are especially likely to enter Evans. The channeling largely reflects the preferences of the applicants coupled with the necessity of filling all vacancies, including the generally nonpreferred Stern project. Clearly, the channeling of applicants was not directed at lessening the racial imbalance of the two projects with the lowest racial integration: Park and Evans.

Remaining in Public Housing

Staying in public housing, like entering, cannot be explained simply by tenants' preferences for such housing. Families may be forced to leave by the housing authority, they may leave the city, or they may move out because of some other change in family circumstances making such a move seem necessary. Reasons for moving out vary in importance in different times and places. For example, the percentage of families found ineligible to remain in public housing because their income was too high has decreased sharply.[9] In 1949 about 22 per cent of the housing tenants in the nation had incomes too high to remain in public housing; the figure fell to 12 per cent in 1951 and 4 per cent in 1956. This decline is not due to an upward adjustment of income limits at a more rapid rate than the general rise in cost of living and wages. Indeed, public housing has tended to serve poorer

9. Public Housing Administration, *Mobility and Motivations. . . op. cit.*, p. 4.

families over the years. The decline may be due to families moving in anticipation of ineligibility or perhaps private housing alternatives for the moderately poor have improved more substantially than they have for the very impoverished families.

Housing alternatives affect remaining in public housing as well as entering. This is clearest when the reason for moving out is by choice of the tenant, but it may also affect other reasons as suggested above. The relative frequency of the major reasons given by tenants themselves for moving out of public housing is provided by a study of families which had moved out of low-income housing projects located in nine communities throughout the United States. About one-third explained their move as due to changes in personal circumstances, including having left the area. Another quarter moved at the request of management. In addition to income beyond the allowed maximum, this includes violation of Housing Authority rules and nonpayment of rent. Only about one in four of the tenants explained their move as one of personal choice, usually meaning dissatisfaction with public housing. Information was lacking on most of the remaining families.

The reasons for move-outs among the Syracuse projects are similar.[10] There are also variations among the projects, however, which are noteworthy. Tenants in Evans and to a lesser extent in Stern are particularly likely to leave because their incomes are high. The tenants in Evans were relatively unlikely to move out because of changed personal circumstances. In all projects, the tenants forced to leave by management, aside from reasons of too high income, is very small. In park and Grant, changes in personal circumstances such as death or illness in the family and taking a job in another city are particularly frequently mentioned reasons for moving out. All this further indicates the differences in the composition of the projects. Tenants in Evans and to some extent in Stern are more likely to be using the projects as a stepping stone to social mobility, and those in Park and Grant

10. The information was provided by the Syracuse Housing Authority and refers to move-outs in 1963, excluding transfers to other projects.

Table 5.1. Per Cent Entrance into Public Housing by Willingness to Take any Project, by Race, and by Marital Status (Panel, Waves I and II)

Entrance Into Public Housing	Willing To Take Any				Not Willing To Take Any			
	White		Negro		White		Negro	
	Husband-less	Married	Husband-less	Married	Husband-less	Married	Husband-less	Married
Evans	0.0	0.0	0.0	0.0	32.1	31.4	2.3	4.2
Grant	50.0	22.2	6.3	7.7	21.4	15.7	18.2	16.9
Park	0.0	0.0	59.4	38.5	0.0	1.4	38.6	25.4
Stern	33.3	22.2	12.5	21.2	17.9	14.3	9.1	26.8
Villa	0.0	11.1	3.1	1.9	0.0	1.4	2.3	1.4
Did not enter	16.7	44.4	18.8	30.8	28.6	35.7	29.6	25.4
Totals %	100.0	99.9	100.1	100.1	100.0	99.9	100.1	100.0
(N)	(6)	(9)	(32)	(52)	(28)	(70)	(44)	(71)

Table 5.2. Length of Residence in Public Housing by Project and by Marital Status (Percentage)

Length of Residence	Project and Marital Status							
	Evans		Grant		Park		Stern	
	Husband-less	Married	Husband-less	Married	Husband-less	Married	Husband-less	Married
1 year or less	23.8	37.1	17.2	11.8	11.4	28.6	27.6	28.3
2 years	19.1	15.7	24.1	19.1	14.3	14.3	13.8	23.3
3-4 years	14.3	27.1	34.5	41.2	31.5	28.6	27.6	26.6
5 years or more	42.9	20.0	24.2	27.9	42.8	28.5	31.0	21.7
Totals %	100.1	99.9	100.0	100.0	100.0	100.0	100.0	99.9
(N)	(21)	(70)	(29)	(68)	(35)	(49)	(29)	(60)

often seem forced by circumstances to move out.

Fatherless families are more likely to be viewed as problem families than are complete families and this is probably reflected in a higher proportion of move-outs at the request of management. Thus, in a study of one public housing project in Syracuse, the project manager was asked to identify his most severe "problem" families and also his most "stable" families.[11] More than three-fourths of the "stable" families were complete and less than half of the "problem" families were complete. Whatever the differences in reasons for staying in or moving out of public housing between fatherless and complete families, fatherless families do tend to remain longer than complete families. In Table 5.2 we can see that in each project except Grant husbandless mothers report having moved in earlier than do married mothers. Using cross-sectional data this way has one major disadvantage. The proportion of fatherless and married mothers admitted to public housing and to particular projects has varied over time. Consequently, if a higher proportion of fatherless families were admitted in recent years, that would inflate the proportion who had short tenure in the projects. This may be the case particularly in Grant (see Table 5.1).

Another indication of the longer tenure of fatherless compared to complete families in public housing projects is given by the intentions of the entrants to remain in public housing. At the time of moving into public housing, most respondents had expected to remain indefinitely or had no plans to leave. After living in public housing, this percentage declines slightly. Both at the time of moving in and at the time of the interview, husbandless mothers are much more likely to say they expect to remain indefinitely in public housing or have no plans to leave (see Table 5.3).

The obvious explanation for these findings is that husbandless mothers are more likely than married mothers to derive benefits from public housing, to enjoy living in public housing, and, in short, to be satisfied with it. The general observa-

11. Charles V. Willie and Janet Weinandy, "The Structure and Composition of 'Problem' and 'Stable' Families in a Low-Income Population," *Marriage and Family Living*, XXV, (November, 1963), pp. 439-447.

Table 5.3. Per Cent Who Had No Definite Plan to Leave Public Housing at Time of Move into Public Housing and at Time of Interview*

Mothers	*At Time Moved In*	*At Time of Interview*
Husbandless	79.8 (114)	75.6 (111)
Married	58.3 (245)	47.4 (234)

* Includes those who expected to stay indefinitely and those who had no idea of how long they would stay.

tions in our first two chapters, and the comments about entering and staying in public housing made in this chapter, however, should caution us against accepting this obvious explanation. As a matter of fact, husbandless and married mothers are equally likely to say they are satisfied with living in the housing project in which they live. About 60 per cent of each category in the cross-sectional survey said they were satisfied when asked whether on the whole they were satisfied or dissatisfied.[12] In the nation as a whole, in 1963, 76 per cent of the whites and 43 per cent of the nonwhites were satisfied with their housing.[13]

The explanation for remaining and expecting to remain in public housing must be viewed in the larger context of available alternatives which fatherless and complete families

12. Respondents were asked to recall their expectations about various aspects of public housing prior to their moving in and their initial responses to public housing. From 30 to 40 per cent felt that the tenants of public housing, the physical appearance, and the management were about what they had expected. Of those whose initial impressions did not fit their expectations, about twice as many were more rather than less favorably impressed with the management and the physical appearance of the project. Reactions to the people in public housing were nearly equally divided between favorable and unfavorable. Married and husbandless mothers did not significantly differ in these respects.

13. The figures are based upon responses to the question: "On the whole, would you say you are satisfied or dissatisfied with your housing situation?" In 1965, 77 per cent of the whites and 29 per cent of the nonwhites said they were satisfied, and in 1966 the figures were 77 and 51 per cent respectively. Data are from Gallup surveys cited in, Hazel Erskine, "The Polls: Negro Housing," *Public Opinion Quarterly,* 31 (Fall, 1967), p. 498.

have. We saw that fatherless families face many difficulties in the private housing market and public housing is consequently relatively attractive: they are more likely to be interested in it and apply for it than are complete families. The entrance of fatherless families may be restricted by housing authority policy; once in, however, they are not so subject to differential implementation of managerial policy. Fatherless families may be more likely than complete families to be seen as troublesome, but this is not a major factor in determining move-outs from housing projects.

Income is a major determinant of alternatives to public housing. In considering whether or not the tenants have any definite plans to leave public housing we must consider their future incomes. Toward the end of the interview, the respondents in the cross-sectional sample were asked, "Five years from now, do you expect that your family income will be *much more* than it is now, a *little* more, about the *same*, or *less*?" Husbandless mothers were less likely to expect their family incomes would be greater five years hence than were the married mothers. Respondents, who expected the family income to be much higher in five years were more likely to have definite plans to leave public housing. This tendency is particularly marked among the husbandless mothers. How much money is a little or much more depends upon what the current income is. Consequently, it is necessary to also take current income into account. In Table 5.4 this is done. We can see that among those with disposable per capita incomes under $500, husbandless mothers are almost as likely as married mothers to have definite plans to leave public housing if they expect their incomes to be much more in five years.

The findings indicate that an important factor accounting for the difference between husbandless and married mothers in their plans to leave public housing is their expectations about future incomes. Impoverished fatherless families with no expectations of any increase in income in the immediate future could hardly be expected to have plans to leave public housing, and they do not. In general, the difference between husbandless and married mothers in the proportion with definite expectations to leave public housing is greater among those with relatively high incomes than among those who are impoverished. This may be explained by considering the sources of income. Husbandless mothers with relatively high incomes are more likely than other husbandless mothers to be employed. Earnings for them are likely to be insecure compared to the income derived from public assistance. Consequently, a more substantial increment in future income should be required to make them feel confident in planning to leave public housing. Thus, as can be seen in Table 5.4, among husbandless mothers whose current income is relatively high, the proportion who have no definite expectation of leaving public housing drops only if future income is expected to be much more than current income. Among husbandless mothers whose current income is low but secure, even the expectation of a modest increment in future income is sufficient to alter their housing tenure plans.

Table 5.4. Per Cent Who Have No Definite Plan to Leave Public Housing, by Expectation about Future Income in Relation to Current Income and by Current Per Capita Disposable Income

	Per Capita Income							
	Less Than $500				*$500 or Over*			
	Expected Future Income				*Expected Future Income*			
Mothers	*Don't Know*	*Same or Less*	*A Little More*	*Much More*	*Don't Know*	*Same or Less*	*A Little More*	*Much More*
Husbandless	*	100.0	80.0	59.1	†	83.3	81.0	60.0
	(5)	(15)	(15)	(22)	(6)	(12)	(21)	(15)
Married	*	58.3	55.0	50.0	70.0	36.3	48.0	37.5
	(4)	(12)	(20)	(16)	(10)	(22)	(75)	(72)

* The percentage is 100.0.
† The percentage is 50.0.

On the whole, income considerations seem to play a smaller role in accounting for the plans for leaving public housing among the married mothers than among the husbandless mothers. This may reflect the special press which economic considerations and their associated conditions have for the husbandless mothers. This interpretation may also help in understanding the responses to another question. The respondents were asked:

> Suppose (you) (your husband) were offered a steady, secure job paying more than the family gets now. The job would pay $40 a month more than your family is allowed to earn while staying in public housing. Do you think (you) (your husband) should take the job and the family move out of public housing or do you think it would be better not to take the job and stay?

Note that married mothers were asked about the job for their husbands; husbandless mothers were asked about taking the job themselves. This seemed the most realistic way of asking the question, but complicates the interpretation of the results.

Presumably, responses to the question indicate the value of remaining in public housing if a particular economic way out were available. Given the hypothetical possibility of such a job, husbandless and married mothers both shifted to moving out compared to the proportion who had definite plans to leave. Thus, although 76 per cent of the husbandless mothers had no plans to leave public housing, only 50 per cent said they would remain if a job were assured paying $40 a month more than the allowable income maximum for staying in public housing. Among married mothers, 47 per cent had no definite plans to leave and 29 per cent said they would remain rather than take the job.

This certainly reveals a widespread interest in getting out of public housing if it were financially possible. Of course, husbandless mothers are less likely to opt for the job and moving out of public housing than are the married mothers. For the husbandless mother, the job entails more difficulties, especially in regard to child care, than for the married mother choosing to have her husband get a better paying job. Therefore, it is even more striking that the decline in percentages from those who had no definite plans to leave public housing was greater among husbandless than among the married mothers. This indicates, again, that financial considerations play a particularly large role in the husbandless mothers' tendency to remain in public housing longer than married mothers. The continuing disparty between married and husbandless mothers also indicates that the private housing alternatives are less attractive for husbandless than for married mothers, aside from financial considerations.[14]

One possibility which needs to be considered is that tenancy in public housing is more acceptable to persons of low socioeconomic origins. Persons raised in poverty and probably with some experience with welfare programs may be more disposed to use public housing for extended periods or as a terminal residence. For the reasons discussed in Chapter 2, we expect little intergenerational effect. Planning to leave public housing, even preferring a job which pays more than what would permit one to remain in public housing, involves too many particular contemporary considerations. Moreover, we would expect that it is even less likely that there be an intergenerational effect among husbandless than among married mothers. Husbandless mothers face more constraining alternatives than do the married mothers and therefore are less able to express their preferences in behavior. Both expectations are borne out. Thus, as can be seen in Table 5.5, among husbandless mothers there is no relationship between socioeconomic origins and plans to leave public housing, and among married mothers there is a moderate relationship. The same is true of the responses to the question asking about the choice between the job and remaining in public housing.

One other way of testing some of the inferences drawn is to see which husbandless and married mothers tend to remain in public housing. Married mothers of low socioeconomic status origins are somewhat more likely to have been in the project for more years than are those of higher origins. This association is slight among the husbandless mothers. This is

14. Additional evidence supporting the significance of external circumstances in affecting tenure in public housing is found in an analysis of expectations about continued residence by overall satisfaction with the public housing projects. The satisfied persons were proportionately more likely to have no definite expectation of leaving, a finding that holds for both married and husbandless mothers. But, irrespective of satisfaction with public housing, husbandless mothers were much more likely than married mothers to report that they had no definite expectation of moving out of public housing.

Table 5.5. Expectations about Leaving Public Housing by Father's Occupational Socioeconomic Status

Expectations About Leaving Public Housing	*Husbandless Mothers Father's S.E.S.*		*Married Mothers Father's S.E.S.*	
	18 or less	*19 or more*	*18 or less*	*19 or more*
One year or less	8.9	2.3	21.2	39.3
Some definite time beyond one year	17.9	20.9	26.0	25.8
Do not know	33.9	34.9	27.9	25.8
Plan to remain indefinitely	39.3	41.9	25.0	9.0
Totals %	100.0	100.0	100.1	99.9
(N)	(56)	(43)	(104)	(89)

consistent with the findings regarding expectations tc leave public housing and responses to the hypothetical choice between taking a job or remaining in public housing.

We have noted that income expectations were related to plans to move out of public housing. We might consider years of schooling as an indicator of income prospects. High education indicates the opportunities for jobs which are likely to provide not only higher income but more reliable income and future increments. It may also mean more ability to cope with housing alternatives in the private sector. For the married mother, education also is related to the education of the spouse and, therefore, to the family's income prospects. We wouldexpect that people who have high education would not stay in public housing as long as do those with less education. As shown in Table 5.6, this is true of both husbandless and married mothers. A higher proportion of long-term tenants than more recent residents have less than a high school education. Since the recent applicants for public housing tend to be the more socially disadvantaged and impoverished families dislocated by urban renewal programs, the cross-sectional data are more likely to understate than overstate this relationship. These findings confirm the often noted tendency for the more upwardly mobile housing tenants to move out of public housing and for the families in desperate straits to remain, increasing the proportion of such families in public housing.

Table 5.6. Per Cent Who Have at Least Graduated from High School, by Length of Residence at the Present Address in Public Housing and in the Neighborhood Outside

	Length of Residence in			
	Public Housing		*Neighborhood*	
Mothers	*Less Than Two Years*	*Two Years or More*	*Less Than Two Years*	*Two Years or More*
Husbandless	50.0 (40)	34.8 (69)	16.7 (12)	53.8 (13)
Married	50.0 (110)	37.9 (132)	52.8 (53)	57.5 (106)

Table 5.6 presents evidence in support of another inference made earlier. Note that husbandless mothers outside of public housing who have moved recently are particularly likely to have less than a high school education. Among the married mothers, residential mobility outside of public housing is hardly related to education and their educational level is not much different than among the married mothers with relatively short tenure in public housing. These findings indicate that husbandless mothers with low education are especially handicapped in finding suitable housing in the private housing market. Outside of public housing they tend to be especially residentially mobile, while public housing provides a haven which is correspondingly more attractive.

A possible basis for the relative attraction of public housing for husbandless mothers is the social support they derive from living there. Living in housing with relatively many other women in similar circumstances should increase the chances of mutual support among them and also reduce the likelihood of being treated as deviant and consequently feeling deviant. The neighboring patterns of husbandless and married mothers in and out of public housing was examined. The analysis revealed that husbandless mothers, even in public housing, had more difficulty in establishing neighborly relations. Presumably, some stigma to the circumstances persists and husbandless mothers are handicapped in establishing and maintaining neighborly relations because the husband's absence means the loss of a possible link to some neighbors. Furthermore, the absence of a husband means the absence of a resource to be exchanged and of a resource which helps free the woman to carry out the exchange involved in neighborly relations. In any case, the husbandless mothers in the neighborhood are less likely to know many neighbors or to think neighbors are helpful than are husbandless mothers in the housing projects or than married mothers in or out of public housing.

Conclusions

The poverty of fatherless families makes finding adequate housing particularly difficult. Obtaining adequate housing is, in itself, a problem for husbandless mothers. The housing actually occupied in turn becomes the possible source for conditions and influences which may affect other ways in which poor fatherless families accommodate to the absence of a husband-father and the way in which the children in the families grow up. In this chapter we have examined one housing option in particular detail: the utilization of low-income public housing. We have found that poor husbandless mothers are more likely to be interested in living in public housing than are married mothers of similar income. It is also clear that the interest in public housing reflects a weighing of the relative merits of housing in the private sector. In weighing the relative benefits, it appears that consideration of the amount of rent and the quality of the housing obtained for the rent are crucial.

We have also seen that interest in public housing is not automatically expressed by moving into a public housing project. The availability of openings in particular projects and the general admission policy of the Housing Authority affects who actually moves into a housing project. We have seen that at least for some periods husbandless mothers were not able to actualize their interest in moving into public housing in Syracuse because of an informal policy which gave them low priority. Furthermore, the race and marital status of the applicants affected their placement in particular projects. Where a particular family moved was a result of a complex interaction between the family's preferences and the Housing Authority's policy of making available certain choices among the available openings. From the point of view of later analysis in this study, this means that the area of residence of the families is not simply an expression of their preferences.

All this affects the social composition of each public housing project. The length of time different kinds of families remain in the projects also affects the composition of the project. We have seen that fatherless families tend to remain in public housing projects longer than do complete families. The analysis also indicates that their reasons for remaining are similar to their reasons for entering in the first place. They continue to weigh the relative merits of their housing alternatives and generally find the public housing alternatives relatively attractive.

The respondents in the panel survey, after about one year's residence in public housing, used certain phrases in expressing their satisfaction. The husbandless mothers referred again and again to the apartment being economical, not being so crowded, the child having a room of his or her own, and of the child having friends nearby and being able to have them visit. Whatever misgivings there may be about some of the areas, for many, the apartments are an improvement. As one husbandless mother said, "I love this apartment, I just wish I could take it and move it somewhere else."

The cross-sectional survey provides some further data on the relative merits of public housing for fatherless families.

The average rent per room, per month, for fatherless families in public housing is $13.04, while in the neighborhoods it is $19.74; among the complete families it is $13.74 and $19.64, respectively.

For a variety of reasons, then, poor husbandless mothers find tenancy in public housing a less objectionable choice than other alternatives. We have seen little evidence that the selection of this housing alternative and the associated conditions is an expression of values and patterns of a subcultural form intergenerationally transmitted. It is true that education is positively associated with shorter tenure in public housing and educational attainment is positively associated with socioeconomic status of the mothers' family-of-origin. But the linkages are weak enough, and so many other forces affect each factor, that the overall connection between family-of-origin and type of housing occupied is small.

6. Work, Welfare, and Other Income Sources

IF THERE is a subculture of poverty, poor families should choose ways of getting money which keep the family in poverty. The choice should express values and predispositions held by persons in poverty and those values and predispositions should have been acquired from the experiences of their early years. Insofar as we find that we can account for the sources of income selected by poor families in terms of contemporary opportunities and constraints, the subcultural explanation of the maintenance and perpetuation of poverty will be weakened.

The examination of these issues in this chapter will be focused upon female-headed families. As discussed in Chapter 3, about half of the fatherless families in the population studied and in the nation as a whole are poor.[1] The alterna-

1. Mollie Orshansky, "Counting the Poor: Another Look at the Poverty Profile, "*Social Security Bulletin*, XXVIII (January, 1965), Table 11, as reprinted in *Poverty in America*, Louis A. Ferman, Joyce L. Kornbluh, and Alan Haber, eds. (Ann Arbor: The University of Michigan Press, 1965), pp. 42-48.

tive sources of income are circumscribed and some limit them to poverty. Yet about half of the families are at least somewhat above the poverty line. Fatherless families in which the mother earns a decent income, has adequate insurance, alimony payments, or investments, or has relatives or friends who can well support the family avoid poverty. Otherwise, the family is wholly or partly dependent upon public assistance and that provides only a subsistence income. The main concern of this chapter is to examine the choice most husbandless mothers must make to meet the financial needs of their families: earn money or accept public assistance benefits. This is a central issue in a consideration of the subculture of poverty. Do families depend upon public assistance as a way of life which is intergenerationally transmitted, or is it a choice made out of desperation arising from contemporary circumstances? We will seek answers to that question in this and the next chapter. In later chapters we will consider the consequences of one or another choice.

Secure Income

The absence of a husband does not necessarily mean that the fatherless family is destitute and must depend either upon the mother's employment or upon public assistance. Social security, private pensions, investments, or alimony, alone or in combination, may provide an adequate, secure income for a fatherless family. Not all husbandless mothers are equally bereft of such secure income. If the former husband earned a high income, the family he has left—by death or divorce—is likely to be decently provided for. Such husbandless mothers need not face the hard choice between welfare or employment; but most husbandless mothers do face this choice. The earnings of the former husband is not the only determinant of having some secure income.

In large part, the type, number, and proportion of fatherless families with secure income reflects the level of social

Also see James N. Morgan, Martin H. David, Wilbur J. Cohen and Harvey E. Brazer, *Income and Welfare in the United States* (New York: McGraw-Hill, 1962), Table 16.3.

security programs. The growth in coverage and size of benefits of the programs has altered the composition of husbandless families dependent upon public assistance. Social security programs provide benefits for the widow and children but not for the divorced, separated, or deserted mother and her children. Consequently, widows and their children make up a shrinking proportion of fatherless families receiving public assistance. Federal grants-in-aid to match state payments for ADC benefits began in 1936. Death of one of the parents was the most important cause for AFDC dependency at that time. By 1948, death was the cause in 24 per cent of the cases and by 1960, in fewer than 11 per cent of the AFDC cases.[2]

In addition, the growth of private insurance plans increasingly can provide secure income for widows and their children. A general rise in the level of income and secure employment would also make available income for the divorced and separated mothers and their children. If the former husband earns a decent income, he is at least able to provide some support for his former family.

In any given year, whether or not a fatherless family has any secure income largely depends upon how the family was disrupted and the occupational level of the former husband. Thus, widows, more than other husbandless mothers, have some secure income. Among the widowed and the divorced, the higher the earnings of the former husbands, the more likely are the husbandless mothers to have some secure income. The proportion of the husbandless mothers receiving such income and its amount, however, is very low. The data presented refer only to husbandless mothers who are not maternal surrogates.

Government and private insurance benefits are generally available only to widows and their children. In the cross-sectional sample, 55 per cent of the widows report receiving some such income in the year preceding the interview.[3] The other basic source of money is alimony and sup-

2. M. Elaine Burgess and Daniel O. Price, *An American Dependency Challenge* (Chicago, Ill.: American Public Welfare Association, 1963), p. 190.

3. In a study of 80 female-headed families in a Boston, low-income area, of the 11 widows, 73 per cent received social security benefits. See Sydney E. Bernard, "The Economic and Social Adjustment of Low-Income Fe-

port payments from the separated or divorced husband. Only about 20 per cent of the separated and 30 per cent of the divorced mothers received such income. The few unwed mothers in the sample received no insurance benefits nor support money from the father of their children.

Among the divorced and separated husbandless mothers, alimony and support payments vary with the income of the former spouse. Among husbandless mothers whose former spouses earned less than $4,000 a year at the time of the marital disruption, only 20 per cent received income from the husband and only 10 per cent of them received more than $1,000 a year. Among the husbandless mothers whose former spouses earned $4,000 or more, 39 per cent received some such income and 31 per cent received more than $1,000 a year. A man earning very little money is unable to make any substantial contribution to his former family's maintenance. Furthermore, it is difficult to enforce legal claims even for small contributions. Men of low occupational status can make themselves difficult to find and evade court-directed claims. Thus, of the former husbands whose occupations were of a socioeconomic index of 13 or lower, none paid any alimony or support money.

None of the husbandless mothers in the sample had savings or investments which provided any income. Although a majority of the widowed received some secure income, they constitute less than 20 per cent of the husbandless mothers in the cross-sectional sample. On the whole, then, few husbandless mothers have substantial secure income. Two-thirds of them received none at all; 9 per cent received less than $500; 18 per cent received between $500 and $1,999; and only 6 per cent received $2,000 or more in the 12 months preceding the interview. Even this small variation in secure income, we shall see, affects the likelihood of getting income from working rather than from public assistance programs.

Although nearly all the husbandless mothers in the sample

---

male-Headed Families" (The Florence Heller Graduate School of Advanced Studies in Social Welfare, Brandeis University, 1964; mimeographed) p. 121. The lower percentage in the study reported upon here may be attributable to a generally lower occupational status of the former husbands of the mothers in the Syracuse sample.

lack a substantial secure income, some may still have another alternative to working or depending upon public assistance. They might rely upon boyfriends, parents or other relatives for financial support. We did not ask the respondents about assistance from boyfriends. Consequently, we cannot estimate the percentage of the respondents who received such aid nor the size of the aid. There is no evidence from the interview data nor the participant observer data, however, that would indicate that such assistance, when it is given, is more than a minor supplement to other sources of income.[4] Financial aid from relatives is reported by only 5 per cent of the husbandless mothers and even among these none received as much as $500 in the year before the interview. They probably do not have wealthy relatives who can provide funds sufficient to raise the fatherless families beyond the level at which they could be supported by public assistance. Even discounting support from relatives, husbandless mothers need not choose only between working or depending upon public assistance. They may combine these sources of income in varying proportions or use one or both to supplement whatever secure income they have.

CONTEMPORY CIRCUMSTANCES AND CHOICE OF ALTERNATIVE

In this chapter, our major concern is to account for the husbandless mothers' choice between employment and public assistance. To do this, we will consider the determinants of each. The two are not mutually exclusive and exhaustive; but to make them at least exhaustive we will sometimes consider the income derived from earnings as a percentage of the income derived only from public assistance and earnings. What complicates the matter is that these sources of income are not independent. Earnings are subtracted from public assistance benefits. For some analytic purposes, this is advan-

4. In the Boston study of female-headed families, half of the mothers reported having a boyfriend. About one-quarter of the mothers reported receiving more than $75 a year from boyfriends; but apparently, the amount received was generally not large (Bernard, *op. cit.*, p. 131).

tageous: we can consider choosing employment to replace public assistance benefits as indicative of evaluations of working and of assistance somewhat separately from purely economic considerations.

Even secure income is not always independent of other sources of income. Thus, at the time of the survey, husbandless mothers earning more than $1,700 a year lost a dollar from their survivor's benefits under social security for every dollar earned. For earnings between $1,200 and $1,700, they lost one dollar for every two dollars earned; earnings below $1,200 did not affect their benefits. The fact that some sources of secure income are not independent of earnings makes for difficulties in analysis, but that is the nature of the world in which the fatherless families live.

Let us consider how some of these sources of income are actually related among the husbandless mothers in the sample. From what has been said, one would expect to find a high inverse relationship between the amount of earnings from employment and the amount of income from public assistance. This is the case; the correlation between the two is -.58 (Pearson product moment correlation). The amount of secure income should also be inversely correlated with the amount of money received from public assistance; the correlation is -.37 (Pearson product moment correlation).

The amount of secure income, however, is not correlated with the amount of earnings. Two opposing consequences of secure income are operating. If the secure income is large enough, employment is not necessary. But a lesser amount of secure income can encourage employment. To test this idea we can see how secure income is related to earned income as a percentage of only earned income and welfare income combined. This excludes persons who depend only upon secure income. Now we find a moderate positive relationship between secure income and earned income (.28, Pearson product moment correlation). The findings are presented in tabular form in Table 6.1. Having some secure income makes employment economically reasonable. If a husbandless mother has some dependable income, her earnings can be combined with this other income to yield more money than would public assistance benefits. If she has no secure income, the chances of earning enough money to place her above the levels of welfare payments are decreased. This interpretation is supported by other findings. Mothers who have some secure income are more likely to work part-time than are those with none; but there is no relationship between secure income and full-time employment. Presumably, in the latter case, some of the full-time workers are earning so much that they cannot collect any money from the secure sources; others without secure income have taken employment which yields enough money to make welfare dependence unnecessary; and some others do combine secure income with full-time employment and even with welfare benefits.

*Table 6.1 Per Cent Earned Income by Amount of Secure Income**

Per Cent of Earned Income	Secure Income None	Secure Income Some
0	48.8	25.0
1–99	12.8	16.7
100	38.4	58.3
Totals %	100.0	100.0
(N)	(86)	(36)

* Maternal surrogates excluded; the husbandless mothers are the natural mothers of their children.

The full interpretation of these relationships must depend upon the consideration of other circumstances and of predispositional characteristics. That will be done. What is particularly intriguing thus far is the indication that even some secure income encourages employment, rather than dependence upon public assistance.

The income sources which a husbandless mother combines to support her family depends upon a variety of circumstances. The number and age of her children are particularly important circumstances. Having several children or having a preschool child makes employment difficult. A mother, particularly one without a husband, finds it very difficult to earn money outside of the home.[5] A few husbandless mothers earn some money by caring for other mothers' children while taking care of their own in their own homes. Day-care centers for three- and four-year-olds, where available, facilitate employment. On the whole, under present conditions, having young children is an important handicap to employment. As can be seen in Table 6.2, among husbandless mothers who have no children under 11 years of age and who receive at least $500 in secure income, more than 80 per cent are

Table 6.2 Percentage of Husbandless Mothers Presently Employed or Employed During the Preceding Year by Age of Children and by Secure Income*

Amount of Secure Income	*Age of Youngest Child* Less than 6	6–10	11–18
Less than $500	37.2 (43)	50.0 (22)	71.4 (35)
$500 or more	50.0 (12)	57.2 (7)	83.4 (12)

* Maternal surrogates excluded.

working or had worked in the preceding year. At the other extreme, among mothers who have preschool children and little or no secure income, only 37 per cent are or were employed.

The child-care responsibilities entailed by having many children interferes with employment. Furthermore, the more children in the family, the greater are the financial require-

5. Of course husbandless mothers are under much greater financial pressure to work than are married mothers and therefore are much more likely to be in the labor force. The age of the children, however, makes more difference for employment among husbandless than among married mothers. Thus, in March, 1962, in the nation as a whole, among married mothers living with their husbands, 42 per cent of those with children 6 to 17 only were in the labor force; of those with children 3 to 5 years old, 28 per cent were in the labor force, and of those with children under 3, 18 per cent were in the labor force. Among widowed, divorced, or separated women, the

ments. Public assistance benefits rise with each child, but this is not so for earnings from a job. Consequently, a mother of many children would have to earn much more than a mother of one or two children to make employment as economically rational. We find that among husbandless mothers with only one child, 83 per cent are or were employed during the preceding year; among those with 6 or more children, none worked. Among married mothers, the corresponding percentages are 51 and 24. For married mothers the number of children is not as severe a barrier to employment since the husband can help in child care; furthermore, her earnings can supplement the earnings of her husband. Among the husbandless, employment would not supplement her public assistance benefits, but replace them. Thus, in this sample, all the husbandless mothers with six or more minor children are entirely dependent upon welfare benefits; but among those with only one child, 11 per cent receive some welfare benefits and only 15 per cent are entirely dependent upon public assistance.

In this sample, the number of children a mother has is highly related to the age of her children: if she has many children, she is almost certain to have preschool age children. As we shall note later, both age and number of children are each independently related to welfare dependence and to earnings as a percentage of welfare and earnings income. The number of children, we shall see, is a more important determinant of the sources of income used to support the family than is the age of the children.

Thus far, children have been considered a circumstance. It might be argued, however, that having many children is part of the subculture of poverty and that husbandless mothers have children in order to receive AFDC benefits. A variety of evidence is counter to the argument. For example, if children

---

percentages were 69, 50, and 29 respectively. Computed from Jacob Schiffman, "Marital and Family Characteristics of Workers, March, 1962," *Monthly Labor Review*, (January, 1963), Table G, as cited in Herman Miller, *Rich Man, Poor Man* (New York: New American Library, 1965), p. 201. Also see F. Ivan Nye and Lois Hoffman, "The Socio-Cultural Setting," in F. Ivan Nye and Lois Wladis Hoffman, eds., *The Employed Mother in America* (Chicago: Rand McNally, 1963), p. 13.

were borne in order to maintain and increase assistance benefits, then one would expect husbandless mothers to remain on the welfare roles for a very long time. In a national study of closed AFDC cases, however, the median length of the time payments were received was less than two years.[6] In a study of the AFDC program in Cook County (Chicago), Illinois, the average length of time on AFDC was found to be 3 years.[7]

The number of children born in a family before the marital union is broken and the number born before marriage or after marital disruption may be related to a subculture of poverty or to some of the circumstances associated with poverty. There seems to be no evidence that husbandless mothers desire to have illegitimate children.[8] Other circumstances of their lives and their values and beliefs may increase the chances of this occurring, but that does not mean that they choose to have illegitimate children in order to remain dependent upon welfare and to make it socially acceptable not to work. In any case, at any given time, the children constitute part of the circumstances facing a husbandless mother.

The findings thus far indicate that husbandless mothers want and achieve independence from welfare when circumstances make this possible and the number and age of her children are important circumstances in this regard. Consider Mrs. Smith. She is separated and has four children ranging from 10 years to 19 months; she is a high school graduate whose father was a toolmaker of western European origin. Asked what her hopes and wishes for the future were, she answered that she wanted her children raised and "then I want my independence; I was never cut out to be a mother, believe me." Yet she does not want to work because "I wouldn't be there when the children needed me and I worry too much." So, even though the mother role is not attractive to her, she feels she cannot relinquish a part of it. Perhaps

6. Burgess and Price, *op. cit.*, p. 51.
7. Arthur Greenleigh and Hazel S. McCalley, "Facts, Fallacies and Future: A Study of the Aid to Dependent Children Program of Cook County, Illinois" (New York: Greenleigh Associates, 1960; mimeographed), p. 15.
8. *Ibid.*, p. 19.

the anxiety it involves for her makes the role unpleasant as well as difficult to reduce. The beliefs and feelings about the maternal role may be an important set of predispositions affecting employment, independent of circumstances. We will turn to that possibility after considering the possible role of other circumstances.

Responsibility for children is a condition which may interact with other circumstances to affect the choice of employment rather than welfare dependence. The fatherless family may live with relatives or friends who can assume some of the child-care responsibility. It is true that among husbandless mothers with at least one preschool child, those living with another adult are much more likely to work full-time than are those living without another adult (67 per cent compared to 17 per cent). But in this sample there are only three mothers with a preschool child who live in a household with another adult. Among mothers with older children, there is no difference in employment between mothers living with or without another adult. Living with another adult does not necessarily free the husbandless mother for employment. She may be baby-sitting for the other adult who is employed or it may simply provide a way of economizing on the limited financial resources available to her.

Care for children may also be purchased. The mother's employment, however, must yield enough money to make this feasible and worthwhile. Even more basically, employment is not an option unless there are jobs which a husbandless mother can obtain. It seems reasonable to expect that the more education a woman has, the higher paying employment she can find; it is not as certain, however, that higher education makes more jobs available for a husbandless mother. In any case, the more education husbandless mothers have, the more likely they are to be or to have been employed within the preceding year. This is particularly marked among mothers whose youngest child is either under six or 11 or older. Thus among mothers of preschoolers, 18 per cent of those with 8 or fewer years of schooling are or were employed; 29 per cent of those with 9-11 years of schooling worked, and 71 per cent of those who completed 12 or more years of schooling are or were employed. Among married mothers, education is related to employment to a much smaller degree.[9] The lack of relationship is due to the fact that among the married mothers with low education employment is relatively high, compared to similar husbandless mothers. This, too, is consistent with the interpretation made thus far. Married mothers with low education can take jobs which do not have to yield enough money to equal what the welfare benefits would be plus payment for baby sitting; the money they earn is an addition to their husbands' earnings.

I wish to consider one other circumstance before examining predispositional factors. Relatives, friends, and neighbors may have strong opinions about the propriety of accepting welfare benefits and of a mother working. Such opinions may constitute a normative climate which increases the social cost of choosing one or another alternative. This might be an important aspect of the world of poverty. The poor may think that welfare dependence is no shame, possibly even an estimable way of gaining an income. Consequently, working rather than taking care of one's children would be considered unworthy.

The study provides some data to examine these possibilities. All the respondents were asked if they think better or worse of someone if "a mother works instead of staying home with her children" and if "someone gets welfare or help from charity." In addition to responses of "better" or "worse," responses of "no different," or "depends" were coded. Only about 5 per cent of *all* the mothers said they would think worse of someone if he or she received welfare benefits. The overwhelming majority said it would make no difference in how they thought of the person and about one-third said it would depend. Even fewer said they would think better of such a person than said they would think worse. Significantly, this distribution does not differ by economic status, including the middle-income married mothers.

On the other hand, a sizeable minority of the mothers, about one-quarter, said they would think worse of a mother if

9. Also see Nye and Hoffman, *op. cit.*, p. 11.

she worked rather than stayed home and took care of her children. About one-third said it would make no difference and another third said it would depend. Again, this distribution does not vary by economic status.

Clearly, the normative pressure against a mother's employment is greater than the pressure against accepting welfare benefits. This is consistent with public policy. Welfare programs such as AFDC are intended to make it possible for mothers to stay home and rear their children rather than leave the home for employment. At the same time, the level of normative pressure *against* a mother's employment is not great. Apparently mothers' employment is common enough, and conditions requiring it sufficiently in line with other values, that we do not find widespread condemnation of it. Finally, there is no evidence that the poverty stricken are particularly supportive of accepting public assistance and condeming employment.

The findings from a study of 80 female-headed families in a low-income Boston neighborhood also bear on this question. On the basis of four interviews, all comments regarding AFDC were considered in coding general orientations toward public assistance. Three categories were distinguished: (1) public assistance as an alternative preferable to working or relying on a husband, (2) public assistance as an acceptable alternative, although they would prefer a husband or employment if available, and (3) public assistance as a last resort, tolerated only if they had no other resources. Even in the population studied, only 10 per cent of the mothers were considered to fall in the first category, while 64 per cent and 26 per cent were considered to fall in the second and third categories, respectively.[10]

All this indicates that the collective or aggregate normative pressure is not likely to be an important determinant of husbandless mothers deciding to work or to accept public assistance. This is not to say that at the individual level, mothers who feel that accepting public assistance is wrong will not tend to find other sources of income or that mothers who feel

10. Bernard, *op. cit.*, p. 79-81.

that leaving their children in order to work outside the home is wrong will not tend to accept public assistance rather than accept employment. These possibilities bring us into the realm of attitudinal factors as possible influences regarding the choice of alternative ways of financially supporting the family.

Attitudes and Choice of Alternatives

The evidence presented thus far indicates that circumstances of the husbandless mother are highly related to her choice of alternative ways of supporting her family. Since, on the whole, the circumstances are external and not easily affected by her employment, it is reasonable to argue that the circumstances affect choosing between employment or public assistance. More specifically, husbandless mothers tend to work if they are in circumstances which permit employment and which make employment a way of earning more than the low income public assistance would provide. This presumes certain values: that public assistance is to be avoided if possible or at least that the low income which dependence upon public assistance entails is to be avoided. Not that working rather than caring for children is positively valued; caring for the children is undoubtedly a primary value. Care, however, also includes providing a decent income. If the children are old enough that maternal attention and supervision is not needed for most of the day, employment is possible and even desired.

This reasoning and evidence, however, does not completely account for the choices which husbandless mothers make. Variations in predispositions may contribute further in accounting for the mothers' choices of alternative ways of supporting their families. A consideration of predispositional variables will test further the possible role of cultural processes in the way of life of the poor. Such a consideration can also serve as a check upon the previous interpretations. Finally, a review of attitudinal variables should precede an examination of the consequences of one or another choice.

In general, mothers who feel more condemnatory of

someone working rather than taking care of her children are somewhat less likely to work and are more likely to depend upon public assistance than are other mothers. For example, among husbandless mothers who say they feel no different about someone if she works than takes care of her children, 38 per cent work full-time while among husbandless mothers who say they think worse of such a woman, 29 per cent are working full-time. Moreover, the relationship is about the same among married mothers. This feeling about working mothers is not related to contemporary circumstances or general background characteristics such as education, race, or former husband's occupational status. This feeling seems to be a relatively independent predisposition which affects the choice between working or accepting public assistance. The contribution which such a feeling makes does very under different circumstances. Thus, among husbandless mothers, it is among those with no children under 11 that the association between this feeling and working is greatest. For example, among these women, of those who say they would not think differently of a mother if she worked, 69 per cent are working full-time; of those who say they would think worse of such a mother, only 31 per cent are working full-time. This feeling, then, acts as a constraint among husbandless mothers who would otherwise be able to be employed.

Feelings about the acceptance of public assistance are related to alternative ways of supporting the family in a more complex manner than are feelings about a mother working. It is true that among husbandless mothers those who condemn someone for receiving public assistance tend to work and not to receive public assistance. However, among married mothers there is no relationship between these feelings and working or accepting public assistance. Among the husbandless, as I have argued previously, supporting the family usually requires a choice between accepting public assistance or employment. In that case, feelings about accepting public assistance are relevant to the choice. Married mothers do not usually face the same choice and feelings about accepting public assistance would not be relevant.

The relationship among husbandless mothers between employment and evaluations of someone who accepts public welfare can be interpreted in different ways. It may be that some people are indifferent to accepting public assistance and therefore themselves do so. On the other hand, it may be that contemporary circumstances largely determine the choice of employment versus public assistance, and that feelings about welfare dependency play no independent role; that is, husbandless mothers who accept public assistance *become* indifferent to doing so. Or, it may be that the conditions which largely determine becoming dependent upon public assistance also determine the person's evaluations about others doing so. With the data available, it is impossible to definitively choose among such interpretations. But it is important to consider alternative explanations with the available data because the interpretation bears directly upon some of the theoretical and substantive issues of major concern in this book.

First, evaluations about accepting public assistance are related to some of the same circumstances that affect whether or not husbandless mothers work. For example, husbandless mothers with younger children are less likely than those with older children to say that "it depends," or that they would think worse of someone who accepted public welfare. Thus, it seems that the conditions that lead a husbandless mother to depend upon public assistance also tend to make her more tolerant of someone who does. In other words, she can understand what might make a mother dependent upon public assistance and therefore she is less likely to judge harshly someone who does.

Background characteristics such as former husband's occupational status, education, and race are also somewhat related to evaluations of accepting public welfare. This suggests that the evaluations have some independence of contemporary circumstances. However, some of these background characteristics are themselves related to husbandless mothers accepting public assistance rather than employment. Taking all this into account in a regression analysis, discussed in more detail later, it appears that evaluations of someone accepting public assistance do not help account for husbandless mothers themselves being dependent upon public assistance. Nearly everyone is tolerant, in varying degrees, of accepting public assistance. The variations in such tolerance are not linked to socioeconomic status so that they help account for welfare dependence. Rather, it is living in circumstances which seem to compel such dependence, or oneself becoming dependent, that increases the tolerance.

The choice of family support through public assistance rather than employment may reflect a willingness to accept a very low standard of living. People differ in their willingness to accept such a low standard. This is difficult to measure directly, but presumably, people who have lived in poverty would be more likely to accept such a standard of living than would persons who previously had a relatively high standard of living. In the case of husbandless mothers, this is particularly clear. A husbandless mother who had a high socioeconomic status before her marriage was broken would be strongly motivated to maintain a high standard of living. A husbandless mother whose former husband had low socioeconomic status may find that dependence upon public assistance gives her a higher regular income than she previously had. For example, one divorced mother, who is dependent upon AFDC, commented about her former husband:

> He was like a grasshopper in his jobs—three months here and never happy or satisfied—hopped from one job to another. So consequently, we were on unemployment more than—or relief—more than we were on a weekly paycheck. It always turned out that when time came for shoes or for clothing, one or the other grandmother was handy. So in all fairness, all the way around, I've got to say my husband never supported me. He worked when he felt like it, and he gave me money when he felt like it and paid the rent when he felt like it. You can't say that he married me and we had a family and he gave me a paycheck every week so that I could, like other women, go to the grocery store and get haircuts for the children, 'cause it wasn't so. Now it's like that, it wasn't then.[11]

11. The quotation was reported by one of the participant observers from one of the public housing projects. Cited in Helen Icken Safa, "Profiles in Poverty: An Analysis of Social Mobility in Low-Income Families" (Syracuse University Youth Development Center, 1966; mimeographed), p. 44.

In the sample as a whole, husbandless mothers whose spouses had relatively high occupational status tend to work and not accept public assistance. The relationship is a moderate one and it is stronger among husbandless mothers with little or no secure income than among those with a substantial secure income (see Table 6.3). Earlier, I argued that having some secure income made the choice of employment rather than assistance economically reasonable. The fact that former economic status is particularly important among those with little or no secure income indicates that high former status has produced expectations about a standard of living

Table 6.3 Percentage of Husbandless Mothers Presently Employed or Employed During the Preceding Year by Former Husband's Status and by Secure Income*

Amount of Secure Income	*Former Husband's Occupational Status†*	
	Low	*High*
Less than $500	37.5 (48)	67.4 (43)
$500 or more	58.3 (12)	63.3 (15)

* Maternal surrogates excluded.
† Occupational status rated according to Otis Dudley Duncan's socioeconomic Index for occupations; *low* refers to occupations with an index of 18 or lower and *high* refers to occupations with an index of 19 or higher.

which is a strong incentive for working rather than living at the poverty level which dependence upon public assistance entails.

Another explanation needs to be considered. Perhaps husbandless mothers whose former spouses had relatively high occupational status tend to have the skills and social contacts which facilitate finding employment that is sufficiently remunerative to warrant their employment. The socioeconomic status of the husbandless mothers' former spouses is directly related to the mothers' educational level. Possibly the relationship between former status and employment is due to the mothers' educational level or it is possible that their educational level may account for the previously noted relationship between educational level and employment. Actually, both educational level and socioeconomic status of the former spouse each have some relationship to employment; but there is an interaction effect. As can be seen in Table 6.4, one out of five of the husbandless mothers who had a high former status and at least completed high school were employed; a majority of those who had high status and some high school or had low status and at least completed high school worked; other mothers were not likely to do so.

Table 6.4. Percentage of Husbandless Mothers Presently Employed or Employed During the Preceding Year by Former Husband's Status and by Education*

	Former Husbands' Occupational Status	
Mother's Education	*Low*	*High*
8 years or less	45.0 (20)	36.4 (11)
9–11 years	34.6 (26)	53.3 (15)
12 or more years	56.3 (16)	81.2 (32)

* Maternal surrogates excluded.

If subcultural processes help account for the choice of ways female heads support their families, we would expect that characteristics of their family-of-origin would be related to the alternatives selected. The socioeconomic status of the family-of-origin is best indicated by the socioeconomic status of the fathers' occupations. This turns out to be unrelated to whether or not the husbandless mother is employed or to how much she earns. It is slightly related, however, to the amount of money coming from public assistance (Pearson product moment correlation: -.15). The socioeconomic status of the family-of-origin contributes little to accounting for the choice of financial support for female-headed families. This is surprising, since it is moderately related to some conditions and predispositions associated with the financial alternative selected. The socioeconomic status of the husbandless mothers' fathers is associated with the husbandless mothers' education (.33), former husbands' occupational status (.19), number of children (-.10), and condemnation of accepting welfare (.19, all Pearson product moment correlation coefficients).

The race of the husbandless mothers might also be indicative of a subculture relevant to the choice of financial support selected. But race is not associated with employment, amount of earnings, amount of welfare, or of earnings as a percentage of income from welfare and earnings. As for socioeconomic status, race is associated with some of the conditions related to the kind of financial support which the fatherless families have taken; but it is not related to condemnation of accepting welfare. Apparently the associations are too small to produce even a spurious relationship between race and the alternatives taken. Presumably, this reflects some of the peculiarities of the sample. But this means that if proper controls were applied in any sample living under similar conditions, we would not find that race contributed importantly to an explanation of the kind of financial support fatherless families select.[12]

One other characteristic of the family-of-origin about which information was collected deserves attention. The experience of growing up in a family in which the mother worked could make a mother's employment seem admirable; it could also make it objectionable. All the respondents were asked whether or not their mother had worked for pay while they were growing up. There is no relationship between the reports about this and the respondent's evaluations of a mother working rather than taking care of her children. Presumably, the experience had opposite influences for different daughters and no influence at all for others. Regardless of feelings about the propriety of working, however, the experience may provide a model which makes employment seem feasible

12. An unpublished analysis of employment among married mothers in the panel sample was made by Grace Q. Vicary. She found that the Negro wives were much more likely than white wives to be employed, even when other variables related to employment were held constant.

and other alternatives more objectionable. Indeed, having had a working mother is negatively associated with the amount of income received from welfare sources and positively associated with the amount of earnings and earnings as a percentage of welfare and earned income.

Whether or not the respondents own mothers worked is not correlated with their fathers' socioeconomic status, race, or education in this sample. Consequently, this modeling process cannot be used to help account for any subcultural pattern of welfare dependence. The association between having had a working mother and choosing one rather than another means of supporting a fatherless family indicates that certain experiences in the family of orientation do affect later-life patterns of behavior. But the connection is quite specific and does not necessarily influence what might be thought to be related attitudes.

Relative Contribution of Determinants of Alternative Sources of Income Support

Thus far we have considered several possible determinants of alternative ways in which fatherless families may be financially supported. We have suggested which determinants are more or less important, but only crudely. In order to assess the relative importance of the determinants considered, we have used a regression analysis.[13] Although some of the variables do not meet all the statistical requirements for use in a regression analysis, I feel that a cautious interpretation of the results, in conjunction with the other statistical analyses made, will be helpful. From the regression analysis we will examine the Beta coefficients and the F ratios. The Beta coefficients indicate the extent to which a given variable accounts for the variance of a given dependent variable, taking into account all the other variables included

13. The multiple regression analysis was done using the TSAR IVAN data processing program developed at Duke University. For an explanation of the regression analysis see Karl A. Fox and Mordecai Ezekiel, 3rd ed., *Methods of Correlation and Regression Analysis, Linear and Curvilinear* (New York: Wiley, 1959).

*Table 6.5. Characteristics Used to Explain Alternative Sources of Financial Support**

Characteristics	*Amount of Welfare*		*Amount of Earnings*		*Earnings as a Percent of Welfare and Earnings*	
	Relative Importance (Beta coefficients)	*Significance (F ratios)*	*Relative Importance (Beta coefficients)*	*Significance (F ratios)*	*Relative Importance (Beta coefficients)*	*Significance (F ratios)*
Secure income	-.435	24.36	-.002	0.00	.284	9.00
Number of children	.450	22.03	-.260	5.76	-.299	8.48
Age of children	.038	0.15	.167	2.41	.175	2.92
Other adults in household	-.066	0.54	.016	0.02	.065	0.46
Education	.045	0.02	.202	3.71	.176	3.10
Condemn accepting welfare	.065	0.48	.082	0.61	.062	0.39
Condemn mother working	.133	2.55	-.180	3.65	-.113	1.57
Former husband's occupational status	-.186	4.45	.087	0.77	.108	1.31
Father's occupational status	-.107	1.40	-.071	0.49	-.074	0.58
Race	.024	0.61	-.094	0.76	-.077	0.58
Own mother worked	-.155	3.13	.100	1.04	.134	2.07
Multiple r	.656		.515		.612	
(N)	(100)		(100)		(95)	

* Maternal surrogates excluded.

in the regression analysis. The F ratios indicate the statistical significance of the Beta coefficients; with the number of cases and variables in the regression analysis, an F ratio of 1.8 or higher is significant at the .05 level and an F ratio of 2.8 is significant at the .001 level.

In Table 6.5 the Beta coefficients and F ratios are presented for the characteristics previously discussed and three dependent variables: amount of welfare, amount of earnings, and earnings as a percentage of welfare and earnings. We are most interested in examining the determinants of the latter variable. Earnings as a percentage of welfare and earnings summarizes the choice which is of most concern here. The degree to which the 11 characteristics considered account for the variance in this dependent variable is indicated by the multiple correlation presented at the bottom of the table. The multiple r is .612; and the amount of variance accounted for is given by r^2; that is, a little more than one-third of the variance is accounted for by the characteristics considered. Obviously, many other characteristics are important. Thus, the mothers' health, stamina, and general energy level probably are important determinants of whether they work or depend upon welfare. Probably, too, the mothers' knowledge of and access to jobs they could profitably hold varies and helps account for the variation in earnings as a percent of welfare and earnings. In addition, using a straight linear regression and treating each characteristic independently also reduces the amount of variance explained. Thus, earlier we noted that the socioeconomic status of the former spouse and the mother's education interacted in affecting employment. In this regression analysis, however, we wish to consider each characteristic separately to assess the relative importance of each.

In terms of the issues of central concern in this book, the results are clear. Contemporary circumstances have a particularly important effect upon the alternative sources of income chosen by the husbandless mothers. Characteristics pertaining to a subculture of low socioeconomic status seems to contribute little or no explanatory power. Among the contemporary circumstances, secure income and the number and age of children explain a relatively large amount of the variance in earnings as a percentage of welfare and earnings. The regression analyses are consistent with the interpretations made earlier. Secure income and number of children are very important in accounting for the amount of welfare received in the preceding year, while the number and age of children are relatively important in accounting for the amount of earnings. Presumably having very young children is a handicap for employment, as are having many children, but a large number of children makes employment a less rational solution to the problem of supporting the family than depending upon welfare. The less secure income one has, the more dependent one is upon welfare, but secure income makes employment reasonable for some, while it makes employment unnecessary if it is large enough.

Education of the mother contributes significantly in accounting for earnings as a percentage of earnings and welfare. The analysis presented earlier suggested that education probably has this effect because it makes possible the holding of jobs which make employment economically competitive with welfare dependence and not because it indicates status considerations regarding accepting public welfare.[14] This interpretation is supported by the finding that education does not help account for the amount of welfare received and does help account for the amount of earnings.

The socioeconomic status of the former spouse contributes markedly in accounting for the amount of income derived from public welfare sources, but not for the amount of earnings, and very little for earnings as a percentage of income from welfare and earnings. Apparently, the former socioeconomic status provides a bench mark so that dependence upon welfare can be an acceptable alternative for someone of previously low status, and unacceptable or unnecessary if the former status was high.

Since education and socioeconomic status of the former

14. This interpretation is buttressed by the finding that education is only slightly, and negatively associated with desire to work. This is true among husbandless and among married mothers.

spouse have some explanatory power, one would expect the same to be true of general background characteristics such as the socioeconomic status of the family-of-origin and race. Yet these characteristics do not help account for the variance in earnings as a percentage of welfare and earnings. Apparently, too many other specific circumstances intervene for these general characteristics to have any significant effect. Whatever effect they may have is explicable in terms of more contemporary and specific characteristics. All this argues against the idea that a general subculture of poverty exists which accounts for choosing to be dependent upon welfare rather than seek employment. Consistent with this interpretation, we do not find that evaluations of accepting welfare help account for the variance in earnings as a percentage of welfare and earnings.

This is not meant to argue that no intergenerational processes are relevant for the issue under discussion. Conceptions of the maternal role, particularly in regard to employment, apparently do play some explanatory part. These conceptions presumably are formed, in some degree, by early socialization experiences. They do not appear, however, to be part of a subculture of poverty; the variations in the conceptions seem to be distributed independently of the socioeconomic status of the family-of-origin, at least in the population studied here.

Conclusions

On the whole, the evidence supports the interpretation that there is no comprehensive subculture of poverty which accounts for husbandless mothers choosing to be dependent upon public welfare rather than upon their own employment. We have seen some evidence that intergenerational processes do affect this choice. Presumably experiences in the family-of-origin affect certain aspects of the mothers' conception of the maternal role and employment. Such aspects, however, are not associated with the socioeconomic status of the family-of-origin.

The socioeconomic status of the mothers in the more immediate past is somewhat related to the choice of financial support. Thus, the mothers' education seem to affect the opportunity for finding a job which makes employment worthwhile; the former husbands' occupational status seem to affect the desire to have income beyond the poverty line provided by public assistance.

The evidence clearly demonstrates the great importance of contemporary situational factors in affecting the choice of financial support for the family. Yet, these conditions are associated with previous socioeconomic status. Socioeconomic status of the family-of-origin is correlated with mothers' education (.33, Pearson product moment correlation), former spouses' occupational status (.19, Pearson product moment correlation), and age of children (.14, Pearson product moment correlation). In other words, family-of-origin status affects the probability of some circumstances which in turn are related to the choice of financial support. The relationships are not very high and the intervening steps numerous; consequently, explaining the choice of alternative as an expression of the subculture of poverty is inadequate.

In Chapter 2 we considered aspects of a phenomenon which makes it explicable in terms of one set of factors and processes rather than another. In general, we argued that behavior more than values would be accounted for by contemporary conditions. Obviously, employment is behavior. It cannot be conducted without permissive conditions, even if employment is desired; on the other hand, some mothers may feel circumstances compel employment despite many contrary values and beliefs. As a matter of fact, among husbandless mothers, employment is not associated with the desire to work. Many working husbandless mothers wish they were not working and many who are not working wish they were. Among married mothers, the pressures for employment and the obstacles against it are less; consequently, there is some association between desiring to work and doing so.

Some aspects of work make it particularly susceptible to contemporary circumstances. It is an activity which can be repeated; a woman can choose to work, leave the labor force, and reenter it. At least some of the consequences of employment are clearly visible; certainly this is true of the monetary return. On the other hand, some aspects of employment make it relatively susceptible to intergenerational processes. Thus, it is not very serially independent; training in skills which would make highly remunerative employment possible are probably related to some intergenerational processes and to previous experience. Finally, employment involves many aspects of critical self-conception. Ideas about the maternal role and female employment may well depend in part upon intergenerational processes.

Within the population under study, furthermore, there appears to be less variation in relevant values and beliefs than in contemporary conditions. Husbandless mothers want to have more money than the low amount available through public assistance. The satisfaction with this amount and the strength of the desire to have more, however, probably vary and are related to some previous conditions. Thus, for husbandless mothers who had been economically deprived before the marital disruption, the public assistance allowances are more acceptable than they are to mothers who had previously had high incomes. This is one way in which poverty may be perpetuated over several years. On the basis of the analysis here, however, this is not an important determinant of the choice of financial support.

Dependence upon public welfare is not positively desired, but there is undoubtedly some variation in tolerance for accepting public assistance. Presumably, persons who know many others who are dependent upon welfare would be more willing to accept such dependence for themselves than would persons who did not know others doing so. This study does not have any evidence bearing directly on this possibility. In any case, the evidence analyzed here reveals that condemning someone for accepting public assistance does not help account for the choice of means of financial support. Furthermore, this indicator of a norm about accepting public assistances is not related to socioeconomic status.

Finally, there seems to be general adherence to the priority of caring for children rather than working. There is some variation about this and presumably it is partly related to experiences in the family-of-origin. The variation contributes something to accounting for the way the family is supported. Again, however, this variation is not related to socioeconomic status and therefore could not be an element in a subculture of poverty accounting for welfare dependency.

The variations in contemporary circumstances largely explain the choice of means of financial support. Since there is so much agreement about many of the relevant standards, this should not be surprising. People who find that employ-

Table 6.6. Per Cent of Husbandless and Married Mothers Who Have Selected Attitudes and Social Characteristics by Work Status*

	Husbandless Mothers			*Married Mothers*		
Per Cent of Mothers Who:	*Work Full-Time*	*Work Part-Time*	*Not Work*	*Work Full-Time*	*Work Part-Time*	*Not Work*
Had per capita income under $500	8.1 (37)	38.6 (31)	89.5 (57)	14.5 (48)	9.3 (96)	24.0 (200)
Had at least one preschool child	25.0 (36)	42.3 (26)	53.3 (60)	45.0 (40)	78.9 (90)	81.9 (177)
Disapprove of working mothers	11.6 (43)	21.2 (33)	25.4 (63)	10.5 (57)	23.9 (113)	32.3 (235)
Had only one child	62.8 (43)	33.3 (33)	12.5 (64)	28.1 (57)	23.5 (115)	16.0 (237)
Whose (former) (present) husband's occupational status score is 30 or more	46.2 (39)	51.7 (29)	24.6 (57)	36.4 (55)	46.8 (111)	38.3 (235)
Whose father's occupational score is over 18	56.1 (41)	48.5 (33)	37.3 (53)	39.1 (46)	55.0 (100)	43.6 (204)
Are nonwhite	46.5 (43)	30.3 (33)	53.8 (65)	35.1 (57)	30.4 (115)	24.5 (237)

* Includes maternal surrogates

ment will enable them to earn more than the welfare allowance, will tend to do so. Having some secure income, having occupational skills which are remunerative, or having few children each makes employment more rational than would be the case without these characteristics. Mothers whose child supervision responsibilities are small will tend to choose employment rather than welfare dependency; thus, having no preschool children or having only a few children is associated with employment.

Certain conditions, then, add together to make one or another choice of financial support probable. Many of these conditions are related to the family situation prior to the marital disruption. Family-of-origin experiences, however, are not of major direct relevance. Too many new conditions intervene to attenuate any relationship. When intergenerational processes play an explanatory role, they do not appear to be significantly associated with socioeconomic status nor is their explanatory role large.

Employment by husbandless mothers is not necessarily desirable. In other chapters of this book, some consequences of maternal employment will be examined. Since employed mothers do differ in many circumstances and characteristics from those who are not employed, it is necessary to keep such factors in mind and incorporate them into the analysis. In Table 6.6 some of the characteristics which have been considered are presented, by marital and employment status.

7. Intergenerational Patterns of Poverty and Broken Families

THE PERSISTENCE of poverty from one generation to another within the same families is a prerequisite for a subculture of poverty. Even intergenerational persistence of poverty does not prove the existence of a subculture, of course; other forces may keep each generation in poverty. But unless there is a high degree of intergenerational poverty, one cannot argue that a way of life is transmitted from generation to generation which helps keep people poor. In this chapter we will examine the available evidence concerning the extent of intergenerational perpetuation of poverty. Since we are especially concerned with fatherless families and poverty, we will also examine the perpetuation of broken families.

THE INTERGENERATIONAL PERSISTENCE OF POVERTY

Despite the considerable discussion of intergenerational perpetuation of poverty, the term is ambiguous. It is necessary to be clear about what the phenomenon is before trying to assess its magnitude or explain its causes. The study of occupational mobility provides a useful analogy for considering the phenomenon and suggests ways in which it may be specified. There are two ways of analyzing intergenerational occupational mobility: inflow and outflow analysis.[1] Outflow analysis means that one asks what the chances are of children of a given occupational stratum remaining in the same stratum or entering a higher or lower stratum. Inflow analysis is an inquiry of the occupational origins of persons in a given stratum. In the study of poverty, similarly, intergenerational persistence of poverty may refer to two different phenomena. First, one may point forward and say that children of poor families are likely to be poor when they grow up—that the children are doomed to live their lives in poverty. Or, one may refer back and say that poor persons generally have themselves grown up in poverty-stricken families.[2]

What is especially noteworthy is that inflow mobility need not equal outflow mobility. It would be equal if mobility were simply an exchange of persons of different origins. That is, for every son of a manual worker who became a white-collar worker, a son of a white-collar worker became a manual worker. Upon reflection, it is clear that mobility between generations can, and does, occur in other ways.[3]

A major determinant of mobility between different strata is the variation between generations in the number of positions in each stratum. For example, there may be more jobs available for white-collar workers in the sons' generation than in

1. S.M. Miller, "Comparative Social Mobility: A Trend Report," *Current Sociology*, Vol. IX, No. 1, 1960; Thomas Fox and S.M. Miller, "Intra-Country Variations: Occupational Stratification and Mobility," in *Class, Status, and Power: Social Stratification in Comparative Perspective*, 2nd. ed., Reinhard Bendix and Seymour Martin Lipset (eds.) (New York: The Free Press, 1966), pp. 574–581.

2. There is another problem in assessing the intergenerational perpetuation of poverty analogous to assessing occupational mobility. Within each generation there is some income and occupational mobility. Data are not always comparable for the two generations to be compared. Presumably, we would want information for both the parental and children's generations when they are both in their early child-rearing years.

3. For a discussion of many of the determinants, see Seymour Martin Lipset and Hans L. Zetterberg, "A Theory of Social Mobility," in Bendix and Lipset, *op. cit.*, pp. 561–573.

the fathers' generation. In that case, children of manual workers will tend to move out to white-collar jobs, but children of white-collar workers are not as likely to move out to manual jobs. Consequently, compared to the white-collar workers, manual workers' sons may disproportionally leave their stratum but the manual workers of the sons' generation may be disproportionally recruited from manual worker families.

Another factor affecting intergenerational mobility is the relative number of offspring in each stratum. For example, if white-collar worker families do not reproduce themselves, all the positions in that stratum cannot be filled by sons of that stratum, assuming no contraction in the stratum. On the other hand, if the families headed by manual workers more than reproduce themselves, at least some of their sons will move out into other strata, unless the manual stratum expands.

The rates of inflow and outflow even vary depending upon the size of the categories being studied. If one category is large and the other small, a few people leaving the small category and entering the large category will appear as a high rate of outflow from the small category and a low rate of inflow into the large category. Suppose, for example, the number of white-collar workers were small compared to the number of manual workers. Then an equal exchange of persons between these categories, between generations, could appear as a low outflow from the manual stratum and a high inflow into the white-collar ranks.

The extent of intergenerational persistence of poverty, similarly, depends upon the relative size of the poor and the nonpoor categories, changes in their relative size, and relative rates of reproduction, as well as the extent to which persons who grew up in poor families exchange positions with persons not reared in poverty. We shall examine these factors before turning to data directly dealing with the intergenerational perpetuation of poverty.

The relative size of the poor and nonpoor categories obviously depends upon the definition of poverty. Definitions can be made using various dimensions and dividing lines. Most students of the subject have used annual dollar income as the basic dimension, and that is used in this discussion.

The division between poverty and nonpoverty is usually made at what is considered a minimally adequate standard of living. The minimally adequate standard is the level at which some social services are provided without charge. What is minimally adequate, obviously, is a societal decision. Below that standard is one which has been called a minimal subsistence standard—the level at which public assistance would maintain a person. (Actual payments, however, are often below budgeted need!) The income amounts selected to define these levels vary somewhat but one set of figures may be used illustratively—these figures are the bases for the proportions of poor households cited later. In 1960 a family of four with less than $2,662 was living below the "minimum subsistence" standard and such a family would need more than $4,348 for a minimally adequate standard.[4]

What is considered subsistence and what is considered adequate certainly changes. In general, the figures have tended to rise. In making comparisons over time, one may use contemporary standards for each period compared or use a constant standard. Since poverty is societally defined and some of the consequences of poverty probably depend upon the relative deprivation entailed by poverty, it seems best to use contemporary standards in making comparisons over time. Even using such standards, the proportion of the American population living in poverty has declined between 1929 and the present. In 1929, 26 per cent of the households had income below the minimum subsistence level; in 1935–36, 27 per cent; in 1960, 11 per cent.[5] The proportion of households with income below the minimum adequacy level for these three periods was 43, 46 and 26 per cent, respectively.

A decrease in the proportion of the population living in poverty in two generations would mean that many of the children of the poor families of a generation ago have escaped poverty but that many of the current poor are likely to have come from poor families.

The relative reproduction rates of the poor and the non-

4. Oscar Ornati, *Poverty Amid Affluence,* (New York: Twentieth Century Fund, 1966), pp. 7–11, 27–33.
5. Ornati, *op. cit.,* Appendix 5, Table A.

poor also may affect the vacancies in each stratum.[6] Low-income families generally have higher birth rates than higher-income families, except for the highest income levels. This difference in birth rates has been declining, but it has not disappeared. Despite higher mortality rates for children of low-income than high-income families, poor families (but not necessarily poor broken families) tend to have more children than do nonpoor families. This, too, would mean that recruitment into poverty is not high from nonpoor families, but many of the children of poor families escape poverty.

Changes in vacancies do not alone account for intergenerational mobility. The other basic way in which mobility occurs is through the interchange of positions. This is the case when a child of the poor rises from poverty and a child of the nonpoor falls into poverty. Such interchange is of special interest because it is at this point that the style of life of the poor may play an important role in the intergenerational perpetuation of poverty.

If children of the poor are raised so that they do not develop the motives and skills necessary for economic advancement, they are obviously handicapped in escaping from poverty. Some evidence of this will be discussed. In addition, the resources available to the children from their families and through the schools and other institutions serving them, may be relatively inadequate. In varying degrees, too, those who are not poor may block advancement of the children of the poor if they do not have the style, color, or other characteristics demanded for acceptance into the nonpoor strata.

Interchange of ranks is also affected by the ability of the nonpoor to prevent their children from falling into poverty. In part, this is the other side of the coin of the difference between the poor and the nonpoor in the skills and motives necessary to maintain an adequate income. The nonpoor parents can sometimes provide, in addition, places of employment or capital resources which can almost insure avoiding

6. William J. Goode, "Family and Mobility," in Bendix and Lipset, *op. cit.*, esp. pp. 596–597; and Robert J. Lampman, "Population Change and Poverty Reduction, 1947-75," in Leo Fishman (ed.), *Poverty Amid Affluence*, (New Haven: Yale University Press, 1966), p. 40.

poverty. Falling into poverty has fortuitous elements, such as the death or old age of the main wage earner, family illnesses, or changes in the labor market in local areas. Persons who grew up in nonpoor families are likely to have friends and relatives with resources which help prevent such events from causing a family to slip into poverty. Friends and relatives may aid in finding new sources of income or directly supplement the family income at least until the immediate crisis is past. In other words, growing up in a well-off family can be a protection against poverty, aside from any bourgeoise virtues which may have been acquired in childhood.

These observations make it clear that the style of life among the poor is only one possible factor among many others in accounting for any intergenerational perpetuation of poverty. Even in accounting for the interchange of ranks as a factor in the intergenerational mobility between the poor and nonpoor, the life style of the poor is only one among other possible determinants. Certainly, generational changes in the proportion of the population which is poor is largely determined by economic developments and public policies regarding income maintenance and distribution. Thus the steady decline in the proportion of the population below the minimum subsistence level, from 27 per cent during 1935-36 to 11 per cent in 1960, may be attributable to the rise in employment levels and the expansion of various income maintenance programs under social security. In addition there has been a marked increase in the proportion of families which have more than one breadwinner. The participation of the wife in the labor force supplements the family's income and lessens the probability of extreme poverty among the low-paid workers' families.[7] These developments have the greatest impact upon the lowest-income category and it is this category that has declined most steadily.

Assessing the role of a culture of poverty in the intergenerational perpetuation of poverty then, is very complex. One issue, as discussed in the first two chapters, is the extent to which there is a way of life associated with poverty and the degree to which that way of life is intergenerationally

7. Ornati, *op. cit.*, pp. 29-30.

transmitted. Another issue is the extent to which particular aspects of the way of life of the poor may be related to the intergenerational perpetuation of poverty. Several aspects of those issues are analyzed in other chapters of this book. Insofar as we find that aspects of the way of life of the poor are not intergenerationally transmitted, we cannot expect that those aspects could play an important role in the intergenerational perpetuation of poverty. In this chapter, however, we are considering the matter from another vantage point. We need to consider the extent to which there is intergenerational perpetuation of poverty and the many possible determinants of mobility into and out of poverty. Such an analysis provides us with the context within which cultural processes can operate to affect intergenerational poverty.

Socioeconomic Origins of the Poor. Evidence of the extent to which the poor are recruited from families of low socioeconomic status is scanty. Nevertheless, by drawing together the available information, some general inferences may be made. Let us begin by considering the evidence regarding the origins of families currently dependent upon AFDC. Such families, of course, are not all fatherless, but they constitute one of the poorest segments of the population and include the segment of particular concern in this monograph—fatherless families.

In a 1960 national study of closed ADC cases, respondents were asked whether or not the family in which *either* the mother or the father of the dependent children were raised ever received ADC, general assistance, or other forms of public welfare. Information was lacking for about one-quarter of the cases. Of the cases for which information was available, more than 40 per cent reported that the family-of-origin of at least one parent of the children received some assistance.[8] Similar findings are reported for the State of Washington in 1964. Among the active AFDC cases in which the father was absent or disabled, 48 per cent of the assistance recipients reported that their parents had received public assistance, but 13 per cent reported this was for only a brief

8. M. Elaine Burgess and Daniel O. Price, *An American Dependency Challenge* (Chicago, Ill.: American Public Welfare Association, 1963), p. 21.

time.[9] Among the current AFDC cases in which the father was unemployed, 39 per cent reported that their families-of-origin had received some public assistance. A study of mothers receiving public assistance in 1966 in New York city found that only 15 per cent reported that their parents had ever received public assistance. This low figure, however, is due to the mothers who migrated to New York from places where public assistance was less readily available, such as the rural south and Puerto Rico. Among New York city-reared whites, 19 per cent report that their parents were on welfare; among New York city-reared Negroes, 45 per cent so report; and among New York city-reared Puerto Ricans, 38 per cent report that their parents received some public assistance.[10]

The previous discussion of the measures and determinants of the intergenerational perpetuation of poverty should make it clear that the interpretation of such figures is not obvious. One must know what proportion of families who do not receive public assistance come from families which had received financial assistance, but this information is not available. We can make some inferences, however, by considering what proportion of the population was impoverished in the parental generation and what proportion received any assistance. The median age of the homemakers in the 1960 survey was 34.5 years and 60 per cent of them were between 25 and 44 years old;[11] therefore, most of them grew up during the Depression. At that time the proportion of the families below the minimum subsistence level was high: 27 per cent. Figures on recipients of assistance during the Depression are not available, but some estimates have been made. In 1935, about 17 per cent of the population were on emergency relief and persons receiving other kinds of aid would increase the total to 20 per cent or more of the population.[12] In some

9. Greenleigh Associates, *Public Welfare: Poverty-Prevention or Perpetuation* (New York: Greenleigh Associates, 1964), pp. 32–33.

10. Lawrence Podell, "Families on Welfare in New York City, Preliminary report No. 5, Welfare History and Expectancy" (The Center for Social Research, The City University of New York, Graduate Center, January, 1968), Table B and pp. 4–6.

11. Burgess and Price, *op. cit.*, p. 18.

12. James Truslow Adams (ed.), *Dictionary of American History* (New York: Scribner's, 1940), Vol. IV, p. 227.

states, 40 per cent of the population were receiving assistance in 1932.[13]

Undoubtedly, many people received assistance for a short time only, but this also means that even if 20 per cent of the population received some form of assistance in 1935 a higher proportion of the population received assistance at one time or another, in the course of the Depression. In the light of these considerations, it is not so shocking that 40 per cent of one or both parents of the ADC-supported families received assistance.

Without question, families now dependent upon public assistance come disproportionally from families which had also been dependent upon assistance. The disproportionate representation, however, does not mean that the dependent come *only* from such backgrounds, nor that those who are not now dependent have not frequently experienced a similar background. Unfortunately, there are no data which permit a straightforward comparison of the welfare origins of families currently receiving and not receiving public assistance.

Some comparative figures are available when we consider low-income families, however. We may begin by considering the origins of poor one-parent families. We must use characteristics such as education and occupation of the head of the families-of-origin, since evidence is lacking about their income. A national survey conducted in 1960 provides pertinent information regarding the origins of poor families.[14] Poverty is defined as having income below a minimum adequate level; according to the definitions used in the study, about 28 per cent of the adult units in the nation were poor. This is a larger strata than would be true if a minimum subsistence level (the level at which families might receive public assistance) were used. As noted earlier, there has been a greater decline in the proportion of the population at the minimal subsistence level than at the minimal adequate level. According to the reasoning presented earlier, we would

13. Arthur Schlesinger, Jr., *The Coming of Roosevelt* (Boston: Houghton Mifflin, 1959), p. 263.

14. James N. Morgan, Martin H. David, Wilbur J. Cohen, and Harvey Brazer, *Income and Welfare in the United States* (New York: McGraw-Hill, 1962), p. 207.

expect families in the more sharply contracting strata to be more highly recruited from low socioeconomic origins than is the case for the less sharply contracting strata.

Among poor single-parent families, 76 per cent came from families with fathers with fewer than nine years of schooling; this compares with 64 per cent for all families.[15] Similarly, 66 per cent of the single-parent families came from families headed by laborers or farmers, compared to 44 per cent for all families. Presumably, poor single-parent families are generally more impoverished than the general strata of poor families.

Consistent with our expectations, *all* poor families are slightly less likely to have low social origins than are poor single-parent families: 66 per cent of all poor families had fathers with fewer than nine years of education and 64 per cent of them came from families headed by laborers or farmers.

Using the sample studied and reported upon in this book, more detailed analyses were made. Among complete families, the differences between the poor and the nonpoor in social origins are similar to those found nationally. Surprisingly, however, we did not find that those with income below the minimum subsistence level were recruited from low socioeconomic origins more frequently than were those with at least a minimum adequate income level. This seems to be a result of the peculiarities of the sample: using occupational status as an indicator, at least, there was no difference in the fathers and sons generation in occupational status distributions. Presumably, the families in the sample include more who have been downwardly mobile, than in the nation as a whole.

All this suggests that falling into poverty is somewhat fortuitous. Obviously, coming from poor families-of-origin increases the likelihood of bad luck and reduces the chances of escaping from the consequences of misfortune. Nevertheless, the relationship between the socioeconomic status of the family-of-origin and the current economic status is not so great that being in poverty can be accounted for simply by the fact that one was raised in poverty.

15. *Ibid.*, p. 207.

The point may be made clearer by considering the fatherless families in the sample. Among the mothers who are husbandless due to separation or divorce, for example, whether or not they are poor is not related to their socioeconomic origins. That is, families at each income level are about as likely to have had fathers of low occupational status, unstable employment, or low education. The findings of the previous chapter should help explain this. The economic fortunes of a husbandless mother are largely determined by contemporary circumstances. Other relevant characteristics such as the occupational status of her former husband and her own education are related to her own social origins, but so many particular circumstances intervene that her socioeconomic origins can have only a tenuous effect upon her avoidance of poverty—once her family has become disrupted.

In short, the poor do tend to be recruited from families which themselves had been poor. But when comparisons are made, with the nonpoor, the tendency is much weaker than is suggested by terms such as "three generations on welfare." The American society seems fluid enough for the poor to include many children of families which had not been poor. The evidence is scanty and indirect, but it does not support the view that the poor are made up only, or even largely, of children of the poor while the rest of the nation was raised in families which had not been poor. Before making any further inferences, let us turn to a consideration of the chances for children of the poor to escape poverty.

Social Mobility of the Children of Poverty. It is difficult to assess the chances children of poor families have to escape their poverty, since information is limited and indirect. There is no information about the income of adults who themselves came from poor families. There is information about educational attainments, however, and education is highly related to income and is a means of avoiding poverty. On the basis of a 1962 national survey, we can compare the educational attainment of children from poor families and from all families. Considering children who have finished school, among families with income below the minimum adequacy level, 45 per cent of their children completed 12 years or more of school, but among *all* families in the nation, 65 per cent at least graduated high school.[16] Obviously the chances of children of poor families to attain the educational level needed to escape poverty are less than for the nation as a whole; but again, the overlap is great and almost half of the children of poverty also are high school graduates.

When we consider the chances of children from AFDC families to escape poverty, we are still limited to considering the educational and occupational achievements of the children. We are now examining a poorer and smaller segment of the population. The child from a very poor family may be handicapped further if he comes from a broken family. We will have to consider these factors in interpreting the sparse data available.

Some evidence is available from the national study of ADC cases terminated in 1951. Of children 20 years or older, 26 per cent had at least completed high school.[17] A similar study, completed a decade later, found that 30 per cent of the 18–24 year old children had completed high school or gone beyond it.[18] These percentages are considerably below the proportion for the nation as a whole: in 1959, 62 per cent of the persons aged 18–24 had at least completed high school. These percentages are even below those for poor families generally. The odds for children of ADC-supported families to attain an educational level that will enable them to escape poverty are not high.

To assess the extent to which children in fatherless families have a particularly reduced likelihood of moving out of poverty, we need to compare equally poor complete and fatherless families. In local studies of different categories of public assistance, there are some indications that the children of ADC families are slightly less likely to complete at least high school than children of families dependent upon other cate-

16. *Ibid.*, p. 211.

17. Gordon W. Blackwell and Raymond F. Gould, *Future Citizens All* (Chicago: American Public Welfare Association, 1952), pp. 100–106, 148–149.

18. Burgess and Price, *op. cit.*, p. 109.

gories of public assistance. Indirect evidence on the national scale is available by considering the *educational* achievement of children of fathers in various occupational strata.[19] In a national survey conducted in 1952, it was found that among adult males whose fathers were in skilled or semi-skilled occupations, 38 per cent had completed at least 12 years of schooling. Among those of unskilled-worker origins, the percentage is 28. This may be compared to the figures for former ADC children of 26 per cent and 30 per cent cited above. It must be noted, however, that many of the adults grew up when completing high school was less widespread; consequently, the proportions are expected to be relatively low. This makes it difficult to conclude that children of families on ADC are as likely to complete high school as are equally poor *complete* families. Presumably, there is a slightly decreased likelihood. Poverty *per se* certainly seems to be a more important factor.

It should be noted that there is considerable variation among children in ADC families. Among the children of such families, almost one-third did complete at least high school, compared to less than two-thirds of similarly-aged children in the population as a whole. Obviously, poverty is not wholly determining of educational outcomes.

Assessing the *occupational* achievements of the children of poor families is also difficult given the very limited data available. Without doubt, sons of families who received AFDC assistance are much less likely to have white-collar and more likely to have service jobs and especially to be in unskilled laborer occupations than is true for the population as a whole. Since many of the children of ADC families studied are still young, one should compare them with young members of the labor force or with new entrants. Doing so improves the relative standing of children of ADC families slightly, but the differences are still great.

Again, to compare fatherless families with equally poor

19. Seymour Martin Lipset and Reinhard Bendix, *Social Mobility in Industrial Society* (Berkeley and Los Angeles: University of California Press, 1960), p. 97.

complete families could tell us something about the incremental disadvantage of coming from a fatherless family. In general, sons of fathers of low occupational status tend to remain in the same occupational strata. If we compare sons of ADC families with sons of fathers in laborer occupations, we still find that they are more likely to be in service or laborer occupations and less likely to be in white-collar occupations. When we look at the first occupations entered by sons of laborer fathers, however, the differences are very small. It would seem that sons of ADC families, then, do about as well as sons of laborer fathers.

The fathers of ADC boys, however, were not all of such low-status occupations. If we examine the intergenerational occupational mobility of sons of ADC families and males in the population at large, the issue is clarified. Although again the data are not strictly comparable, the findings indicate that sons of ADC families are as likely to have a higher occupational status than their fathers as are males in the population at large. The sons of ADC families, however, are more likely to have been downwardly mobile. Clearly, a son of a white-collar father, if the family is broken and is poor, is much less likely to be able to attain his father's occupational status, than he would be if the family were not poor and broken.

A comprehensive national study of occupational structure and mobility conducted in 1962 provides information about the effect a broken family has upon the occupational and educational achievement of sons. Controlling for the fathers' education and occupation, the authors conclude that "living in a broken family or with parents with disrupted marriages has some adverse effect on educational attainment partially because of the association with socioeconomic background factors but partially for other reasons.... The educational handicap is, in turn, translated into poorer than average occupational achievement, but there is little or no direct effect of rearing in a broken family on occupational success apart from this."[20]

20. Peter M. Blau and Otis Dudley Duncan, *The American Occupational Structure* (New York: John Wiley, 1967), p. 336.

The same data were used in a more detailed analysis bearing on this issue and the findings modify these conclusions. Sons of intact families were found to be somewhat more efficient in translating educational attainment into occupational achievement than sons of female-headed families.

In other words, the analyses "lend some support to the notion that the son raised in a family headed by a female is handicapped with respect to occupational success, even when allowance has been made for . . . his education and point of entry into the occupation structure."[21]

On the basis of the variety of evidence reviewed, we can make a few inferences. Poor families disproportionally come from poor families and children of poor fatherless families are disproportionally likely to remain in poverty. Heads of poor fatherless families are slightly more likely than other poor families to have come from poor families-of-origin. Children of very poor fatherless families are somewhat less likely than the children of other poor families to gain the education and enter the occupations which would enable them to escape poverty.

The data also make it clear that most of the poor did not come from poverty-stricken families. Even the poor fatherless families are not homogenously of poor origins. It is more difficult to assess the chances of children from poor families to escape poverty. Most of them seem to lack the educational and occupational characteristics associated with at least income comfortably beyond poverty. But the evidence refers to a relatively early stage in their lives. Some occupational advancement in their own lifetimes is likely. Certainly a continuing contraction in the proportion of the population which lives in poverty must mean an increase in the odds of a child of poverty to escape from it. Children from fatherless families seem to have some incremental handicap. In the next section of this chapter we will examine the extent of broken families, trends in broken families, and the degree to which there is an intergenerational perpetuation of broken families.

21. Beverly Duncan and Otis Dudley Duncan, "Family Stability and Occupational Success," *Social Problems*, 16 (Winter, 1969), pp. 273–285.

The Intergenerational Persistence of Broken Families

Concern with the plight of broken families should not lead to an exaggeration of their number or rate of increase. The U.S. Census Bureau provides the basic data about the number of broken families. Yet selecting different definitions and ways of calculating percentages can yield results which have different implications. Thus, in 1960 there were more than 9,000,000 female-headed households in the United States; that is 17 per cent of all households.[22] But this includes widows living alone—not in any family. Even figures on female-headed families includes families without children. If we consider only families with children under 18 related to the head, nearly 2,000,000, or 7 per cent, of such families were headed by a female and 1 per cent was headed by a male without a wife. The figures on families do not include "subfamilies"—families living in the same household with a related family. For example, a mother and her children may be living with her parents. Such families should also be considered. If we do so, the percentage of broken families is slightly greater: about 9 per cent of all families *and* subfamilies are female-headed and, again, 1 per cent have a male head without a wife.

On the basis of these percentages, the problem posed by broken families cannot be considered of vast magnitude. Yet in absolute terms we are still concerned with large numbers of families. Several other considerations increase the significance of broken families. We have already discussed the close relationship between broken families and poverty. In addition it should be remembered that census figures about broken families refer to the number at a given time. Broken families are reconstituted, however, and a much larger percentage of children have lived at least part of their lives in broken families than are doing so in any given year. For example, about one-third of the cross-sectional sample and

22. Calculated from U.S. Bureau of the Census, *1960 Census of Population, Families,* PC(2)-4A (Washington, D.C.: U.S. Government Printing Office, 1963), Table 9.

one-half of the panel sample did not live with both their parents until they reached 15 years of age. In the United States, as a whole, about one in six adults did not live in intact families through early adolescence.[23]

Moynihan, in his famous report, drew widespread public attention to another consideration: the relatively high concentration of broken families among American Negroes.[24] Calculating percentages as we did earlier, we find that in 1960, 27 per cent of all nonwhite families and subfamilies with children under 18 related to the head were broken: 24 per cent had female heads and 3 per cent had males without wives as heads.[25] Even among American Negroes, however, note that almost three-fourths of the families and subfamilies are complete.

Finally, the number of broken families is rising. The increase in broken families may be calculated in different ways and with different results. Before considering that issue, let us examine changes in the source of broken families. The divorce rate has been increasing as has the rate of illegitimacy.[26] Furthermore, there is a trend for divorces to occur when children are still minors. Consequently, it is reasonable to expect that broken families are increasing relatively as well as absolutely. On the other hand, death rates have

23. Blau and Duncan, *op. cit.*, p. 331. Also see Raymond Illsley and Barbara Thompson, "Women from Broken Homes," *The Sociological Review*, New Series, 9 (March, 1961), pp. 27–54. They studied about 3,000 Aberdeen women having their first pregnancy and delivery in the years 1952–54. About 18 per cent of the women came from broken families. Since either marriage partner, or both, could have come from a broken family, the proportion of married couples with at least one spouse who came from a broken family would be higher. In another English study, about one-third of the persons in each of three social classes were found to have come from broken families. See Thomas S. Langner and Stanley T. Michael, *Life Stress and Mental Health* (London: Free Press of Glencoe, 1963), p. 151.

24. Office of Policy Planning and Research, U.S. Department of Labor, *The Negro Family: The Case for National Action* (Wshington, D.C., U.S. Government Printing Office, 1965).

25. Calculated from U.S. Bureau of the Census, *1960 Census of Population, Families PC(2)-4A*, *op. cit.*, Tables 9 and 21.

26. Paul H. Jacobson, *American Marriage and Divorce* (New York: Rinehart, 1959), p. 131; and Office of Policy Planning and Research, U.S. Department of Labor, *op. cit.*, pp. 8–9.

declined and families broken by death of one of the parents are less frequent than in earlier decades.[27] Data from the sample used in this study show that over many decades these two major trends have about balanced each other. As can be seen in Table 7.1, the proportion of the respondents who had their family of orientation disrupted in some manner before they were fifteen is not markedly different, regardless of the decade in which they were born.

*Table 7.1. Intactness of Family-of-Origin by Age of Respondents**

Family of Origin	*29 or Younger*	*30 to 39*	*40 to 49*	*50 to 59*	*60 to 69*	*70 or Older*
Broken by divorce or separation	13.0	12.7	6.3	6.1	2.6	0.6
Broken by death of a parent	17.3	16.2	25.2	23.1	29.3	20.8
Other disruption†	2.3	1.5	2.7	4.1	1.7	3.5
Respondent lived with both parents at least until age 15	67.3	69.7	65.8	66.7	66.4	75.1
Totals %	99.9	100.1	100.0	100.0	100.0	100.0
(N)	(346)	(346)	(222)	(147)	(116)	(173)

* All respondents, male and female, with and without children are included.
† Includes respondent left home before 15, living in foster home, or institution.

The U.S. Census provides other data on changes in broken families over time. In comparing 1950 and 1960, we will consider only families with children under 18 related to the head. In 1960, 7 per cent of such families were headed by a female, compared to 6 per cent in 1950.[28] In 1960 and in 1950, 1 per cent of such families were headed by a male

27. Paul H. Jacobson, "The Changing Role of Mortality in American Family Life," *Lex et Scientia*, 3 (April-June, 1966), pp. 117–124.

28. 1960 figures calculated from *1960 U.S. Census of Population* previously cited; 1950 figures calculated from U.S. Census Bureau, *1950 U.S. Census of Population Report P-E, No. 2A* (Washington, D.C.: U.S. Government Printing Office, 1955), Table 4.

without a wife. This hardly indicates a rapid increase in the rate of broken families. It is true that if one calculates the *percentage increase* of such families, the results are more startling. Thus, while complete families with children under 18 related to the head increased by 28 per cent between 1950 and 1960, female-headed families increased by 51 per cent and families with a male head without a wife increased by 26 per cent.

One other possibility affecting changes in the proportion of broken families over time must be considered. A broken family to appear in the census data requires not only the disruption of a marriage or illegitimacy, but also the retention of the child in the same family with the parent. It is possible that in the past, once a family was disrupted, the children were less likely than presently to remain with either parent—they may have received institutional care, gone to live with other relatives, or started an independent household if at all possible. In other words, the existence of a fatherless family does not simply mean that children are not living with both parents—it also means that they are living with their mother rather than in an institution, foster home, or foraging on their own.

Data from the present study bear on this possibility. Respondents whose family of orientation had been disrupted were asked to report with whom they lived afterward. Their reports, by the year in which the family of orientation was disrupted, are presented in Table 7.2. Certainly since the beginning of this century there has been a trend for the children of disrupted families to remain with at least one of their parents. In part this may be attributable to changes in the causes of parental disruption, as shown in Table 7.1. Children usually stay with the mother. In the event of divorce or separation, an option exists—either the mother or the father is available. In the event of death (about equally likely for the mother and father in this sample), the possibility of staying with the mother is cut in half. As Table 7.1 shows, death of one of the parents was slightly more likely to be the cause of parental disruption in earlier decades than in more recent ones. The magnitude of the shift in Table 7.2, however, cannot be explained by the shift in the causes of marital disruption. The decline in the proportion of families broken by the death of one of the parents is very slight compared to the decline in the per cent of children of disrupted homes who managed to stay with one of their parents. Perhaps the general rise of the standard of living, urbanization, and to some extent welfare measures have played major roles in the change.

Table 7.2. Type of Child-Parental Relationship by Year of Disruption of Parental Marriage

Type of Child-Parental Relationship	*Year of Disruption*						
	1900 or Earlier	*1901 to 1910*	*1911 to 1920*	*1921 to 1930*	*1931 to 1940*	*1941 to 1950*	*1951 or Later*
Stayed with parent who did not remarry	44.4	32.4	26.2	29.0	30.2	44.4	55.6
Stayed with parent who did remarry	41.7	20.6	28.6	33.3	38.4	33.3	33.3
Did not stay with either parent	13.9	47.1	45.2	37.7	31.4	22.2	11.1
Totals %	100.0	100.1	100.0	100.0	100.0	99.9	100.0
(N)	(36)	(34)	(42)	(69)	(86)	(81)	(9)

The evidence in Table 7.2 bears on another issue. There appears to be a tendency, particularly in the decades after 1930, for the parent with whom the respondent stays not to remarry. This may be attributable to the same factors suggested above for explaining the increased likelihood of a child staying with one of his parents after their marital union was disrupted. It may be alleged particularly that the growth of welfare programs makes it easier for a husbandless mother to rear her children and therefore contributes to family instability. As noted in discussing Table 7.1, there was a marked increase in divorce or separation as the source of family disruption. The steady, long-run trend is such, however, that one can hardly attribute the relatively recent growth of public welfare measures as an explanation. The explanation must be sought in long-run trends of a more general nature affecting marital relations: the employment of women, sexual equalitarianism, and underlying processes of urbanization and technological developments.

The data presented suggest that welfare programs may contribute to the increasing likelihood that a child of a broken home remains with one of his parents; welfare programs may also reduce the need and therefore the likelihood of the parent remarrying. These findings must be considered tentative. The sample from which they are drawn is a peculiar one: residents of four public housing projects and the surrounding areas in one upstate New York city. Additional evidence and analysis would be necessary before one could conclude that the trends noted here are correct. Even if the trends are correct, much additional information is needed to account for them.

Now we can turn to the question of the extent to which children of broken families are themselves likely to have their marriages disrupted or to have illegitimate children. That there should be such a relationship would appear to be obvious. Yet, there is no clear evidence that this is the case.[29] In a national study it was found that neither Negro nor non-Negro men who grew up in broken families were more likely than those from intact families to be unmarried or living apart from their wives.[30]

In the sample reported upon here, there is no relationship between the mothers' marital status and the marital stability

29. Robins and O'Neal in one study found that subjects who had come from unbroken homes were slightly less likely themselves to have been divorced than was true of those who came from broken homes; but the differences were far below significance. See Lee N. Robins and Patricia O'Neal, "The Marital History of Former Problem Children," *Social Problems*, V (Spring, 1958), p. 351. Studies of courtship behavior of children of broken families do not yield consistent findings. See Robert F. Winch, "The Relation Between Loss of a Parent and Progress in Courtship," *Journal of Social Psychology*, 29 (1949), pp. 51-56; and Robert O. Andrews and Harold T. Christensen, "Relationship of Absence of a Parent to Courtship Status: A Repeat Study," *American Sociological Review*, 16 (August, 1951), pp. 541-544.

30. Duncan and Duncan, *op. cit.*, pp. 274-275.

of their family-of-origin. Thus, as can be seen in Table 7.3, mothers who came from intact families are as likely to have been divorced or separated as are mothers whose parents

Table 7.3. Marital Status of Mothers by Marital Status of Their Parental Home*

Mother's Marital Status	Marital Status of Parental Home: Married	Broken by Death	Broken by Divorce or Separation
Married: once	69.2	59.2	68.1
Husbandless: widow	2.9	9.2	1.5
Married: more than once	7.6	10.0	10.1
Husbandless: divorced separated, never married	20.4	21.7	20.3
Totals %	100.1	100.1	100.0
(N)	(344)	(120)	(69)

* In this table, mothers refers to natural mothers; women who are maternal surrogates such as grandmothers or aunts are excluded.

were divorced or separated. Of course the categories are crude, but other kinds of analyses do not reveal different results. For example, disregarding the reasons for the disruption of the parental home, we compared mothers who (1) lived with both parents at least until age fifteen, (2) did not, and did not stay with either parent, (3) stayed with one parent who did not remarry, and (4) stayed with one parent who did remarry. There is no relationship between these conditions and the mothers' marital status.

Furthermore, the stability of the family-of-origin does not seem to affect the current income of the husbandless mothers. That is, husbandless mothers who came from families broken by divorce or separation are no more likely to be poor than are husbandless mothers who grew up in complete families.[31] Moreover, husbandless mothers from broken families

31. This should not be too surprising. The income of a husbandless mother is affected by her former husband's occupation by way of social security and insurance benefits and by her own employability. The latter is affected by the factors discussed in Chapter 6. Intactness of the family-of-origin would not materially affect all the conditions.

are slightly less likely to be living in public housing than are those from complete families.

There are poor husbandless mothers who came from poor fatherless families but these findings all indicate that the intactness of the family-of-origin is not a major determinant of the mothers' marital status. Furthermore, most husbandless mothers grew up in complete families (this can be seen in Table 7.3 by noting the number of families-of-origin who were intact, broken by death, and broken by divorce or separation while the mother was growing up). In addition, the daughters of families broken by divorce or separation are more likely than not to be maritally stable. In other words, there may be a hard core of fatherless families that is intergenerationally perpetuated, but most children of broken families establish stable marital unions, and the mothers who do not cannot be accounted for by the marital condition of their parents.

Upon reflection, these findings should not be surprising. A broken family need not be a traumatically damaging experience working against sons and daughters having a stable marriage of their own. Living in a home with an intact marriage but in which the mother and father are estranged can be more damaging to the children than a divorce. Furthermore, the consequences of a broken family depend upon the living arrangements afterwards. This is well illusstrated by the findings of a study by Illsley and Thompson of about 3,000 Aberdeen women who had their first child.[32] They found, for example, that illegitimate or premarital conceptions were more likely among daughters of families that had been broken by divorce or separation or in which the daughters lived with unrelated persons or in institutions, than among daughters who grew up in intact homes. But a daughter whose mother died and who lived then with her father and a step-mother or whose father died and who remained with her mother who did not remarry was no more likely to have conceptions outside of marriage than was a daughter of an intact home.

Even if coming from a broken home is related to later marital instability, this need not be explicable in terms of

32. Illsley and Thompson, *op. cit.*

psychological damage. Having one's family-of-origin disrupted increases the likelihood of being educationally and economically handicapped and the resulting low income may have more to do with impairing later marriage than any psychological handicap. There is much evidence that divorce and separation rates are lower as socioeconomic rank rises.[33] Goode points out several reasons for the differences in marital stability among different economic strata.[34] He has argued that the predispositions are likely not to be very different, but the external support for union and the internal strains are likely to vary in ways which account for socioeconomic status differences in divorce and separation. Those in the upper occupational strata live in networks of "interdependent social groups whose livelihoods and ways of life are based upon great continuity of social relations. . . . Divorce is never an anonymous matter in these strata. Furthermore, child support can almost never be evaded. . . ." Internal stresses are likely to arise from the material circumstances of the lower occupational strata. Persons here not only lack many of the material comforts they want, but the higher proportion of working wives in such strata cause extra strain because the men are presumably less willing than middle- or upper-strata husbands to share housekeeping burdens, and the wife's employment has few intrinsic satisfactions.

The inverse relationship between socioeconomic rank and marital stability is not very marked among the mothers interviewed in this study. Mothers of lower socioeconomic

33. For studies regarding divorce rates, see H. Ashley Weeks, "Differential Divorce Rates by Occupation," *Social Forces*, XXI (1943), pp. 334–37; August B. Hollingshead, "Class Differences in Family Stability," *Annals of the American Academy of Political and Social Science*, CCLXXII (1950), pp. 39–46; William A. Kephart, "Occupational Level and Marital Disruption," *American Sociological Review*, XX (1955), pp. 456–65; William J. Goode, *After Divorce* (Glencoe, Ill.: Free Press, 1956), Chapter IV. Contrary evidence is presented in Karen G. Hillman, "Marital Instability and Its Relation to Education, Income, and Occupation: An Analysis Based on Census Data," in *Selected Studies in Marriage and the Family*, rev. ed., Robert F. Winch, and others, eds. (New York: Holt, Rinehart and Winston, 1962), pp. 603–608.

34. Goode, *op. cit.*, esp. pp. 64–67.

origins are only slightly more likely than those of higher status origins to be husbandless because of divorce or separation or to have been married more than once. The relationship is more marked with measures of current socioeconomic status. Thus, the mothers' educational attainment, as shown in Table 7.4, markedly affects marital stability. The mothers' educational attainment may be related to the kind of social networks and social support for continued marriage which surrounds her. However, education is also an indicator of social skills and competence. In addition, it is related to the occupational status of her husband or former husband. We do not have information about the occupational status or income of the former husbands of mothers who were married more than once. We can only use the occupational status of the

Table 7.4. Marital Status of Mothers by Years of Education Completed*

Mother's Marital Status	*Years of Education*				
	7 or Fewer	*8*	*9 to 11*	*12*	*13 or More*
Married: once	53.1	53.6	64.4	73.8	78.3
Husbandless: widow	6.1	5.4	4.0	1.7	5.8
Married: more than once	10.2	21.4	8.5	4.7	4.4
Husbandless: divorced, separated, never married	30.6	19.6	23.2	19.8	11.6
Totals %	100.0	100.0	100.1	100.0	100.1
(N)	(49)	(56)	(177)	(172)	(69)

* Maternal surrogates excluded.

former spouses of the husbandless mothers and that of the husbands of the currently married mothers. Doing so, we find only a small relationship between husbands' occupational status and marital stability. Thus, among husbands (former spouses of husbandless mothers and current spouses of married mothers) with occupational status indices of 18 or less, 25 per cent of the mothers are husbandless by reason of divorce or separation; among those with higher occupational statuses, 15 per cent of the mothers are husbandless for those reasons.[35]

The ancient Greek adage that a person's life cannot be judged happy until it has been completed should be kept in mind in interpreting these data. As we have noted, the husbandless mothers are somewhat older than the married mothers. Many of the married mothers will become husbandless before all their children reach maturity. Using a cross-sectional sample, as we have done here, obscures the factors which may account for marital instability.

In summary, the immediate circumstances of the marriage, particularly those associated with current socioeconomic status, more directly affect the likelihood of a stable marriage than whether or not one of the partners grew up in a broken home. On the whole, a broken home may not be directly related to the children's own marital instability. The consequences of a family break-up depend upon the social, economic, and psychic conditions which are then experienced.

Conclusions

The evidence regarding intergenerational persistence of poverty does not demonstrate that the poor or even that poor female-headed families have offspring doomed to poverty or

35. The same difficulties in comparing income of the stable marital unions with the broken ones exist as in comparing occupational status. In addition, fewer husbandless mothers were able to report on the former husband's earnings than on his occupation. On the basis of the limited data, it appears that income is more highly related to the marital break-up of the mothers than is the husbands' occupational status. Husbands with low incomes are more likely to be former husbands of presently husbandless mothers than are husbands of currently married mothers. In making this interpretation, several points affecting such a comparison have been noted. First, the former husbands' earnings refer to earlier years and, since there have been some general increases in wage levels, the former husbands' earnings are relatively underestimated. Furthermore, failure to report the former husbands' earnings is probably more likely among women whose former husbands' earnings were relatively low. On the other hand, the former husbands' earnings reported by the husbandless mothers probably refers to a higher point in the husbands' careers, compared to the current husbands of married mothers, who are generally younger. This would tend to overestimate the relative earnings of the former husbands.

that these families all came from poor families themselves. Children of the poor rise out of poverty and children of the nonpoor fall into destitution; many of the poor were not always impoverished. Of course this does not mean that there is no relationship between poverty in one generation and the next. If one is born into a poor family, the chances of being poor when an adult are much greater than if one were born into a not-so-poor family.

The evidence of discontinuities in poverty between generations, however, has several implications for the subcultural explanation of poverty and the way of life of the poor. Insofar as the poor share a way of life, but poverty is not inherited, neither can the way of life be inherited. That way of life must be acquired in response to current circumstances. On the basis of evidence considered thus far, then, the patterns of life of poor people in many cases are not intergenerationally transmitted.

Although there is intergenerational poverty, this is not necessarily because a way of life is transmitted which prevents the children of the poor escaping poverty. The same circumstances which resulted in the parents' poverty also can constrain the children: for example, residence in an economically depressed area or discrimination against minority groups. Thus, educational achievement yields less economic benefits to Negroes and other minorities in the United States than it does to the white majority.[36] The evidence of movement out of poverty indicates that growing up in poor families does not doom the children to impoverishment—if other conditions are conducive to moving out of poverty. We need to look for more direct evidence about the intergenerational transmission of the way of life of the poor. That will be done in the next two chapters.

Of course the evidence assembled in this chapter cannot rule out the existence of subcultures of poverty. Within the heterogenous stratum of the poor, families may inter-

36. See, for example, Walter Fogel, "The Effect of Low Educational Attainment on Incomes: A Comparative Study of Selected Ethnic Groups," *The Journal of Human Resources,* I (Fall, 1966), pp. 22-40, and Paul M. Siegel, "On the Cost of Being a Negro," *Sociological Inquiry,* 35 (Winter, 1965), pp. 41-57.

generationally transmit a way of life which makes escape from poverty almost impossible and thus the poverty is also transmitted. Such subcultures must be associated with a bounded, intergenerationally stable, community. The community may be geographically or ethnically bounded, and probably must be both to be self-perpetuating. The evidence in this chapter certainly indicates that the stratum of the poor is more extensive than are such communities.

The connection between broken families in one generation and the next is non-existent or small. Having lived part of one's childhood in a broken family does not mean having had a single set of experiences so different from growing up in an intact family that marital stability as an adult is markedly affected. Who one lived with after the break-up and under what specific conditions, the conditions prior to the disruption, and the intact families with which comparisons are made, all affect the relationship between marital stability in one generation and the next.

Although broken families tend to be poor, there is no clear relationship even between the stability of the family-of-origin and later life in poverty. According to one study, comparing persons of three different social classes did not reveal any significant differences in the proportion not only of broken families-of-origin, but of mentally ill parents, physically ill parents, or parental quarrels.[37]

Having come from a poor family that was also broken appears to be incrementally handicapping in escaping from poverty. This is the point. Conditions such as poverty or broken families are heterogenous. The outcomes of such conditions depend upon their interaction with each other and with many other specific conditions. It is necessary to examine the way a variety of circumstances jointly affect the way people live. Even the initially surprising finding that broken families are not self-perpetuating cannot be understood with-

37. The study also found that childhood economic deprivation was related to social class position: 30 per cent of the lows and 15 per cent of the highs came from deprived backgrounds. See Langner and Michael, *op. cit.*, p. 151.

out paying attention to the processes occurring in different combinations of specific conditions. In the remaining chapters of this book, particular conditions and combinations of conditions will be examined. The findings from such an examination should help explain how the degree of association and lack of association of poverty and broken families between generations occurs.

8. Rearing Children for Independence and Achievement

THE CONTINUITIES and discontinuities in the intergenerational patterns of poverty and broken families described in the preceding chapter require explanation. Does a subculture of poverty provide such an explanation? In this and the next chapter we will examine some possible linkages in a subcultural explanation, as well as alternative explanations.

If there is a subculture of poverty, we would expect (1) that the way children are raised effects their later achievement of an adequate income, (2) that these child-rearing ways differ markedly between the poor and the nonpoor, and (3) that those ways were acquired by the parents in their own childhood and youth and are maintained. Subcultural explanations do not specify how determining the childhood experiences must be of later achievement, to what extent poeple in poverty differ from others in rearing their children, nor to what extent the ways must have been acquired earlier. But if the links at each stage are weak, a subcultural explanation cannot be powerful. In order to assess the strength of the links, it is also necessary to consider other explanations.

In this chapter, the focus of concern is upon child-rearing patterns that are presumably relevant for independence and achievement in general. In the next chapter the focus is upon patterns relevant for educational achievement. In both chapters, then, we will be examining directly some possible intergenerational links in the way of life of the poor. Much of the analysis will focus upon fatherless families. They constitute a specially significant category of the poor. Furthermore, in this way we can analyze the role of intergenerational links in poverty for people in different circumstances.

In order to assess intergenerational linkages, we must know what child-rearing patterns affect the independence and achievement of children. Although there has been considerable research on this topic, our knowledge is still incomplete. We know that we cannot single out a particular pattern of conduct or parental value or belief that has a specific effect upon the future life of a child. A brief review of the reasons for this will also indicate some of what is known about the effects of child-rearing patterns and the caveats to be kept in mind in the ensuing analysis.[1]

Children learn by direct inculcation *and* by implicit accommodation. Certainly values, beliefs, and orientations may be inculcated through the child's identification with parents and through the directed rewards and punishments of the parents. But, in addition, the children react to the beliefs, feelings, and conduct of their parents in ways not intended by the parents. Children learn by observing what really is going on as well as by what they are told. The child is formed in part by the generalizations he makes based upon his experience and by the patterns he develops in accommodating to the circumstances in his family. Meanwhile, the other members of his family develop ways of reacting to his accommodations.

1. For reviews of the literature on socialization, see Irwin L. Child, "Socialization," in Gardner Lindzey, ed., *Handbood of Social Psychology,* (Cambridge, Mass.: Addison-Wesley, 1954), Vol. II, pp. 669-672 and Wesley C. Becker, "Consequences of Different Kinds of Parental Discipline," in M.L. Hoffman and L.W. Hoffman, eds., *Review of Child Development Research,* Vol. I, (New York: Russell Sage Foundation, 1964), pp. 169-208.

Furthermore, the effects of any particular activity depend in part upon the emotional context and meaning of the activity. Similarly, feelings may be interpreted variously depending upon their mode of expression. This is illustrated in McClelland's summary of a number of studies pertaining to the patterns of child-rearing that are related to the development of what he calls the achievement motive. He writes that the optimal pattern is "reasonably high standards of excellence imposed at a time when the sons can attain them, a willingness to let him attain them without interference, and real emotional pleasure in his achievements short of overprotection and indulgence."[2]

This suggests additional cautions in relating particular patterns to particular outcomes. A particular pattern has different consequences when it is pursued too far or not far enough. Permissiveness can be carried to the point of neglect and rejection. Guidance can be carried to the point of overprotection and domination. In part, what is overprotection and what is neglect depends upon the age and the characteristics of the child himself.

Finally, it must be recognized that the evidence about the effects of child-rearing patterns is still very incomplete. One can point to apparent inconsistencies and many gaps in information. For example, some studies have found that children reared with warmth and permissiveness tend to be independent and creative.[3] Other studies have found that high-achieving adults and high-aspiring students disproportionally report unhappy family life and rejecting parents.[4] Presumably, with further specification, these findings

2. David C. McClelland, *The Achieving Society* (Princeton, N. J.: D. Van Nostrand, 1961), p. 356. Also see F. L. Strodtbeck, "Family Interaction, Values, and Achievement," in *Talent and Society*, D. C. McClelland, and others, eds. (Princeton, N. J.: D. Van Nostrand, 1958), pp. 135-194.

3. See studies cited in Becker, *op. cit.* Also see Elizabeth Douvan and Joseph Adelson, "The Pschodynamics of Social Mobility in Adolescent Boys," *The Journal of Abnormal and Social Psychology*, 56 (1958), pp. 31-44; they found that upward-aspiring high school boys tended to come from warm, permissive families.

4. See, for example, W. Lloyd Warner and James C. Abegglen, *Big Business Leaders in America* (New York: Harper, 1955); Russell R. Dynes, Alfred C. Clarke, and Simon Dinitz, "Levels of Occupational Aspiration: Some Aspects of Family Experience as a Variable, " *American Sociological Re-*

would not be inconsistent. But we lack those specifications. Furthermore, we lack information connecting childhood independence, aspirations, achievement fantasies, and the actual attainment of occupational success.

In the analysis that follows, we will examine particular aspects of child-rearing, bearing in mind these limitations. We will discuss some of the evidence indicating the relevance of the patterns for later independence and general achievement. We will examine parental values, beliefs, and conduct pertaining to rearing children for independence and achievement. Although we will look at specific aspects of child-rearing patterns, the entire complex of maternal-child relations must be borne in mind. In order to do this it will be useful to sketch the major ways in which poverty and the absence of a husband may affect the way a mother rears her children.

The absence of a husband-father may increase or decrease the salience of the mother-child relationship. She may become more emotionally involved with her children as they are used to compensate for the social and emotional gratifications the husband no longer provides. This could be expressed by indulging the child—giving him freer reins than he would otherwise have; or, it might be expressed by excessive supervision, interference, and control. On the other hand, the mother may withdraw from the child, rejecting him for the burdens he embodies or the disliked qualities of the father he represents. This may be expressed by hostile neglect or even by aggressive overcontrol. In addition to this dimension, since a husbandless mother is especially subject to competing demands upon limited resources of time, money, and energy, she may encourage her child toward early independence; this may even go to the point of pushing the child faster than he is able to move successfully or it may be expressed in neglect.

It is also possible, however, that the child-rearing patterns

---

view, 21 (April, 1956), pp. 212-215; William A. Rushing, "Adolescent-Parent Relationship and Mobility Aspirations," *Social Forces*, 43 (December, 1964), pp. 157-166; and the review of such studies in Seymour Martin Lipset and Reinhard Bendix, *Social Mobility in Industrial Society* (Berkeley and Los Angeles; University of California Press, 1960), pp. 250-254.

of the mother are little affected by the absence of the husband-father. These patterns may be largely the result of the mother's own socialization experiences and will be continued whether or not a husband-father is around. In addition, the general societal rules about child-rearing may be constraining of all mothers, and variations in the rules among different subgroups in the society will be supported by neighbors, friends, and kin. Furthermore, some of the regularities and variations in child-rearing patterns are the result of the inherent and idiosyncratic character of the relationship with the child. Particular patterns may develop in interaction with particular children and this is a source of variation somewhat independent of the other factors mentioned.

One further consideration must be stressed in interpreting the findings. Even if we should find little difference between married and husbandless mothers in child-rearing patterns, fatherless children may still have different socialization experiences than children of complete families. The absence of a father with whom they can interact and identify may have consequences independent of the mother's accommodation to the father's absence.[5] Teachers, police,[6] and other children

5. Thus some studies indicate that boys from father-absent families have special difficulty in their sex identification. See, for example, George R. Bach, "Father Fantasies and Father-Typing in Father-Separated Children," *Child Development,* XVII (1946), pp. 63-80; David B. Lynn and William L. Sawrey, "The Effects of Father-Absence on Norwegian Boys and Girls," *Journal of Abnormal and Social Psychology,* LII (1959), pp. 5-19; and Allan G. Barclay and D.R. Cusumano, "Testing Masculinity in Boys without Fathers," *Trans-action* 5, (December, 1967), pp. 33-35. Other studies have found no differences, at the aggregate level, between children of broken and complete families. See, for example, F. Ivan Nye, "Child Adjustment in Broken and Unhappy Homes," *Marriage and Family Living,* XIX (1957), pp. 356-361, and Joan McCord, and others, "Some Effects of Paternal Absence on Male Children," *Journal of Abnormal and Social Psychology,* LXIV (1962), pp. 361-369.

6. For example, policemen in one city were asked, "What are some of the factors that you take into consideration in determining how you will handle and dispose of contacts that you have with juveniles?" In the sample, 38 per cent of the policemen mentioned the marital status of the parents. This compares with the following proportions for other factors: (1) attitude of juvenile, 80 per cent; (2) attitude of parents, 56 per cent; (3) time of day of contact, 50 per cent; (4) dress and manner of juvenile, 44 per cent; (5) seriousness of danger of behavior, 38 per cent; (6) type of offense, 24 per cent; (7) address of parents, 16 per cent; (8) past record of juvenile, 16 per

may treat fatherless children differently. They may grow up in different social settings, particularly those associated with poverty. Although these possibilities will not be studied directly, they also are conditions which may affect the mother's child-rearing patterns and thus are a matter of concern in this analysis.

Husbandless Mothers' Views of Absence of Fathers

Before beginning an analysis of the husbandless mothers' socialization of their children, let us see how the mothers themselves view the consequences of the fathers' absence upon their children. To minimize stereotypical responses, respondents were often asked about *one* of their children; we refer to the child as the "study child."[7] Children under six are excluded. Husbandless mothers were asked, "Do you think (study child) would be any different if (his) (her) father were around?" When respondents answered "yes," they were then asked if the child would be better or worse off. Almost half of the mothers thought the child would not be better off, and almost one in five thought the child would be worse off. (In this discussion we are considering only the mothers; the maternal surrogates are not included.)

In other words, most of the mothers do not feel that the

---

cent, and (9) age of juvenile, 4 per cent. Data from Lyle W. Shannon, "The Distribution of Juvenile Delinquency in a Middle-Sized City," *The Sociological Quarterly*, 8 (Summer, 1967), pp. 365-383, note 9. In a study of self-reported juvenile delinquent acts and police disposition of juveniles contacted, it was found that children of fatherless families had a higher risk of being treated as delinquents than did children of complete families (from personal communication by Robert Hardt and Sandra Peterson). Nathan Goldman has made the same observation on the bases of his analyses (also personally communicated).

7. In trying to ascertain parents' actual conduct, by interviewing, we sought to make the questions as specific as possible to maximize accuracy of reporting. Some questions were asked about children in general, others about any child of the respondent, and other questions were about one of the respondent's children, whom we call the "study child." The study child was chosen by a method to maximize comparability. The interviewer selected the study child from among all the respondent's children according to the following priorities: (1) boy between ages 9-11; (2) boy, 12-14; (3) boy, 6-8; (4) girl, 9-11; (5) girl, 12-14; (6) girl, 6-8; (7) boy, 15-18; and (8) girl, 15-18.

child suffers because of the absence of the father. Among those mothers who do feel that the child would be better off if the father were around, the majority explain that the father would help discipline the child, and several mention the value of the father's companionship: only one mother mentioned that there would be more money for the child's care. Among the mothers who thought the child would be worse off, nearly all of them talked about the father as a bad example, or of poor father-child relations. As one mother said:

> George (study child) lived in fear of his father. His father ignored him. His father didn't finish high school, is a vegetable, he didn't help with school work but was displeased when the report card came. His father has a good mind but doesn't use it. He has no real drive or stick-to-it. He didn't do anything with George. Raising the children was 100 per cent my job.

A few mothers also mentioned that the father wasted money or did not earn money, and a few mentioned the poor marital relationship they had with their husbands.

Of course, one might be suspicious of many of these replies—particularly if one is a father. A mother undoubtedly wants to believe that she is doing an adequate job of raising her children without the father; saying the child would be no different is self-protective. But the responses have a specificity which indicates that our question was considered concretely by the mothers. Furthermore, the reasons given bespeak the child's welfare in terms of immediate social relations with the child. Analysis of the mothers' evaluations does not support the idea that they are simply self-justifying defenses.

Thus, neither the mother's employment nor income is related to whether or not she feels the child would be better off, worse off, or no different. Mothers with former husbands of higher occupational status tend to think the child would be worse off if the husband were present; mothers whose husbands had lower occupational status tend to say the absence has not made the child any different. Widowed mothers do not say the child would be worse off and 46 per cent say he would be better off; among the other husbandless mothers,

20 per cent say the child would be worse off and 37 per cent say he would be better off.[8]

All this indicates that the husbandless mothers are particularly concerned with the social influence of the father upon the child, and are evaluating that influence in terms of the father's character. In the analysis which follows, we are not trying to assess the accuracy of the mothers' judgments. We are trying to see how husbandless mothers, compared to married mothers, raise their children.

Values and Beliefs

In analyzing the mothers' values and beliefs pertaining to the development of independence and achievement of their children, we assume the values and beliefs may effect the children in several ways. First, the mothers may try to teach them to their children. Second, parents with their values and beliefs serve as models for the children. The values and beliefs may also be reflected in the conduct of the mothers toward their children. Finally, they may be indicators of the emotional and cognitive world to which the children must accommodate.

We begin this analysis by considering the maternal valuation of children acting independently of the parents. One consistent finding in the study of child-rearing patterns by socioeconomic rank is that low-ranking parents place particular emphasis upon obedience.[9] There is some evidence that an overemphasis upon obedience restricts the development of independent, creative children.[10] As an indicator of the mothers' valuation of independence rather than obedience, the mothers were asked several questions.

8. For an analysis of divorced mothers' concern about the way their children would be without the father and their problems with their children, see William J. Goode, *After Divorce* (Glencoe, Ill.: The Free Press, 1956) pp. 307-330.

9. For a review of such studies, see Urie Bronfenbrenner, "Socialization and Social Class through Time and Space," in *Readings in Social Psychology*, 3rd ed., E.E. Maccoby, T.M. Newcomb, and E.H. Hartley, eds. (New York: Holt, Rinehart and Winston, 1958), pp. 424-425.

10. W.C. Becker, *op. cit.*

The meaning and relevance of this dimension can be sensed by noting the responses the mothers made to a series of open-ended questions asked in both waves of the panel interviews. The mothers were asked,

1. Some people think children who respect their parents would not talk back to them. How do you feel about this?
2. When you ask (study child) to do something, does (he) (she) talk back—always, usually, rarely, or never?
3. What do you do when (study child) talks back?

Consider the responses of Ruth M., a 31-year-old separated mother of five children, three of whom are still living with her. A Negro, she grew up in Georgia, where her father was a sharecropper; she had eight years of education and her former husband was a car washer. She answered the questions, "I feel the same way Bible say, 'Honor thy father and thy mother'—I'm with the Bible. Child has no business talking back." The study child, she reports, usually does, however; and she says that when he does, "I whips him and punishes him too." These responses, of someone who lived in the area around Park homes and who then moved in Park, were essentially the same in both interviews. The responses of Nancy K. reveal a somewhat different orientation. She too is a Negro who grew up in the South; her father was a farmer and then became a construction worker. She had ten years of education; her former husband was a construction worker. She too had lived in Park neighborhood and then moved into Park project and her answers were also the same at both interviews. She said "Kids these days know so much and if you say something wrong they gonna tell you back—but not 'cause they don't respect you; they gotta say their side." The study child rarely did talk back, but when she did, the mother said, "Sometimes I tell her if she don't stop, I'll whip her."

The analysis in this section will be concentrated upon the answers to forced-choice questions asked in the cross- sectional survey. The questions were:

1. Some people say parents should try to make a child, say a 10-year-old boy, do what they ask without arguing or talking back. Do you agree very much with that idea, agree somewhat, or *disagree* somewhat, or disagree very much?

> 2. Some people say parents should encourage a child, say a ten-year-old boy, to talk up and decide for himself what to do. Do you agree very much with that, agree somewhat, or *disagree* somewhat, or do you disagree very much?

Valuing obedience and valuing autonomy may be considered two aspects of valuing children's independence in general.

Consensus was relatively high in regard to the child's obedience: about 60 per cent of the mothers agree very much that the 10-year-old boy should do what he is told without talking back; another quarter agree somewhat; only 4 per cent disagree very much. There is a little less consensus about encouraging a child to talk up: almost one-half of the mothers agree somewhat with the statement and another quarter agree very much; about 10 per cent disagree very much.

Several questions concern us about valuing obedience and not autonomy. Are these values associated with poverty? What conditions, related to poverty, help account for variations in these values? In particular, are socioeconomic origins related to these values and do the values differ between husbandless and married mothers? Answers to these questions will contribute to an assessment of the possible role of intergenerational processes in accounting for the way of life of the poor and its possible perpetuation.

In the aggregate, married mothers and husbandless mothers do not differ in their distribution of responses to these questions. This may be the result of their different circumstances. Employment is related to marital status and to poverty; is it related to these values? On the whole, it is not. There is only a small tendency for nonworking mothers to agree very much that a ten-year old boy should do as he is told without talking back and not to agree that he should be encouraged to talk up. This tendency holds for married and husbandless mothers and, holding employment status constant, does not reveal any differences between the two categories of mothers.

Area of residence is another contemporary circumstance related to poverty and marital status. Poor people tend to live among other poor persons and are subject to influences arising from that condition. There is some variation in the proportions of residents agreeing with the statements about obedience and autonomy among the four housing projects and the surrounding neighborhoods. Most notably, the tenants of Park housing projects are most likely to agree very much that a boy should do as he is told. This is particularly marked among the husbandless mothers. On the whole, however, we still find no systematic difference between husbandless and married mothers in their responses. There is no discernible pattern of responses by area in regard to the statement about encouraging a ten-year-old boy to talk up. These values appear to be relatively unaffected by the contemporary conditions studied.[11]

Let us turn to the most crucial variables for our concern. The impoverished mothers in the sample do tend to value obedience more than other mothers. Using gross income, 68 per cent of the poor agree very much that a boy should not talk back, while 53 per cent of the others agree very much. Using per capita disposable income, the differences are somewhat greater: 73 per cent of the impoverished agree compared to 52 per cent of the other mothers. Income has a variety of meanings; gross income has particular relevance for income as a social status indicator, while per capita disposable income has special relevance for income as an indicator of economic well-being or access to the commercial market. Therefore, the findings suggest that the financial strains of poverty, rather than the social status of poverty, is conducive to valuing children's obedience.

Disagreement with the statement that a boy should be encouraged to speak up is not related to either income measure. It may be that the tendency for low-status persons to agree with statements propounded by interviewers counter-

11. An analysis of several other values also fails to reveal differences between husbandless and married mothers. The other values investigated were importance for children of (1) having many friends and being popular, (2) being careful about spending money, and (3) being satisfied with whatever they have. Controls by age of children, race, income, and maternal employment did not reveal any differences between married and husbandless mothers. See Laurence T. Cagle, "Child-Rearing in Fatherless Families: Maternal Values, Beliefs, and Aspirations" (unpublished Master's thesis, Department of Sociology and Anthropology, Syracuse University, 1965).

acts any tendency there may be for the poor to be less likely to value autonomy and therefore disagree with the statement. It may also be, however, that valuing autonomy simply is not associated with poverty, unlike the small association noted with obedience. We cannot be certain which interpretation to make, but the more cautious interpretation will be taken here, that there is no relationship between this value and poverty. Holding income constant, there is only a suggestion that husbandless mothers are less likely to value obedience and more likely to value autonomy than are married mothers.

Even finding some association between poverty and valuing obedience, we need to consider intergenerational processes to assess the role of a subculture of poverty in regard to this value. We should expect the value to be held more frequently among mothers of low socioeconomic origins than among those of high socioeconomic origins if a subculture of poverty plays an important role. Furthermore, we have argued that for attributes whose expression does not depend upon conditions associated with being married, husbandless mothers are more likely to maintain attributes acquired in their families of orientation than are married mothers. Married mothers are subject to the current influence of their husbands. Values are one kind of attribute that should exemplify this reasoning.

As can be seen in Table 8.1, only among husbandless mothers is the social status of the family-of-origin highly associated with valuing obedience. Comparing married and husbandless mothers, holding constant both fathers' status and current income, reveals the variations underlying the aggregate similarity between the married and husbandless mothers. If the husbandless mother had a high socioeconomic background, she is unlikely to value obedience, compared to the married mothers. The pattern is the same for the responses to the question about a child talking up: husbandless mothers of high socioeconomic origins are likely to value autonomy.[12] (For simplicity, I am using the words "low"

12. Although the relationships are still statistically significant (at the .05 level by the Chi Square test and Kendall Tau), the relationships are not as strong as in the case of the value about obedience. Among the husbandless,

versus "high" socioeconomic origins; actually, the dichotomy is between low and not-low.)

Table 8.1. Per Cent Who Agree Very Much that Boy Should Obey Without Talking Back by Fathers' Occupational Status, by Income, and by Marital Status

Father's Occupational Index	*Husbandless Mothers Per Capita Disposable Income*		*Married Mothers Per Capita Disposable Income*	
	Less Than $500	*$500 or More*	*Less Than $500*	*$500 or More*
18 or less	75.8 (33)	65.5 (29)	77.8 (36)	57.5 (134)
19 or more	50.0 (22)	26.9 (26)	70.6 (17)	52.5 (118)

All this indicates that mothers of *high socioeconomic origins* toward a high valuation of independence if the husband father is missing. Evidence presented later in this chapter bears on the possibility that this value is expressed by appropriate promotion of independence rather than by overindulgent permissiveness or by abandonment of efforts at control. At this point it is sufficient to note that there is no evidence that mothers, in accommodating to the absence of a husband-father, modify their values about children's independence and obedience to that found among low-status parents.

On the whole, mothers living in poverty are more likely than other mothers to value obedience from their children. Among married mothers, however, this value is barely related to the socioeconomic status of their family-of-origin. Presumably, the valuation of obedience is a response to current income more than to childhood experiences in low-status families. Among the husbandless mothers, however, there is a marked interaction between current income

only the relationship between social origins and the value of talking-up is marked. Among the married mothers, neither income nor social-status origin is related to valuing talking-up.

and social origins. It is those who are currently impoverished *and* who had high status origins who are particularly likely to value autonomy and unlikely to value obedience. Intergenerational processes in accounting for this value, then, depend upon marital status and current income.

One aspect of child rearing which seems to be clearly related to the achievement motive of children is the promotion of early mastery of skills and responsibility for personal functions.[13] Studies of differences in child-rearing patterns by socioeconomic status often find that middle-strata parents, compared to lower-strata parents, encourage their children to take care of themselves and help in the house at an earlier age than do lower-strata families.[14] This aspect of child- rearing is particularly worth examining for another reason. Information on the division of labor in the household shows that the husbandless mother generally substitutes herself for most tasks that the missing husband usually performs; in many activities, others in the households, usually the children, also provide some substitution.[15] It might seem reasonable, there-

13. McClelland, *op. cit.;* there is also evidence that being responsible for home duties does not result in children having an attitude of responsibility. See D. B. Harris, K. E. Clark, A.M. Rose, and F. Valasek, "The Relationship of Children's Home Duties to an Attitude of Responsibility," *Child Development,* XXV (1954), pp. 29-33.

14. Bronfenbrenner, *op. cit.*

15. A series of questions on household tasks was included in the interview schedule. Mothers were asked to report those persons in and out of the households who took part in carrying out a sample of tasks or in making decisions about them. In the great majority of households, mothers have some assistance with one or more tasks from their husbands. On the whole, in the absence of a husband, the wife substitutes herself for most tasks which the missing husband usually performed. For example, 75 per cent of the husbandless mothers assume sole responsibility for paying bills, compared with but 29 per cent of the married mothers. In tasks in which husbands rarely participate (for example, cleaning the apartment or washing the dishes), virtually identical percentages of husbandless and married mothers perform the job without assistance. The proportion of mothers, both husbandless and married, who have assistance from others than their spouse, presumably children, increases substantially as the children grow older; it is lowest among those whose youngest child is of preschool age and highest among those who have no children under eleven years of age. It is also important to note that husbandless mothers are as likely as married mothers to maintain a clean, orderly home and to keep furniture in good repair. The interviewers rated each home they visited on each of these characteristics. The distribution of ratings does not differ between married and husbandless mothers.

fore, that husbandless mothers would expect their children to assume responsibility for certain activities at an earlier age than married mothers. The respondents were asked:

> Parents feel differently about when—that is, what age—children should be able to do different things. Tell me, at what age would you expect a boy to be able (1) to stay out after 10 at night, (2) to help out around the house, (3) to play outside without being watched, (4) to be able to tell right from wrong, (5) to get married, (6) to make up his mind on whether to stay in school, (7) to go downtown by himself.

The same series of questions was asked about a girl. As can be seen from Table 8.2, husbandless mothers differ very little from married mothers in the age at which they expect boys and girls to engage in these activities.

There is a slight tendency for husbandless mothers as a group to give a younger average age than married mothers. However, the differences approach statistical significance only for the age at which the boy is expected to be able to help around the house or go downtown by himself, or at the age at which the girl would be expected to get married or go downtown by herself. Apparently, there is enough societal consensus about the proper age for children to engage in various activities that not having a husband does not alter the mother's situation so markedly that she will modify her expectations. It might be argued that husbandless mothers vary greatly in accommodating to the husbands' absence and some would push for too early independence while others would be overprotective. The data do not support this idea. Thus, as can be seen in Table 8.2, the standard deviations for the age expectations of the husbandless mothers are the same as for the married mothers; there is no greater variability among the husbandless than among the married mothers.

The evidence suggests that the absence of a husband induces some modification in age expectation only for activities directly relevant to the mother's needs. The husbandless mother may expect a boy to help out in the house at a younger age than do married mothers. Going downtown at

Table 8.2. Mean Age at which Child Is Expected to be Able to Engage in Various Activities by Sex of Child and by Mother's Marital Status

		Boy		Girl	
*Activity**		*Husbandless Mother*	*Married Mother*	*Husbandless Mother*	*Married Mother*
1. Stay out after 10 at night	M	15.7	15.7	16.1	16.0
	(N)†	(132)	(400)	(132)	(400)
	SD	1.62	1.65	1.68	1.45
2. Help out around the house	M	7.2	7.6	7.1	7.2
	(N)†	(134)	(398)	(132)	(404)
	SD	2.68	2.68	2.75	2.66
3. Play outside without being watched	M	5.9	6.0	6.0	6.1
	(N)†	(132)	(399)	(133)	(400)
	SD	2.24	2.51	2.29	2.73
4. Be able to tell right from wrong	M	5.1	5.2	5.2	5.4
	(N)†	(132)	(398)	(132)	(398)
	SD	2.56	2.76	2.60	2.93
5. Get married	M	22.0	22.0	19.2	20.1
	(N)†	(132)	(397)	(132)	(402)
	SD	2.70	2.36	2.18	2.22
6. Make up (his) (her) own mind on whether to stay in school	M	16.9	17.1	16.8	16.9
	(N)†	(122)	(390)	(124)	(390)
	SD	1.68	1.81	1.50	1.73
7. Go downtown by (himself) (herself)	M	11.1	11.6	11.3	11.9
	(N)†	(133)	(402)	(134)	(401)
	SD	2.06	2.07	1.95	2.08

* None of the differences in the means between husbandless and married mothers are statistically significant at the .05 level, using the T-test.

† The number of cases upon which the means are based varies from one activity to another because differing numbers of mothers were unable to give a specific age.

age eleven or twelve also suggests the ability to shop and do errands, thus releasing the mother for other activities. If this is the case, we can also expect a working mother to give earlier age expectations for these activities than will a nonemployed mother. There is a tendency in this direction. As can be seen in Table 8.3, it is among husbandless mothers working full-time that the average age at which a boy is expected to go downtown himself is youngest. The differences are still small. Working and being without a husband combine to induce younger age expectations for activities which aid the husbandless mother. This is not true, however, for activities such as playing outside without being watched. The intrinsic imperatives of that responsibility are not easily modified by the mothers' marital or employment situation.

Table 8.3. Average Age at which Boy Is Expected to go Downtown by Himself by Mother's Work Status and Marital Status

	Work Status		
Mother	*Work Full-Time*	*Work Part-Time*	*Not Work*
Husbandless	10.4	11.1	11.5
(N)	(39)	(30)	(63)
SD	1.74	1.97	2.21
Married	11.4	11.3	11.8
(N)	(57)	(110)	(397)
SD	2.07	1.91	2.11

Residential areas may provide a set of circumstances that affect the husbandless mothers' expectations about the proper age for their children to engage in certain activities. Suppose, that children in slums generally behave in ways which the mothers think reprehensible. The mothers will try to keep their children from being exposed to this conduct. Of course, they may not succeed in doing so and they may even abandon their efforts after a time. Some indications of the efforts might be discernible if we compare areas which differ in the frequency with which young persons engage in disreputable behavior. The residential areas under study do differ in this regard.

The majority of tenants in Park project think that nearly all the children in the project get into trouble with the police or adults. Two-thirds of the tenants in Park and in Grant think that it is not safe to go out alone at night in their projects; in the other two projects only a third have such beliefs. These beliefs roughly parallel the juvenile delinquency rates of the areas. The juvenile delinquency rates were computed as an annual rate per 1,000 based upon the number of delinquents and the number of juveniles age seven to fifteen in each census tract. The rate for the census tract in which Park project is located is 82.9. The project adjoins two other census tracts—they have rates of 105.8 and 113.8, the highest in the city. Grant is located in a census tract with a rate of 50.8. Evans is in a tract with a rate of 22.4. Stern is in a tract with a rate of 26.7 and adjoins another tract whose rate is 36.6.[16]

Attempting to explain these variations among the areas would take us far afield from our concerns here. Given their existence, the analysis of maternal child-rearing practices may help account for their perpetuation. Under the circumstances, it is reasonable for a mother to try to control her child against the bad influences and dangers she sees all around. It is also reasonable for the child to assert himself against what appears to be overcontrol. Such revolt may then be met with greater suppression and attempted coercion which further estrange the child. Caught in such a cycle, the mother may feel hopeless and despairing, and the husbandless mother may be particularly vulnerable to such a cycle. Husbandless mothers could be particularly concerned about their children and yet lack the resources for indirect supervision.

By this reasoning, we anticipate variations by area for age expectations in regard to one of the activities about which the mothers were questioned. This is the age at which a child should stay out late at night. We do find some area variation in regard to age expectations for this activity, but no others.

16. Data drawn from George E. Bodine, *A Delinquency Profile of Syracuse and Onondaga County N.Y., 1962* (Syracuse, N.Y.: Syracuse University Youth Development Center, 1964).

Mothers in Park project expect children to be a little older before they can stay out after 10 at night, compared to the mothers in the other areas (see Table 8.4). Mothers in Grant project have the next oldest average age expectation for their children. The cross-sectional data, however, does not reveal any difference between husbandless and married mothers in these expectations.

Table 8.4. Mean Age at which Boy Is Expected to be Able to Stay Out After Ten at Night by Area and by Mother's Marital Status

	Residential Area				
Mother	*Evans*	*Grant*	*Park*	*Stern*	*Neighborhood**
Husbandless	15.3	15.8	16.1	15.5	15.5
(N)	(21)	(23)	(34)	(28)	(26)
SD	1.71	1.53	1.57	1.43	1.88
Married	15.5	15.9	16.2	15.6	15.7
(N)	(68)	(62)	(49)	(60)	(161)
SD	1.53	1.60	2.16	1.51	1.58

* In this table, and in Tables 8.5, 8.7, 8.8, 8.10, and 8.11, "neighborhood" refers to the four neighborhoods surrounding each project; there are too few husbandless mothers in each neighborhood to permit separate calculation of percentages.

The panel survey permits further testing of the ideas presented. In the panel, respondents were asked about one particular child of theirs, the study child. The age at which the study child would be expected to stay out late was compared between the first and second interviews. The analysis indicates very marked differences in the age expectations among the persons who moved into the different projects. Thus, the mothers who later moved into Park had especially high age expectations at the time of the first interview. Since they generally lived in the area around the project, movement into the project was not a marked change. The results are clear for the mothers who moved into Grant project. Their age expectations were not high at the first interview, but increased after a year's residence (on the average, an increase of .45 years). On the whole, however, we must conclude that selective factors were sufficiently important to obscure changes in age expectations as a result of residence in the various projects.

In general, age expectations for various kinds of activity are not markedly affected by the absence of a husband-father. Only for two items which may involve direct assistance to the mothers is there some indication that lacking a husband contributes to an earlier age expectation; the effect is increased when the mother is working. Residential areas may have some effect upon age expectations pertaining to the vulnerability of the child to what the mothers consider pernicious influences.

Finally, we must consider the possible significance of different social origins and current income levels. We noted earlier that husbandless mothers of low status origins were likely to value obedience. Consistent with this, there is a slight tendency for husbandless mothers of low status origins to expect their children to be older before independently engaging in various activities, compared to husbandless mothers of high status. The same tendency is found among the married mothers. This suggests that a pattern of inhibiting independence is related to socioeconomic rank and is intergenerationally transmitted. But the pattern of maternal expectations is not consistently related to current income. Among the married mothers there is little relationship between current income and age expectations; insofar as there is any, it is those with high income who have the older age expectations.[17] Among the husbandless mothers, the pattern is more inconsistent, and therefore in some activities we do find that those of high status origins and high current income are particularly likely to have young age expectations. For example, the average age expectation for a boy to help out around the house, in this category of mothers is 5.7 years (compare with Table 8.2, item 2). We must conclude that any subculture in regard to age expectations is overwhelmed by

17. The pattern is different for the one other item about which husbandless and married mothers appear to have somewhat different age expectations—the age at which a girl could marry. Among the husbandless mothers, those with low current income and low socioeconomic origins have particularly young age expectations.

the general societal agreement. A subculture could only make a very small contribution to accounting for age expectations related to children's independence.

Mothers may affect their children's independence and achievement not only by their values and expectations in these regards, but also by the means they use to influence their children and the socioemotional environment they provide. We begin our examination of these aspects of child-rearing by considering what the mothers believe to be good ways of influencing and controlling their children. As Bronfenbrenner writes, studies of child-rearing practices among different social strata regularly reveal that "in matters of discipline, working class parents are consistently more likely to employ physical punishment, while middle-class families rely more on reasoning, isolation, appeals to guilt, and other methods involving the threat of loss of love."[18] Empirical evidence generally supports the idea that "power-assertive techniques of discipline tend to be used by hostile parents, and in this context, tend to promote aggression in young children, resistance to authority, power assertion to other children, and externalized reactions to transgression (fear of punishment, projected hostility). There is suggestive evidence that, in time, consistent use of power-assertive techniques leads to an inhibition of overt aggression, but the hostility generated is still detectable . . . "[19] There is consistent evidence that internalized reactions to transgression in the form of guilt or acceptance of self-responsibility results from the use of praise and reasoning and low use of physical punishment.

We do not have observations of how the mothers actually discipline their children. The mothers were asked to report about their conduct, their childrens' behavior, and their beliefs about how they thought children should be raised. In expressing their beliefs, they are probably indicating their tendencies in conduct or at least their intentions. Since the feelings are also communicated to the child, such beliefs are

18. Bronfenbrenner, *op. cit.*, p. 424.
19. Becker, *op. cit.*, p. 189.

pertinent data. The mothers in the cross-sectional survey were asked, "People have different ways of raising their children. What do you think are the best ways to get a child to behave?" Overall, there are no differences between husbandless and married mothers in the answers they give to this question.[20] Over half of both categories of mothers mention physical punishement; almost a third mention isolation or denial of interaction; more than a quarter mention withholding toys, food, or other objects; almost a third mention explaining and reasoning with the child; and a wide variety of other actions were less frequently mentioned. Some of the circumstances under investigation do at least slightly affect the husbandless mothers' choice of ways to make a child behave, but no real differences between husbandless and married mothers emerge.[21]

Husbandless mothers who are not employed and have not been employed within the last year are less likely to mention reasoning with the child and more likely to mention denying interaction, compared to other husbandless mothers. Among married mothers no relationship was found. Socioeconomic status origins are not related to these beliefs; there is only a suggestion that husbandless mothers of low status origins are more likely to mention denial of interaction than are husbandless mothers of higher socioeconomic origins.

Surprisingly, the use of reasoning to influence children is not less widespread among the impoverished married mothers than among the other married mothers. Among the husbandless, those who are not living in poverty are more likely to use reason and less likely to deny interaction as a punishment than is true among the poor husbandless mothers or the married mothers in general. Even among the husbandless mothers, however, there is no consistent relationship between these ways of influencing children and their social

20. Some of the evidence is also reported and discussed in Cagle, *op. cit.*

21. The discussion is limited to mentions of denial of interaction and explanation, although other responses were also analyzed. However, references to physical punishment and denial of access to things are related to the age of the mothers' children, and this complicates the analysis. This is not true for the belief about the importance of spanking, which is considered later as a separate item.

origins. Current circumstances seem to be more important in accounting for these patterns than the intergenerational transmission of ways associated with the status of the family of origin.

The area differences are of particular interest. As can be seen in Table 8.5, there is some area variation in the proportion who mention explaining or reasoning with a child; this is especially marked among the mothers without husbands.[22] In Evans and Stern, husbandless mothers are particularly likely to mention this method of control. It is true, as shown in Chapter 5, that selective and self-selective processes play an important role in who lives in Evans. But that is not an adequate explanation of the findings, since selection did not

Table 8.5 Per Cent Who Mention Explanation or Reason as One of the Best Ways to Get a Child to Behave by Area and by Marital Status

	Areas				
Mother	*Evans*	*Grant*	*Park*	*Stern*	*Neighborhood*[*]
Husbandless	42.9 (21)	17.2 (29)	14.3 (35)	48.3 (29)	16.0 (25)
Married	32.9 (70)	16.2 (68)	22.5 (49)	31.7 (60)	30.3 (162)

[*] See note to Table 8.4.

operate in the same manner in Stern project and the findings are similar in both projects. In Park, Grant, and in the neighborhoods, the references to explaining and reasoning are very low. This indicates that where husbandless mothers do not fear the influences from the neighborhood they tend to choose less suppressive methods of control than do married mothers. However, in areas of greater potentially undesired influences, the husbandless mothers are less likely than the

22. The area pattern for the denial of interaction complements the pattern for references to explanation or reasoning, with one exception. Married mothers in Evans are very likely to mention denial of interaction (50 per cent do); among the husbandless mothers, about one-third of those in Evans do—equalling the to-be-expected relatively high proportions in Park, Grant, and the neighborhood.

marrried mothers to believe that explaining and reasoning is the best method of control. This interpretation is supported by the analysis of the responses to a question about the belief in spanking.

The mothers were asked, "Do you think that spanking them if they did something wrong is very important for your children, somewhat important, or don't you believe in that?" About half of the married and husbandless mothers replied that spanking is very important. But when we compare husbandless and married mothers under various circumstances and backgrounds, differences begin to emerge. Among the married mothers, belief in spanking is affected by current income, but hardly by social status origins; among the husbandless mothers, the relationships are trivial.

Other evidence indicates that the husbandless mothers' attitudes are especially likely to be influenced by their family of orientation. The respondents were asked not only how important they thought spanking to be, but to report how important their mothers and fathers thought it to be.[23] The association between the respondents' beliefs and the beliefs they attribute to their parents is substantial, as shown in Table 8.6. The association is greater between the respondent and her mother than between the respondent and her father. More pertinent to our concern, the association is slightly higher among the husbandless mothers than among the married.

We have argued that husbandless mothers, lacking the additional source of influence which a husband may provide,

23. We examined the relationship between their fathers' socioeconomic statuses and their reports of their mothers' beliefs in the importance of spanking. The relationships are small, even if statistically significant. This explains the lack of association between belief in spanking and social status origins. Respondents were classified into five categories depending upon their fathers' occupational socioeconomic index. Belief in spanking was divided into three categories: (1) believe it to be very important, (2) somewhat important, and (3) do not believe in it. The association was calculated for both married and husbandless mothers. The association between reported mother's belief and father's occupational index, according to the Kendall Tau C is −.14 (based upon 448 cases, $p=.001$); the association between the respondent's father's belief about spanking and his occupational index is −.09 (based upon 420 cases—fewer respondents could report knowing their fathers' beliefs—$p=.01$).

are likely to be more influenced by their family-of-origin than are married mothers. We also expect husbandless mothers, however, to be more subject to influence from directly relevant current circumstances. Income is a circumstance, but we

Table 8.6. Associations Between Mother's Belief about the Importance of Spanking and Her Mother's and Father's Belief about Importance of Spanking by Marital Status

	Mother	
Kendall Tau C.	*Husbandless*	*Married*
Between respondent's belief and her mother's	.38 (110)	.30 (332)
Between respondent's belief and her father's	.31 (100)	.26 (316)

found that belief in spanking was not related to current income among the husbandless mothers, while it was among the married mothers. Income, however, is not a circumstance which is directly relevant to the belief about spanking. Furthermore, income is not only an economic circumstance but is also an indicator of social-class position for the married, but less so for the husbandless mothers. Therefore, we would expect that current income, indicating the husband's class position would be related to the married mothers' beliefs about spanking.[24]

By this reasoning, we expect that husbandless mothers, more than married mothers, will have their beliefs about spanking affected by the area in which they live, if the areas differ in ways relevant to control of children. The data support this (see Table 8.7). We see considerable variation by residential area among the husbandless mothers. In Evans and Stern the proportion who believe spanking is very important is quite low. On the other hand, the husbandless mothers in Park and Grant are especially likely to think it is very important to spank children. These are the projects, as we have noted, seen as having a possible detrimental in-

24. Mother's work status is not related to the belief about spanking.

fluence upon the children. These area patterns persist when income and social status of family-of-origin are held constant.

Table 8.7. Per Cent Who Think Spanking Children Is Very Important by Area and by Marital Status

	Areas				
Mother	*Evans*	*Grant*	*Park*	*Stern*	*Neighborhood*°
Husbandless	14.3 (21)	65.5 (29)	65.7 (35)	28.6 (28)	72.0 (25)
Married	51.4 (70)	45.6 (68)	59.6 (47)	46.7 (60)	42.1 (164)

° See note to Table 8.4.

As suggested earlier, in areas in which other children are thought to be behaving improperly, parents will make special efforts to counter the disliked peer influences. Husbandless mothers are particularly disadvantaged in applying that pressure since they lack support from a spouse in providing it; they cannot count on another parent also applying some pressure; they have fewer resources with which to distract or reward their children; and they may even be accorded less legitimacy by their children in the exercise of parental authority. Consequently, they tend to resort to more coercive forms of pressure in a rising crescendo. This interpretation may also be relevant for the general finding that low-income families are more likely to employ physical punishment than are middle-income parents. One explanation for this is that the failure to achieve status in the larger society induces a sense of frustration which is expressed in aggression against the children.[25] It is also possible that the processes described above operate for parents in complete families, even if to a less marked extent. In other words, poor parents generally face greater problems of control of their children than do more well-to-do parents and feel constrained in the resulting interaction to resort to physical punishment.

25. Donald Gilbert McKinley, *Social Class and Family Life* (New York: Free Press of Glencoe, 1964).

Physical punishment in disciplining children is more widespread among the impoverished families in the study than among the others. Although reliance upon physical punishment may have some deleterious effects upon the later achievement of the children, we have no evidence that the practice can be accounted for by a subculture of poverty which is intergenerationally transmitted. Social origins are not related to the practice. This does not mean that all intergenerational processes are irrelevant (see Table 8.6). What one's parents thought about spanking is related to one's own beliefs, but the relationship between those beliefs and socioeconomic status is so weak that socioeconomic status origins do not help account for current beliefs about spanking.

Another aspect of child-rearing which may affect children's achievement is the mother's own sense of competence and control. Perhaps a mother who feels that what she does largely determines the future of her children will have definite goals and will exert effort to realize them; in any case, her sense of responsibility and control may be transmitted to her children. Studies indicate that a mother's sense of potency in influencing her children and their future is associated with the adjustment of children in school.[26]

The respondents were asked, "Do you think how a child turns out is *mostly* due to his own nature, mostly due to how his parents raise him, or mostly due to the children he goes around with?" Here we find a difference between the married and the husbandless mothers: 74 per cent of the married mothers replied, "How parents raise him;" 57 per cent of the husbandless mothers made the same response.[27] Further-

26. A review of studies of maternal attitudes and children's adjustment (M. C. L. Gildea, J. C. Glidewell, and M. B. Kantor, "Maternal Attitudes and General Adjustment in School Children," in *Parental Attitudes and Child Behavior,* John C. Glidewell, ed. [Springfield, Ill.: Charles C. Thomas, 1961], p. 89) concluded that lower-class mothers, compared to upper- or middle-class mothers, are "least confident about their methods, least responsible for the behavior of their children, saw their children as in need of close parental control, but most often felt impotent to influence the outcome of behavior problems in their children.... Mothers with the best adjusted children could see multiple influences on child behavior, felt themselves to be one of the influences, and felt potent to exercise influence."

27. Respondents were also asked who largely determined how intelligent, how ambitious, and how popular a child becomes. On these more specific

more, the husbandless mothers in Park project are relatively unlikely to choose this response; while in Evans they are likely to do so (see Table 8.8). It may well be that peers play a relatively larger role in influencing children in fatherless than in complete families, particularly in some neighborhoods.[28] It is also conceivable that some husbandless mothers try to protect themselves from a sense of failure in raising children by shifting some of the responsibility to the child's peers and some to the child himself.

Table 8.8. Per Cent Who Think How Child Turns Out is Due Mostly to How Parents Raise Him by Area and by Marital Status

	Areas				
Mother	*Evans*	*Grant*	*Park*	*Stern*	*Neighborhood*°
Husbandless	80.0 (20)	58.6 (29)	35.3 (34)	62.1 (29)	61.5 (26)
Married	81.2 (69)	77.6 (67)	77.6 (49)	61.7 (60)	72.1 (161)

° See note to Table 8.4.

The findings from the panel survey cast some light on these possibilities. On the whole, there is a tendency among married and husbandless mothers to be less likely to say that parents are responsible for how their children turn out in the second interview than in the first. This is not the case among those who did not move between the first and second interviews. Among the husbandless mothers, the shift is toward viewing the neighborhood in which the child grows up as having responsibility, and among the married mothers, the shift is slightly toward the child's own nature. Moreover, it is particularly in Park and Grant that husband-

beliefs, husbandless and married mothers usually, and in about the same proportion, said the child himself. See Cagle, *op. cit.*, pp. 81-84.

28. This interpretation is supported by the finding that among husbandless mothers the proportion who say the parent is largely responsible markedly declines when they have only older children at home; there is no relation between age of children and this belief among the married mothers. The pattern of area differences persists when income or socioeconomic origin is held constant.

less mothers shift toward believing that the neighborhood is responsible for how a child turns out. These diverse findings can be explained in terms of the parents' experiences. Belief in parental responsibility for how children turn out declines as children become older and the parents see how the children develop. Changing neighborhood residence makes more visible how much a neighborhood affects the children and this affects the parents' belief in the relevance of the neighborhood. This would be most marked among husbandless mothers. The peer pressures upon fatherless children may be particularly important, and especially in areas where the age-mates pursue activities the parents do not like.

Finally, neither income nor socioeconomic origins are related to the belief that parents are responsible for how a child turns out, among the married mothers. Current income is not related to this belief among the husbandless mothers either. There is a small association among the husbandless with the socioeconomic status of the family of origin: those with low status origins are less likely to say the parents are responsible than are those with high status origins (47 per cent compared to 64 per cent). This suggests that the lack of a husband induces some mothers to eschew parental responsibility if they come from families of low socioeconomic status. This interpretation is supported by analysis of the responses to another question. The mothers were asked if they agreed or disagreed with the statement, "It is impossible to plan the future of a child because one doesn't know what the future will bring." Overall, there is no difference between husbandless and married mothers in response to this question (over 60 per cent of each category agree). But the overall similarity between husbandless and married mothers obscures important variations, particularly among the husbandless. We again find evidence that family-of-origin has a marked effect upon this belief among the husbandless mothers, and origins interact with current income to affect the belief about the possibility of planning (see Table 8.9). If the husbandless mother had low socioeconomic origins and is currently impoverished, she is very likely to think that it is impossible to plan for the future of her children; but if she did not come from low socioeconomic origins and is not currently impoverished, she is even more likely to think it is possible to plan than similarly situated married mothers.

The impoverished mothers in this study are not much more likely than the others to think planning is impossible. Among the married mothers, it is only those who are impoverished *and* had low socioeconomic status origins who are likely to think planning is impossible.

Table 8.9. Per Cent Who Agree That it Is Impossible to Plan Future of Child by Father's Occupational Status and by Mother's Income and Marital Status

	Husbandless Mothers		*Married Mothers*	
	Per Capita Disposable Income		*Per Capita Disposable Income*	
Father's Occupational Index	*Less Than $500*	*$500 or More*	*Less Than $500*	*$500 or More*
18 or less	79.4 (34)	72.4 (29)	75.0 (36)	56.8 (132)
19 or more	59.1 (22)	46.2 (26)	55.6 (18)	57.9 (121)

The panel survey reveals that the responses to this question change from one time to another. About three-fourths of those who agreed to the impossibility of planning at the time of the first interview said the same thing a year later. Only about one-half of the persons who disagreed with the statement did so a year later. There is no major net change by neighborhood, however, except among married mothers who moved into Evans: at the time of the first interview, 80 per cent agreed with the statement but at the second interview this had fallen to 45 per cent. All this indicates that the belief is modifiable, but the change in circumstances entailed by moving from one neighborhood to another are not great enough to produce a general shift in this belief. The lack of perfect stability in responses to the question does not invalidate the question. It does indicate that the responses, to some extent, reflect contemporary conditions as well as internalized predispositions.

In summary, most husbandless mothers have the same values and beliefs about control and independence of their children as do most married mothers. Attitudes about child-rearing are not radically affected by losing a husband. Some accommodation to his absence, however, does seem to occur. In general, the findings indicate that husbandless mothers have a heightened concern about the well-being of their children. The expression of this concern assumes different forms for husbandless mothers of different forms for husbandless mothers of different socioeconomic backgrounds in different circumstances. Husbandless mothers of relatively high socioeconomic origins tend to value independence, do not eschew responsibility for the way their children turn out, and believe that they can plan for the future of their children.

Among the circumstances under study, the area of residence appears to be of particular importance. Husbandless mothers living in areas perceived as potentially dangerous for their children seem to value obedience, have slightly older average age expectations for certain activities for their children, are less likely to believe that reasoning and explaining is the best way to make a child behave, are more likely to believe in spanking, and are less likely to feel responsible for the way their children turn out. The data also suggest that being employed is associated with valuing independence and believing that reasoning is the best way to control children. Income *per se* does not markedly affect husbandless mothers' child-rearing attitudes; insofar as it does, it appears to be associated with a smaller likelihood of valuing independence and believing in reasoning as a way to get a child to behave, and a greater likelihood of mentioning denial of interaction as one of the best ways of controlling a child.

Intergenerational processes play a role in accounting for some of the values and beliefs analyzed. Their importance, generally is greater for the husbandless than the married mothers. Current income, on the other hand, often is more associated with the values and beliefs studied among the married than among the husbandless mothers.

DIRECT AND INDIRECT CONTROL OF CHILDREN

When we consider the mothers' actual conduct in relationship to their children, we do not expect predispositions learned in the family-of-origin to be as important, even among husbandless mothers, as was the case for attitudes. The competing demands upon the husbandless mothers' limited time and energy resources should play a greater explanatory role. The analysis of the mothers' conduct will also help resolve some ambiguities in interpreting and explaining the previous findings. With increased importance of the mother-child relationship, do husbandless mothers, in circumstances which are not threatening, overindulge their children, or do they use the opportunity to promote appropriate early independence? Under conditions of stress, do these mothers despair of control so much that they abandon their efforts, or do they try to compensate—even to the extent of overcontrolling their children and thus perhaps facing a different kind of threat as the child seeks his independence? Or is being husbandless simply not a very important factor in explaining the way mothers act toward their children?

To assess the actual independence allowed the children, we are using the mothers' reports of whether the parents or the study child decides about various activities. The question was:

> Parents differ on the things they allow their children to decide for themselves. Do you (and your husband) allow (study child) to make up (his) (her) own mind or do you (and your husband) decide about (1) the amount of time (he) (she) spends watching TV or listening to the radio? (2) the things he reads and the movies he goes to? (3) whether or not (he) (she) goes along when you visit friends or relatives? (4) the amount of time (he) (she) spends with (his) (her) friends?

Note that in this question the married mother could answer about the husband as well; thus we can see the extent to which the husbandless mother decides activities for her child compared to both the father *and* mother in the case of complete families.[29]

Obviously, the age of the study child is highly associated with whether he or his parents decide about these activities. Therefore, we have standardized the responses by the age of the study child. This standardization also permits us to compare mothers who report deciding things for a child when he is older, somewhat younger, much younger, or the usual age at which most parents decide about the particular activity.

For each activity we studied the distribution of responses for both married and husbandless mothers with a study child at each age (one-year intervals were used). We found a clear discontinuity in the age at which parents did or did not decide upon each activity.[30] The break in continuity served as the dividing line in setting up categories for types of control. If the parents decided upon the activity and the child was older than the age at which *most* parents no longer decided upon the activity, the parent is overcontrolling the child. Control at the usual age includes two possibilities: (1) the child was at the age at which most parents still decided the activity *and* the mother reported deciding upon the activity or (2) the child was older than the usual age at which parents decided the activity *and* the mother reported that the

29. Four possible responses to the question were coded: (1) child decides, (2) parent(s) decide, (3) both parent(s) and child decide, and (4) sometimes child and sometimes parent(s). Only a small proportion of the respondents volunteered the last two responses. The preliminary analysis did not reveal differences not shown by simply dichotomizing the responses into the categories of parent decides or parent does not.

30. For the amount of time watching TV or listening to the radio, 64 per cent of the mothers with a study child of eleven years report the parent decides; among parents with a 12-year-old child, only 38 per cent so report. Furthermore, the percentage reporting the parent decides ranged from 64 to 82 among mothers with study children age 6 to 11 years, and the percentages ranged from 48 to 0 among mothers with children 12 to 18 years old. For the things read and movies seen, 56 per cent of the mothers of 13-year-olds decide, while only 16 per cent of those with study children aged 14 do so. For going along on visits to friends and relatives, age 13 also marks the discontinuity: 64 per cent of the mothers of the 13-year-old study children report the parent decides, compared to 26 per cent of the mothers of 14-year-olds. On controlling the time spent with friends, 64 per cent of the mothers with study children age 13 decide this, compared to 37 per cent of the mothers with children age 14.

parent did not decide upon the activity. If the parents did not decide and the child was at the age at which the parents still usually decided upon the activity or was only one or two years younger, the parent is categorized as promoting early independence. If, however, the child was three years or more below the age at which most parents controlled the child and the mother reported not doing so, she is categorized as exercising undercontrol.

A difficulty remains with this measure. Since the distribution of ages of study children varies by marital status, employment, and other conditions, the opportunity to overcontrol, undercontrol, or allow early independence varies by such conditions. Therefore, it is still necessary to control for the age of the study child. For example, we must see whether or not mothers with study children age fourteen or older report exercising usual control or overcontrol. The results of such an examination are considered in making all interpretations. Of course, the number of cases for certain comparisons are very few; therefore, the results must be considered as suggestive rather than definitive.

We will discuss the decision about the time the study child spends with his friends as a prototype of the conditions affecting parental control of the study child's activities. Taking into account the age of the study child, we find that husbandless mothers are much more likely to overcontrol than exercise usual control.[31] The two categories of mothers do not differ in the proportion who undercontrol or allow early independence rather than exercise usual control.

We are especially interested, however, in how particular conditions may affect the mothers' conduct. First, we wish to consider the consequences of the early socialization experiences, as indicated by their fathers' socioeconomic status. The patterns of association are complex. Husbandless mothers of low socioeconomic origins are more likely to overcontrol and less likely to undercontrol than are husbandless mothers of higher socioeconomic origins. There is

31. Thus, among mothers with study children 14 or older, 47 per cent of the husbandless mothers overcontrol, compared to 19 per cent of the married mothers.

no difference in relationship to early independence. Among the married mothers, those of low socioeconomic origins are also somewhat more likely to overcontrol, but they are less likely to promote early independence compared with married mothers of higher socioeconomic origins. When we hold socioeconomic rank constant, husbandless mothers are still much more likely to overcontrol than are married mothers. However, husbandless mothers of low socioeconomic rank are less likely to undercontrol than are married mothers. Among mothers of high origins, the husbandless are more likely to undercontrol than are married mothers.[32]

Several interpretations can be offered for these findings. We noted earlier that husbandless mothers of high socioeconomic origins tend to value independence; now it appears that such valuation may be expressed in excessive permissiveness. But other evidence indicates that the process and meaning may be different. It is the husbandless mothers of high socioeconomic origins *and* current poverty who are particularly likely to undercontrol. This suggests that undercontrol reflects an abandonment of effort among mothers of formerly high status who now face particularly difficult circumstances. On the whole, then, all this indicates that husbandless mothers tend to overcontrol, but some of them, under certain conditions, do withdraw from efforts at direct control. We need to examine the effects of other conditions before we can fully interpret these findings.

In the analysis of values and beliefs relevant to indepen-

32. Among mothers with study children aged 6 to 10, 26 per cent of the husbandless of low socioeconomic origins exercise undercontrol rather than usual control. Among husbandless mothers who are not of low socioeconomic origins, 73 per cent exercise undercontrol. Among the married mothers, the percentages are 46 and 39, respectively. Among mothers with study children aged 11 to 13, 41 per cent of the husbandless mothers of low socioeconomic origins and 46 per cent with high socioeconomic origins report allowing early independence rather than usual control. But among the married, the percentages are 27 and 53, respectively. Among mothers with study children 14 to 18 years old, 75 per cent of the husbandless of low socioeconomic origins exercise overcontrol rather than usual control. Among husbandless mothers who are not of low socioeconomic origins, 33 per cent report overcontrol. Among the married mothers, the percentages are 31 and 6, respectively.

dence, we found little or no effects of employment. There was only a suggestion that working mothers tended to favor earlier independence for their children than did nonemployed mothers. Now we find that among husbandless mothers there is no relationship between employment and type of parental control over the time the study child spends with his friends. Among the married mothers there is a tendency unlike that found in the case of values and beliefs: the employed married mother is less likely to promote early independence than the nonemployed. Perhaps the working mother verbally supports early independence but her absence results in her attempting to exercise more control than she would otherwise attempt.

We did not find a marked relationship between current income and those values and beliefs among the husbandless mothers. There are no statistically significant relationships between income and reports of actual control—only indications. Among husbandless mothers, those who are poor are somewhat more likely to undercontrol and less likely to promote early independence than are those who are not poor. Among the married, there is a tendency for the poor to be less likely to overcontrol, as compared with the nonpoor.

On the whole, there is little or no relationship between income and the degree of parental control. In itself this indicates that this pattern of conduct cannot be accounted for by a subculture of poverty. We have seen that under certain combinations of circumstances, variations in degree of control do occur. Poor husbandless mothers show some tendency to either overcontrol or undercontrol their children. Undercontrol is most marked for the poor husbandless mothers who came from low socioeconomic status backgrounds. Intergenerational processes, then, can play a role in the perpetuation of child-rearing practices relevant to later achievement *if* certain specific contemporary conditions exist.

We found that mothers' values and beliefs are affected by residential area, particularly if the mother is without a husband. The findings, however, were not always consistent and unambiguous. An examination of the possible area differences in type of control clarifies the ambiguities. As can be seen in Table 8.10, there is little area variation among married mothers in type of parental control, but there is considerable variation among the husbandless mothers. Husbandless mothers in Grant, Park, and Stern appear to be disproportionally likely to overcontrol, but when age of the study child is held constant, this is only true for Grant and Park. Undercontrol is particularly unlikely in Park and likely in Stern; when age of children is held constant, undercontrol is also relatively high among the husbandless mothers in Grant. Early independence is relatively high in Evans and Grant.

Table 8.10. Type of Parental Control of Time Study Child Spends with Friends by Area and by Marital Status

	Husbandless Mothers Area				
Type of Control	*Evans*	*Grant*	*Park*	*Stern*	*Neighborhood*°
Under-control Parent does not decide and child is 6–10	12.6	16.6	5.8	32.0	11.1
Early independence Parent does not decide and child is 11–13	18.8	25.0	8.8	4.0	11.1
Usual control Parent decides and child is 6–13 or parent does not decide and child is 14–18	62.5	33.3	73.5	48.0	72.2
Over-control Parent decides and child is 14–18	6.3	25.0	11.8	16.0	5.6
Totals %	100.2	99.9	99.9	100.0	100.0
(N)	(16)	(24)	(34)	(25)	(18)

	Married Mothers				
	Area				
Type of Control	*Evans*	*Grant*	*Park*	*Stern*	*Neighborhood*[*]
Under-control Parent does not decide and child is 6–10	21.6	25.0	18.8	20.0	21.9
Early independence Parent does not decide and child is 11–13	5.4	10.7	12.5	2.9	11.8
Usual control Parent decides and child is 6–13 or parent does not decide and child is 14–18	70.3	62.5	68.8	77.1	61.3
Over-control Parent decides and child is 14–18	2.7	1.8	0.0	0.0	5.0
Totals %	100.0	100.0	100.1	100.0	100.0
(N)	(37)	(56)	(32)	(35)	(119)

[*] See note to Table 8.4.

Additional information can be gained by considering the married mothers as a standard of comparison in each area. Holding constant the age of the study child, we find that in Evans, husbandless mothers are more likely to promote early independence than are married mothers. In Grant, the husbandless are more likely to either over- or undercontrol than are the married mothers. In Park, the husbandless mothers are more likely to overcontrol and less likely to undercontrol or promote early independence than are the married mothers. In Stern, husbandless mothers are much more likely than married mothers to undercontrol, somewhat more likely to overcontrol, and even somewhat more likely to promote early independence rather than exercise usual control. In the neighborhoods, husbandless mothers are somewhat less likely than married mothers to promote early independence.

These findings are generally consistent with the earlier findings and interpretations, but they permit further specification. We reasoned earlier that in areas which are viewed as sources of undesired influence upon the children, husbandless mothers would be especially likely to try to control their children. We also noted signs that in such areas some husbandless mothers despair of effectively controlling and directing their children. We could not conclude whether efforts at control would persist or be abandoned. We also reasoned that in areas which are considered safe and possibly of beneficial influence upon the children, the husbandless mothers would be less likely to exercise stringent control. The data before did not allow us to determine whether that freedom would be excessive—indicating withdrawal or indulgence—or be the promotion of early mastery.

The additional data help to resolve some of these issues. In areas which are generally thought of as being safe and in which the children are not viewed as getting into trouble with police, husbandless mothers are somewhat more likely to promote early independence and are not likely to simply undercontrol the children, compared to married mothers. This is clearest in the case of Evans; Stern requires special consideration.

The diversity of responses to the circumstances of Stern, and also Grant, probably reflects the differences among the husbandless mothers and the diversity of the area. Park husbandless mothers are overwhelmingly of low socioeconomic origins and the area is viewed as most threatening. Despite despair and lack of confidence about controlling children, these mothers do not, on the whole, abandon their efforts at control, at least for preadolescents. In Grant, there are favorable beliefs about most of the children in the area, as we shall see in our discussion of education in the next chapter. This may help account for the relatively high proportion of husbandless mothers who report what we call promoting early independence. In Stern, there is a diversity among the husbandless mothers—and it is the poor husbandless mothers who are likely to undercontrol while it is the not-so-poor ones who overcontrol. This also is in response to an area which has great diversity. As described in Chapter 4, Stern neighborhood is comprised predominantly of very high socioeconomic status families, but there are also families of low status. The mothers' children, then, can select or be selected into groups that are quite different.

This last point, as well as others, can be illustrated by the observations made of one group of boys of Stern neighborhood and public housing project.[33] During one summer an observer participated in the activities of a group of teenagers, about half of whom lived in Stern housing project. This was a loosely knit group whose membership and social relationships changed in the course of the summer. At one time or another ten boys were members. Three of the five boys from Stern project came from fatherless families; the boys from the neighborhood were from complete families. But, with the exception of one whose father owned a neighborhood store, the boys' fathers were unemployed or worked at unskilled, manual jobs.

The group did not regularly congregate at any meeting place. Rather, one boy found another and they looked for a third member and then a fourth and so on. They avoided the formal activities of the available recreational centers, preferring to play at the neighborhood playground or swimming pool. The activities were unorganized and even unconstrained by the structure of being home for meals. Parental supervision was minimal, as was any organization of activities from outsiders. What we have classified together as "usual control" includes a broad spectrum of supervision. Among children of families of middle and higher socioeconomic status, there is probably more supervision in the form of checking in at home for meals and keeping the parents informed about their movements. If this is not the pattern, parents who want to maintain supervision must intervene more directly.

33. The observations, by David Cumming, are summarized in Helen Icken Safa, "A Case Study of Adolescent Boys in Public Housing," Social Mobility and Housing Case Studies in Participant Observation #1 (Syracuse University Youth Development Center, 1965; mimeographed.) and in David Cumming and Elaine Cumming, "The Everyday Life of Delinquent Boys," in *Among the People: Studies of the Urban Poor,* Irwin Deutscher and Elizabeth J. Thompson, eds. (New York: Basic Books, 1968), pp. 146-160.

The type of parental control of the three other activities the mothers were asked about were (1) the amount of time the study child spends watching television or listening to the radio, (2) the things he reads and the movies he goes to, and (3) whether or not the study child goes along when the parent visits friends or relatives. The pattern of relationship for these activity spheres are similar in some ways to those noted for control of the amount of time the study child spends with his friends. Again, we find that husbandless mothers of low socioeconomic status origins are more likely to overcontrol than are those of higher status origins. Holding socioeconomic status origins constant, husbandless mothers are more likely to overcontrol than are married mothers. Among mothers of low status origins, the husbandless are less likely to undercontrol; among those of higher status origins, the husbandless are somewhat more likely to undercontrol.

Employment does seem to have some effects upon the three activity spheres. Among the husbandless mothers, those who work are less likely to undercontrol than are those who do not work. This is consistent with the interpretation that if indirect control or supervision is difficult, more direct control is attempted. Among the married mothers, the employed are more likely to undercontrol, compared to the nonemployed. Income is related differently to each of these spheres of parental control. The associations are too complex for brief summarization and not sufficiently large to make a lengthy exposition worthwhile.

There does not appear to be any real area variation in parental control on these items among married mothers. Even among the husbandless mothers the area variations are not as marked as was the case for control over the time the study child spends with his friends. In the case of type of control over whether or not the study child goes along when the parent visits friends or relatives, the area variations, controlling for the age of the study child, are essentially the same as those noted for the time the study child spends with his friends. In general, area effects are clearest for the sphere of activity most obviously related to the characteristics of the area: the time a child spends with his friends and areas which differ in safety and presumed bad influences.

We noted earlier that husbandless mothers did not differ, in the aggregate, in their likelihood of valuing obedience from their children. Now we find some tendency for husbandless mothers to overcontrol their children. This suggests that if there is any relationship between the value and the conduct, the relationships are different for the husbandless and for the married mothers. This appears to be the case. We analyzed, for each of the four areas of possible control, the relationship between valuing obedience and the reports of under versus usual control, early independence versus usual control, and usual versus overcontrol; age of study child was held constant. Thus, twelve relationships among husbandless and then among married mothers were examined. Although a few relationships are large, most are not even statistically significant. Among the married mothers, 10 of the 12 relationships were in the direction indicating congruence between values and conduct and 4 of the 10 were statistically significant (at the .05 level or better, using the Kendall Tau). The largest of these relationships was in the area of control over the things read and movies seen: mothers who valued obedience tended not to report early independence (Kendall Tau $C = .23$). On the other hand, among the husbandless mothers, only 5 of the 12 relationships were in the direction of presumed consistency between the value and conduct. Of the three statistically significant relationships, two were in relationships indicating inconsistency, for example, in the area of control over the things read and movies seen. Those who did not value obedience highly tended to report usual control rather than early independence (Kendall Tau $C = -.42$, $p. = .001$).

On the whole, the findings indicate little overall relationship between the valuation of obedience and type of control practiced. Among the married mothers there is a tendency for the relationships found to be in the direction of presumed consistency between the value and conduct. Relationships are less frequent among the husbandless mothers and when they exist, are in a direction indicating inconsistency between the value and the conduct. We shall see more of this pattern in the next chapter when we examine educationally relevant values and conduct.

We have already suggested an explanation for the husbandless mothers' tendency to overcontrol and exert direct control of their children and that explanation also helps account for the lack of congruence between valuing obedience and the type of control reported. The explanation lies not only in the heightened concern for their children's welfare, but in the fewer opportunities for the indirect control which married mothers exercise. Control of children may be exercised in many indirect ways. If the children play at each other's homes, the parents can implicitly, if not explicitly, affect the selection of friends and the activities of the children. To exercise similar influence upon street activities would require direct and explicit efforts at control. Among older children, participation in formally organized activities can also be more easily regulated than the informal group activities of adolescents.

Answers to one of the questions asked of the mothers in the cross-sectional survey provide information about one aspect of such indirect parental influence. The mothers were asked, "Does (study child) spend time with his friends here at home—often, once-in-a-while, or never?" Husbandless mothers are less likely to report that the study child plays at home with his friends than are married mothers.[34] Apparently it is difficult for husbandless mothers to provide the facilities or the necessary exchanges with other mothers that would make their homes places in which their children could play with friends. This seems to be intrinsically related to

34. Mothers with an older study child are less likely to report that he spends time with his friends at home, compared to mothers with a younger child. Since husbandless mothers tend to have older children than do married mothers, it is necessary to control for age of the study child to see if the difference between husbandless and married mothers remains. The relationship is reduced, but does not disappear. Thus, the percentage of mothers who report that the study child often spends time at home with his friends is as follows: among mothers with children aged 6 to 11—54 percent of the husbandless and 67 per cent of the married mothers; among mothers with children 12 to 18—48 per cent of the husbandless and 58 per cent of the married mothers.

marital condition. Thus, among married mothers, working is slightly associated with less frequent reports of the children often playing at home with friends; this association is not found among husbandless mothers.

Again we find that poverty *per se* does not have simple determining effects. Among the fatherless families, income is not related to the frequency with which children play at home with their friends. Only among the complete families do we find some relationship; but the relationship is direct or inverse, depending upon the income measure used. That is, using per capita disposable income we find that the impoverished are less likely to have their children play at home with their friends. But using gross income, the relationship is just the opposite. This indicates that it is income as access to the commercial market rather than as an index of social status or a way of life which affects this pattern of conduct. Furthermore, there is no relationship between social origins and this pattern of conduct among the husbandless mothers. Among the married mothers, it is true we find a small tendency for those of high socioeconomic status origins to have their children play at home with friends, even holding per capita disposable income constant.

The extent to which children play at each other's homes varies considerably among the areas studied (see Table 8.11). On the whole, the practice is high in Evans and low in Park. On the basis of observations made of Park tenants, the exclusion of children from the home may take extreme forms.[35] In some cases children are allowed into the house only to eat or go to the bathroom, and sometimes they are left unattended even overnight. Since the entertainment of children at each other's homes is generally reciprocal, the nonengagement of mothers in the practice has a multiplier effect and reduces the practice generally. In addition, the practice is a part of general neighborly activity and Park tenants engage in neighboring activities to a much lower extent than do the tenants in other projects. In part this is attributable to their

35. Helen Icken Safa, "An Analysis of Upward Mobility in Low Income Families" (Syracuse, N.Y.: Syracuse University Youth Development Center, 1967), pp. 91-92.

greater involvement with relatives and friends in the immediate area.[36]

Table 8.11. Per Cent of Mothers Reporting that Study Child Often Spends Time with his Friends at Home by Area and by Marital Status

			Area		
Mother	*Evans*	*Grant*	*Park*	*Stern*	*Neighborhood*[*]
Husbandless	62.5 (16)	54.2 (24)	48.5 (33)	44.0 (25)	50.0 (18)
Married	77.8 (36)	75.0 (56)	37.5 (32)	57.1 (35)	64.4 (118)

[*] See note to Table 8.4.

In every area except Park husbandless mothers are less likely to engage in such mutual entertainment of children than are married mothers. Among the other areas, the relative proportion of husbandless mothers reporting this activity mirrors the proportion of married mothers doing so. This is indicative of the reciprocal character of the activity and the dependence of each person's actions upon the general level in the area. The high proportion of husbandless mothers in Park may contribute to the reduced general level of the activity, but it places the husbandless mothers at a lesser relative disadvantage compared to married mothers.

There is considerable evidence that children who interact a great deal with adults tend to have higher intelligence, greater motivation, and attain higher occupational levels, compared with children who have less interaction with adults. Thus, several studies have found that children of small families, within various occupational levels, tend to have higher intelligence test scores than do children of large families.[37] Other studies have found that eminence in various

36. The data are reported in Louis Kriesberg and Seymour S. Bellin, "Fatherless Families and Housing: A Study of Dependency" (Syracuse, N.Y.: Syracuse University Youth Development Center, 1965), pp. 157-208.

37. The studies are reviewed in Lipset and Bendix, *op. cit.*, pp. 238-243.

occupations was related to having been only children, oldest children, or children with longer than average distance between them and the next older child. A study of occupational aspirations of high school boys found that high aspirers were more likely to share leisure activities with their parents than were the boys without higher aspirations.[38]

Not only are husbandless mothers less likely than married mothers to have their children spend time at home with their friends, but the mothers are less likely to engage in activities outside of the home with their children. Husbandless mothers may be very concerned about their children and even want to spend time with their children as companions, replacing the missing husband. Nevertheless, mothers without husbands, are less likely to engage in activities which might involve older children. Furthermore, even considering only mothers who engage in a given leisure-time activity, there is no greater likelihood that husbandless mothers participate with their children than do married mothers.[39] Presumably the desire for adult companionship competes with spending extra time with the children; a married mother can more often avoid the necessity of choosing.

A fatherless child is cut off from, or at least has sharply reduced interaction with his father. Furthermore, the evidence from this study indicates that husbandless mothers

38. Douvan and Adelson, *op. cit.*

39. This varies considerably for different leisure-time activities. Respondents were queried about (1) visiting or going to parties, (2) going to picnics, beaches, zoos, or parks, (3) going to dinner in a restaurant, (4) sitting outside, (5) going to concerts, plays, or museums, (6) going to bars, (7) hunting, fishing, or camping, (8) bowling, golfing, or engaging in some other sport, (9) watching sports, and (10) going to the movies. For each of these activities except going to bars and watching sports, husbandless mothers are less likely to engage in the activity than are married mothers. Considering only those who do engage in the activity, husbandless and married mothers are equally likely to visit, dine out, or go to a bar with their children (neither category of mother goes to bars with her minor children). Husbandless mothers are less likely than married mothers to engage in the following activities with their children: picnic, sit outside, and especially camp or hunt. Husbandless mothers are slightly more likely than married mothers to engage in the following activities with their children: go to concerts, plays, or museums; watch sports; go to movies; and bowl, golf, or engage in some other sport.

usually are not able to compensate for this and may even—in many cases—have fewer opportunities for companionate interaction with their children than married mothers. On the whole, however, the evidence from this study is inconclusive. Probably for some husbandless mothers the absence of the husband-father, under certain conditions, does result in a relatively intense involvement and frequent interaction with the children. Furthermore, the number of children in the fatherless family tends to be smaller than in complete families and this too facilitates parent-child interaction rather than interaction between children and their age-mates.

CONCLUSIONS

The findings presented in this chapter complement those presented in the previous chapters. They help explain why we have not found great overall differences between children of fatherless and complete families in occupational achievement or marital stability. The findings also help to explain how being reared in a poverty-stricken fatherless family is handicapping. The findings are often inconsistent with a subcultural explanation of the life style of people in poverty.

One concern in this chapter has been to assess the differences between married and husbandless mothers and accounting for them. This attention should not obscure the fact that on the whole we have not found large differences between husbandless and married mothers in values, beliefs, or actual conduct pertaining to the independence and achievement of their children. After all, many aspects of the relationship between the mother and child are intrinsic to the relationship. Furthermore, the relationship is markedly affected by many factors other than the presence or absence of a husband-father. The similarity in the outcomes of children from complete and broken families is only in part, however, a consequence of the similarity in the maternal-child relationship in both categories of families. In addition, the children in both cases are subject to many influences aside from the parental ones.

Our interest in husbandless mothers is part of our general interest in poverty and explanations of the life style of the poor. We have examined certain conditions associated with poverty; residence in low-income areas and low socioeconomic origins; we have looked at these and maternal employment and family income in conjunction with marital status to see how particular conditions and combinations of conditions affect selected aspects of child rearing.

On the whole we have found that husbandless mothers do not withdraw from or reject their children, compared to married mothers. Indeed, there is evidence that the mother-child relationship assumes more salience. The consequences of this for the independence and achievement of the children, however, depends upon the way this increased involvement is expressed, upon its meaning in the context of other feelings and conduct, and upon conditions outside of the home affecting the children. We need to review the findings to draw out such implications.

In the aggregate, husbandless mothers do not differ much from married mothers in their valuation of obedience, expectations regarding the proper age for a child to do various activities, nor beliefs about the proper way of raising and disciplining children. They do differ on a few items. Husbandless mothers are *less* likely to feel that parents are responsible for how their children turn out and are less likely to exercise indirect control and supervision, but are *more* likely to overcontrol their children, compared to married mothers. I have argued that these various findings indicate that husbandless mothers, being concerned about the well-being of their children and facing more difficulty in rearing them, actually engage in some activities which unintentionally have an adverse effect, and consequently the mothers feel more despairing about their ability to cope with the developments. All this is clearer when we consider the specific background and current circumstances of the mothers.

We found a moderate relationship between the family-of-origin of the husbandless mothers and their values, beliefs, expectations, and some conduct relevant to the autonomy, achievement, and independence of their children. Having had low-status origins seems to have given them experiences which result in beliefs, values, expectations, and patterns of conduct which are not conducive to the independence and achievement of their children. This is particularly marked in valuation of obedience. We have also seen that these family-of-origin effects depend in large part upon an interaction with current circumstances. Thus, it is among the husbandless mothers of high status origins who are not impoverished that the valuation of obedience is particularly rare. Similarly, husbandless mothers of high-status origins who are not impoverished are especially likely to believe in the possibility of planning for the future of their children. The implications of being impoverished, therefore, depend upon the mothers' backgrounds *and* marital status. The family-of-origin experiences provide a repertoire of values, beliefs, and practices which may be called upon when they seem appropriate. The family-of-origin experiences also may help give meaning to current circumstances; this is indicated by the findings that among husbandless mothers, having had low-status origins is associated with the belief that parents are not responsible for the way children turn out and with the belief that it is impossible to plan the future of a child.

We have seen evidence of some intergenerational transmission of values, beliefs and practices among the husbandless mothers. This does not, however, reveal a clearly bounded subculture. Whether or not husbandless mothers of low-status origins tend to hold values and beliefs and carry out activities typical of low socioeconomic levels depends in large part upon their current circumstances, such as income levels. And, as we have seen in previous chapters, those current circumstances are not determined by their family-of-origin.

Among the married mothers, current income is related to some values, beliefs, and conduct which may affect the later achievement of their children. But this is not true for all the aspects of child-rearing analyzed thus far. Even when we have found some relationships, they have not been very large. Furthermore, it seems that it is income as access to the commercial market, rather than as a social status indicator, that is particularly relevant. Socioeconomic origins were found to be related to only a few of the aspects of child-rearing studied, and in interaction with current income.

One of the current circumstances that affect the way mothers rear their children is their area of residence. There seems to be little or no effect upon the age at which children are expected to decide for themselves about doing various activities or upon values regarding obedience. The husbandless mothers' beliefs about how to raise children and about parental control of the results, however, are affected by the area. Under circumstances of potential harmful peer influence upon their children, they emphasize, more than do married mothers, the use of direct controls and imposition of parental will.

These findings fit together. The husband-father is not available to aid in direct and indirect supervision. The husbandless mother is usually less able than even the married mother to utilize indirect and informal control. (These two matters were particularly mentioned by the husbandless mothers in explaining why they thought their children would be better off if the children's fathers were present.) Usually, the husbandless mother does not abandon efforts at control, but is more likely to try to overcontrol her children. This is probably a method which creates new problems; but the alternatives under the circumstances may not be better. Some husbandless mothers—for example, the poor husbandless mothers in Stern—do give up trying to control the time their children spend with peers when their children are still relatively young.[40]

40. One item of information from the survey pertains to the actual obedience of the children. The mothers were questioned, "When you ask (study child) to do something, does (he) (she) talk back—always, usually, rarely, or never?" The mothers' reports do not differ by income or socioeconomic origins, but there are some significant area differences. Half of the husbandless mothers in Stern project report the study child talks back always or

Under more favorable circumstances—a good neighborhood and one in which there is informal parental control—the husbandless mothers can express their concern for their children in appropriate ways. For example, husbandless mothers in Evans, compared to husbandless mothers in the projects or the neighborhood, disproportionally think they are largely responsible for the way their children turn out, do not believe spanking children is very important, are unlikely to under- or overcontrol but are relatively likely to promote early independence, and are likely to have their children play at home with their friends. The heightened concern for the children does not seem to lead to parental overindulgence among husbandless mothers even when they live in supportive circumstances.[41]

Another circumstance which is associated with being husbandless and which might affect values, beliefs, and conduct related to the children's independence is the mothers' employment. We have noted a small tendency for employed, husbandless mothers not to value obedience and to have lower age expectations for a child to engage in some activi-

---

usually. In every other project and in the neighborhoods, and among both married and husbandless mothers, between one-fifth to one-third report such frequent talking-back. The exception is Park project, where both married and husbandless mothers rarely report this (12 and 5 per cent, respectively). Apparently the Park mothers are generally successful in imposing their will, at least in direct confrontations with their children. In Stern project, many of the husbandless mothers seem to allow more outspokenness or have lost control.

41. In one study of the material, educational, and occupational ambition of high school students, it was found that there was a positive relationship between complete families and high ambition only in high socioeconomic neighborhoods; no relationship was found in the other neighborhoods. See Ralph Turner, "Some Family Determinants of Ambition," *Sociology and Social Research*, 46, No. 4 (July, 1962). This seems to be contrary to the implications of this study. The evidence of this study suggests that it is in the low socioeconomic neighborhoods that the conduct of the husbandless mother is most likely to be different from the married mother and most likely to be detrimental to the ambition of the child. We cannot resolve the discrepancy, but it raises the possibility that the maternal patterns reported here are not very powerful determinants of children's ambition. Rather, the treatment of children from broken families, by extrafamilial persons, is more discriminatory in high socioeconomic neighborhoods than in other neighborhoods and that impedes the children's ambition.

ties. We also noted that working husbandless mothers tended to believe that reasoning was the best way to get children to behave, but there was no relationship with the belief about the importance of spanking. Finally, we saw that working husbandless mothers were less likely than other husbandless mothers to undercontrol in three of the four activities analyzed. On the whole, the relationships were not very marked. Interestingly, however, insofar as any relationships were found, they all indicated that employed husbandless mothers tended to hold values and beliefs and conduct themselves in ways that presumably would promote the independence of their children.

In short, we have found no general tendency for husbandless mothers to differ from married mothers in values, beliefs, and conduct that adversely affect the children. We have found, however, that some of the conditions associated with being husbandless interact with the absence of a father-husband to handicap the children. Of course, aside from whatever accommodations the husbandless mother may make, the absence of a father-husband may directly affect the social-emotional independence of the children. There is some evidence that sons in fatherless families are handicapped in forming socially appropriate sex identities. That this is necessarily handicapping in educational and occupational achievement, however, is not certain. Furthermore, there is even evidence that if the father is typically authoritarian, his absence from the household frees the son to develop a high achievement motive. Where the absence of the father leads to strong mother-son ties and the son's dependency upon his mother, overindulgence, and low standards, the result is a low achievement motive.[42]

The findings of this chapter reveal many limitations to a subcultural explanation of poverty. It is true that some parental values, beliefs, and practices in child-rearing that are presumably not conducive to the children's later independence and achievement are associated with poverty. This is a necessary component of a subcultural explanation, but it is

42. McClelland, *op. cit.*, pp. 374-376.

not sufficient. First of all, poverty does not have consistent, uniform effects for all the items anlyzed. In addition, we have noted some incongruence between values and conduct, as in the discussion of obedience and controlling of children among the husbandless mothers.

It is also important to recognize that even when some relationships are reported, they are small, and therefore the overlap is great. Thus, even on valuing obedience, about three-fourths of the impoverished agree very strongly that a boy should do as he is told, but so do about half of the nonimpoverished mothers.

The findings also clearly indicate that the effects of poverty depend upon particular other conditions, notably marital status. The consequences of being a poor husbandless mother, in turn, depends upon area of residence, employment, and socioeconomic origins. These various conditions have different implications for different aspects of child-rearing.

Finally, the several steps in the intergenerational links are tenuous. The aspects of child-rearing studied are not largely determined by the socioeconomic origins of the mothers, particularly not of the married mothers. This suggests that the children reared by the mothers in this study will not perpetuate a child-rearing style typical of people in poverty. After all, we have already noted the great overlap in styles between mothers in poverty and out of it. The consistency between generations will depend upon the degree to which the circumstances between the generations are similar. Those circumstances, as the preceding chapters have indicated, are not the result of personal preferences of the individuals involved. Nor can one forget that having been reared in a particular way as a child does not completely determine later achievement. In any case, we have analyzed only some aspects of child-rearing experiences that may be relevant to later achievement. In the next chapter we will examine parental values, beliefs, and practices that have a more direct relationship with occupational and therefore income attainments: those related to educational achievement.

9. Training for Educational Achievement

ATTAINING an adequate, secure, and independent income does not depend only upon an individual's desire for it or even the possession of relevant social and emotional resources. The resources need to be channeled in ways that others in the society reward financially. This channeling is accomplished largely through formal education. Even the appropriate social and emotional resources coupled with educational skills, however, do not insure avoidance of poverty and welfare dependence. Obviously the level of economic activity in the society sets limits and provides opportunities for members of the society. Even within these limits, an individual's own skills and resources are not the sole determinants of economic independence. Discrimination by race, sex, age, the misfortunes of illness and accident, and economic changes in particular occupations or localities—all affect family income.

In this chapter, the analysis is focused upon one phase of

this complex, intertwined set of relationships.[1] It is a crucial phase—educational achievement. There is considerable evidence that certain parental values, beliefs, and conduct markedly affect children's educational achievement. This is true whether educational achievement is measured in the number of years of schooling completed or the academic mastery attained while in school.

The task of this chapter is to examine some possible determinants of educationally relevant parental values, beliefs, and conduct. We want to know to what extent poverty and the conditions associated with it result in parents rearing their children in ways that inhibit educational achievement. Insofar as the children of the poor are reared in ways that inhibit educational advancement, a link in the intergenerational perpetuation of poverty is indicated. Insofar as the parental values, beliefs, and conduct are the result of the parents' own origins in poverty, evidence of the importance of a subculture of poverty in accounting for the maintenance of poverty and a particular way of life associated with it is demonstrated.

Before examining what aspects of the home environment affect educational achievement, we should note that extrafamilial influences also have important effects. This is relevant in order to place the evidence about the home environment in its proper perspective. Furthermore, since parental behavior is not independent of what the children think and do, whatever affects the children affects the home environment.

Undoubtedly, genetic factors play some role in intelligence and, of course, intelligence is related to educational achievement. But intelligence cannot be assessed apart from environmental factors. Every human being grows up in a particular social environment and every intelligence assessment instrument uses a limited range of possible indicators. There is abundant evidence that whatever intelligence tests measure,

1. Some of the findings reported here were previously published in Louis Kriesberg, "Rearing Children for Educational Achievement in Fatherless Families," *Journal of Marriage and the Family*, XXIX (May, 1967), pp. 288-301.

their results are markedly affected by the subjects' home environments.[2] Furthermore, although IQ scores are related to academic achievement, various aspects of the home environment affect educational achievement, even holding IQ scores constant. In addition to genetic factors, the children's age peers and their schools also affect their educational achievement.[3]

In this chapter we are interested in parents' values, beliefs, and conduct which may inhibit, facilitate, or promote the educational attainments of their children. As in the case of independence and achievement in general, parents may affect their children's educational attainment through two major processes: through direct inculcation of relevant values, aspirations, and skills and through providing conditions to which children accommodate. Thus there is evidence that children's educational aspirations are related to parental expectations and encouragement of educational attainment.[4] Several studies report that the parents of dropouts are more often indifferent to continuing education, compared to par-

2. Bloom has summarized the various studies on the intelligence measurements of twins as well as siblings. The intelligence scores of identical twins reared together correlate very highly with each other (+.90 to +.94), but when the twins are reared apart, the correlations are much lower (+.67 to +.84), although still somewhat higher than nonidentical twins reared together (+.54 to +.70). Nevertheless, the correlation of IQ scores between identical twins raised in very different educational environments is quite low. Bloom also calculated the correlation for two groups of separated twins. For 11 pairs with similar educational environments, the rank correlation of IQ scores was +.91; for 8 pairs that had the least similar educational environments, the rank correlation was only +.24. See Benjamin S. Bloom, *Stability And Change In Human Characteristics* (New York, John Wiley, 1963) pp. 68-80.

3. See, for example, Alan B. Wilson, "Residential Segregation of Social Classes and Aspirations of High School Boys," *American Sociological Review*, XXIV (December, 1959), pp. 836-845; John A. Michael, "High School Climates and Plans for Entering College," *Public Opinion Quarterly*, XXV (Winter, 1961), pp. 585-595; and Robert H. Hardt, "The Impact of School Milieu on Pupils' Educational Plans," paper read at the annual meeting of the Eastern Sociological Society, New York City, April, 1961.

4. Robert E. Herriott, "Some Social Determinants of Educational Aspiration," *Harvard Educational Review*, XXXIII, 2 (1963), pp. 157-177; and William H. Sewell and Vimal P. Shah, "Social Class, Parental Encouragement and Educational Aspirations," *The American Journal of Sociology*, 73 (March, 1968), pp. 559-572.

ents of high school graduates.[5] They are also less likely to believe that the lack of a high school education is a disadvantage.[6] Another study found that parents' "achievement press" (aspirations for the child and for themselves, their interest in, knowledge of, and standards of rewards for the child's educational achievement) is correlated highly with grade achievement test scores.[7]

There is also much evidence that the nature of parental activities provide an environment that affects the children's educational achievement. Thus, parents of high school dropouts are less likely to participate in school activities than are parents of children who have completed high school.[8] Dropouts less often report having reference books, newspapers, or a quiet room for study at home than do graduates.[9] In one study a whole set of characteristics were used to construct an index of educational environment. In addition to the "achievement press" mentioned above, the index included:

1. language models (the quality of parents' language and the standards they expect in the child's language);
2. academic guidance (the availability and quality of educational guidance provided in the home);
3. activeness of the family (the extent and content of indoor and outdoor activities of the family);

5. William Evariff, "How 'Different' Are Our Dropouts?," Bulletin of the National Association of Secondary-School Principals, XLI (February, 1957), pp. 212-218, cited in S. M. Miller, Betty L. Saleem, and Harrington Bryce, *School Dropouts: A Commentary and Annotated Bibliography* (Syracuse, N.Y.: Syracuse University Youth Development Center, 1964); also see other studies cited in Miller, Saleem and Bryce.

6. Alvin L. Bertran, "School Attendance and Attainment: Function and Dysfunction of School and Family Social Systems," *Social Forces,* XL (March, 1962), pp. 228-253.

7. Ravindrakumar H. Dave, "The Identification and Measurement of Environmental Process Variables that Are Related to Educational Achievement," (unpublished Ph.D. dissertation, Department of Education, University of Chicago, 1963), cited in Bloom, *op. cit.*, pp. 124-125. See also Esther Milner, "A Study of the Relationship Between Reading Readiness in Grade One School Children and Patterns of Parent-Child Interaction," *Child Development,* XXII (June, 1951), pp. 95-112.

8. Bertran, *op. cit.*

9. Parlett L. Moore, "Factors Involved in Student Elimination from High School," *Journal of Negro Education,* XXIII (1954), pp. 117-122.

4. intellectuality in the home (the nature and quality of toys and the opportunity provided for thinking in daily activities);
5. work habits in the family (the degree of routine in home management and the preference for educational activities).

This index of educational environment correlated very highly with the fourth-grade achievement test scores (+.80).[10] Interestingly, the correlation between social status and the achievement test scores was much lower (about +.50). Presumably, the often found relationship between socioeconomic status of parents and the educational achievement of their children is mediated by the existence of favorable educational environments in the home.[11] Such home environments, however, are not perfectly associated with socioeconomic status. We are only beginning to learn more about the way in which the socioeconomic position of a family affects the home in ways that are educationally relevant.[12] The quantity and quality of parent-child interactions related to the children's educational achievement. For example, need achievement has been found to be related to school grades.[13]

In Chapter 7, I cited some of the evidence indicating that

10. Dave, *op. cit.*

11. For further discussion of the relationship between socioeconomic status and educational achievement, see Joseph A. Kahl, *The American Class Structure* (New York: Rinehart, 1953); W. H. Sewell, A. O. Haller, and M. A. Straus, "Social Status and Educational and Occupational Aspiration," *American Sociological Review*, XXII (February, 1957), pp. 67-73; S. M. Lipset and R. Bendix, *Social Mobility in Industrial Society* (Berkeley: University of California Press, 1960), pp. 227-259; and Louis Kriesberg, "The Relationship Between Socio-Economic Rank and Behavior," *Social Problems*, X (Spring, 1963), pp. 334-353.

12. See Fred L. Strodtbeck, "The Hidden Curriculum in the Middle-Class Home," in C. D. Hunnicutt, ed., *Urban Education and Cultural Deprivation* (Syracuse, N.Y.: Syracuse University Press, 1964), pp. 91-112 and B. Bernstein, "Some Sociological Determinants of Perception," *British Journal of Sociology*, IX (June, 1958), pp. 159-174.

13. Bernard C. Rosen, "The Achievement Syndrome: A Psychocultural Dimension of Social Stratification," *American Sociological Review*, XXXI (April, 1956), pp. 203-211. There is evidence that achievement motivation has different outcomes for boys and girls; see James V. Pierce, "Sex Differences in Achievement Motivation of Able High School Students" (University of Chicago Quincy Youth Development Project, 1961; mimeographed).

children of fatherless families do not attain the same levels of educational achievement as do children of complete families. More specifically, many studies report that children of broken families are more likely to be high school dropouts than are children of complete families. The effect of having come from a broken family may be spurious, however, or at least exaggerated, because broken families are much more frequently found in the lower socioeconomic levels and factors associated with such levels, rather than with broken families, may account for the findings. Studies of dropouts usually have not controlled for this possibility.[14] Nevertheless, the review of evidence about the educational attainments of poor female-headed families in Chapter 7, and other studies, do indicate some differences in educational ability and achievement between children of complete and broken families, within the same major socioeconomic stratum. For example, Deutsch and Brown studied pupils in the first and fifth grades of school and found that children in families without a father had slightly lower IQ scores than did those in families with a father present.[15] This difference was more marked within the lower socioeconomic stratum. In this chapter we will seek an explanation for such interaction effects. We will examine the possible consequences of various conditions associated with poverty.

Values and Aspirations Regarding Educational Achievement

Parental values regarding education and parental educational aspirations for their children affect the aspirations and achievements of children. On the bases of the discussions

14. Miller, Saleem, and Bryce, *op. cit.*, p. 14. In one study a variety of control groups were used; see Evariff *op. cit.* Continuation students (dropouts who attend special classes) were matched with students on sex, grade, scholastic aptitude, age, and father's occupation. More continuation students than regular students come from broken homes—but perhaps continuation students are a special category of dropouts. Dropouts from broken families may be particularly likely to return to school to try to complete their education.

15. Martin Deutsch and Bert Brown, "Social Influences in Negro-White Intelligence Differences," *Social Issues* (April, 1964), p. 27.

and analyses already presented, we would not expect to find—on the aggregate level—much difference between married and husbandless mothers in their values and aspirations regarding their children's education. On the one hand, it is true, husbandless mothers may place greater emphasis upon education, given their greater concern about their children; but on the other hand, facing more difficulties, their valuation and aspirations regarding education for their children may be tempered.

Being in favor of education, in the abstract and aside from possibly competing values, is universal. Asked how important it is to obtain a lot of education or to work hard in school, at least 95 per cent of both husbandless and married mothers replied each was *very* important. Given such universality, further analysis does not reveal any subgroups which devalue education. When educational goals are more specific and related to other values, some differences emerge.

The respondents in our cross-sectional sample were asked their valuation of education in competition with another value: "Which of these two ideas comes closest to the way you feel?

1. Even if a child of mine becomes estranged from me, I wish he'd get much more education than me.
2. I would rather my child feel close to me than have him get more education than me."

Most mothers still say they value education. The significance of this, however, is reduced when we consider the response to the follow-up question, "If a child of yours got a lot more education than you did, do you think it actually is very likely, fairly likely, or unlikely that he would become strange from you?" Most mothers think it is unlikely that a child would become estranged; husbandless mothers do not differ from married ones in the proportion who hold this belief. Husbandless mothers are somewhat more likely than married mothers to wish the child would get much more education than they did (87 per cent, compared to 75 per cent).[16]

16. Another series of questions required a forced choice between education and other valuable goals. The questions were: There are many things

The value attached to and belief about education were combined to form a single index of four categories: (1) respondents who wish for more education and think it actually unlikely that the child would become estranged; (2) those who wish for more education and think it likely that the child would become estranged;[17] (3) respondents who do not wish for more education and think it unlikely that the child would become estranged even if he did obtain more education than the respondent; and (4) those who do not wish for more education and think it likely that the child would become estranged. Mothers in the first category (those who wish the child to obtain much more education than they received and who do not believe this will lead to estrangement) are probably most likely consistently to support the child's educational efforts. Husbandless mothers are somewhat more likely to fall into the first category than are married mothers (77 per cent, compared to 64 per cent).

---

that a man can do with his time, but he cannot do everything. Suppose there is a man in his early thirties; he has a wife, a daughter—8, a son—6, and a daughter—3. He has steady work as a helper on construction jobs.

A. Now, which one of the following three things should he give his time to especially? Which is next most important? (1) Stay home with his family. (2) Go out with his friends. (3) Take an extra job.

B. Suppose *this* man takes an extra job, should he save the extra money he earns for his son's college education *or* spend the money on things for the whole family?

C. Finally, do you think it would be better for *this* man to take an extra job to earn money *or* should he study to get a better job?

The questions, obviously, are not strictly comparable in significance for a married and for a husbandless woman. In any case, husbandless mothers do not differ significantly from married mothers in their responses. In answer to B, 51 per cent of the husbandless reply "Save for son's college education," compared to 46 per cent of the married mothers. In answer to C, 90 per cent of the husbandless mothers say the man should study, compared to 85 per cent of the married mothers.

17. The term "think it likely," refers to all respondents who do *not* think it *un*likely; that is, persons who say they do not know are grouped together with those who say it is likely. Mothers who believe the child will become estranged are less likely to wish the child would get more education than they did. This relationship is slightly more marked among the husbandless than the married mothers. Among the husbandless mothers, 68 per cent of those who think the child will become estranged wish for more education, compared to 90 per cent of those who do not think the child will become estranged. Among the married mothers, the comparable percentages are 64 and 77.

Neither social-status origin nor race is related to the index—nor, on the whole, are residential areas— but employment status among husbandless mothers is. As can be seen in Table 9.1, the employed husbandless mothers are particularly likely to desire more education for a child, while believing he will not become estranged as a result. Employed

Table 9.1. Index of Wish for Education and Belief that Child Will Become Estranged by Work Status and by Marital Status

	*Husbandless Mothers**			*Married Mothers**		
Index	*Work Full-time*	*Work Part-time*	*Not Working*	*Work Full-time*	*Work Part-time*	*Not Working*
1. Wish for more education and believe unlikely child become estranged	90.2	78.8	67.8	66.7	58.2	66.8
2. Wish for more education and believe not unlikely child become estranged	4.9	6.1	13.6	14.0	11.8	9.5
3. Do not wish for more education and believe unlikely child become estranged	4.9	15.2	8.5	14.0	24.6	17.2
4. Do not wish for more education and believe likely child become estranged	0.0	0.0	10.2	5.3	5.5	6.5
Totals %	100.0	100.1	100.1	100.0	100.1	100.0
(N)	(41)	(33)	(59)	(57)	(110)	(232)

* Work full-time means being employed full-time when interviewed; work part-time refers to part-time employment or any employment in the previous 12 months but not currently employed full-time; not working means not currently employed and not employed during the preceding 12 months.

husbandless mothers tend to have more income than those who are not employed, and having relatively high income seems to make the husbandless mother believe her child would *not* become estranged. Employment is also associated with greater participation in the larger world of the labor market and with experience in coping with the financial maintenance of the family by such efforts. All this may increase their sense of value of education for their children and their own sense of competence in maintaining relations with their children if they do attain much education. Among the married mothers, as suggested in Chapter 2, employment does not have the same consequences.

In addition to these general values regarding education, we can consider specific educational aspirations. The respondents were asked two questions which indicate educational aspirations for their children. One question asked (first about a son and then about a daughter) whether or not the respondent would be *disappointed* if the child went only as far as grade 6, 7, 8, etc., stopping at the grade at which the respondent would no longer be disappointed.[18] Since the grade at which a mother would be disappointed for a son is very highly correlated with the grade at which she would be disappointed for a daughter,[19] we will discuss responses to only one question, about the son. The other aspirational question asked about the marks which would be disappointing for a child in junior high school – D's, C's or B's. As might be expected, aspirations about grades are correlated with aspirations about years of education.[20] The respondents were also asked about income and occupational aspirations for their children. Though the same analysis was made as for

18. Pearson product moment correlations for husbandless and married mothers combined, excluding weighted cases, were computed for several of the educationally relevant attitudes and behaviors. The correlation between the age at which the mother thinks a boy is old enough to decide for himself about leaving school and the number of years of education she aspires to for a son is +.15 based upon 505 cases.

19. The correlation is +.79, based upon 512 cases. See note 18.

20. The correlation between the aspirations for the marks of a child of the respondent and aspirations for the years of education a son completes is +.22, based upon 528 cases.

the aspirations about marks and years of schooling, we will not report the results in equal detail, but simply refer to them to reinforce, qualify, or help explain the findings regarding aspirations about marks and about years of education.

Husbandless mothers do not differ from married mothers in aspirations about school marks, nor in income or occupational aspirations.[21] Nearly all the mothers would be disappointed if a son did not complete high school. Husbandless mothers, however, are less likely to aspire for more than a high school education for their sons than are the married mothers. The difference is small, but statistically significant.[22] Among the husbandless mothers, 8 per cent would be disappointed if a son completed fewer than eleven years of school, 72 per cent would be disappointed if he did not finish twelve years, and 20 per cent would be disappointed if he did not finish more years; among the married mothers, the comparable percentages are 10, 60, and 30.

Many studies have found an association between socioeconomic status and educational aspirations for children, but it is not clear, whether that results from an accommodation to current circumstances or from the intergenerational transmission of values. The evidence reported earlier about educational values supports the former interpretation. Other evidence bears on this issue more directly. The respondents were asked if their mothers (and then if their fathers) thought (1) getting lots of education and (2) working hard in school was very important, somewhat important, or not important. Between 75 to 85 per cent of the respondents reported both mothers and fathers feeling each value was very important. Strong agreement with the value of education is widely attributed to the parental generation, but not as widely as the respondents assert it for themselves. When we look at the

21. Of course the children may also be influenced by the father's aspirations. The husbands of the married mothers have about the same level of aspiration for education, marks, and occupations as do the married mothers. The husbands, however, do have higher aspirations for income for their children, compared to the married mothers.

22. Chi Square is 6.66, 2 d.f., $p=.05$; Kendall Tau C is +.06, $p=.05$, based upon 544 cases.

distribution of the parental educational values by the fathers' occupational status, we find no relationship. Only in the case of the mothers' evaluation of the importance of education do we find a small, but statistically significant, relationship with socioeconomic status.[23] On the basis of all this, we would not expect to find a marked relationship between mothers' socioeconomic origins and aspirations regarding education and, in fact, we do not.[24] This supports the interpretation that valuing education is so widespread that differences in aspirations must be explained largely in terms of accommodation to current circumstances.[25]

Mothers' aspirations involve consideration of what is attainable as well as what is valued. Current income, then,

23. Chi Square is 17.31, 8 d.f., p=.05; Kendall Tau C is -.09, p=.05, based upon 441 cases. The Kendall Tau C. for fathers' socioeconomic status and mothers' valuation of the importance of working hard in school is -.02; for fathers' socioeconomic status and fathers' valuation of getting lots of education, -.04; and for fathers' socioeconomic status and valuing working hard in school, -.02.

24. This is based upon cross-tabulating fathers' occupational socioeconomic status and the respondents' aspirations for the son among husbandless and among married mothers. Persons of high socioeconomic origins are slightly more likely than those of low status origins to have high aspirations. We also calculated Pearson product moment correlations, (for husbandless and married mothers together); between fathers' socioeconomic status and aspirations, the correlation is only +.13, based upon 460 cases. In the panel sample, the correlation among the married mothers is -.08; among the husbandless it is +.04. The intergenerational transmission of values, aspirations, and expectations about education becomes attenuated when we consider three generations. The correlations between education attained and aspirations is higher than between socioeconomic status, measured by the occupation, and aspirations about education. There is a high correlation between the number of years of education attained by the respondent herself and the number of years she desires for her son—+.39, based upon 521 cases. The correlation between aspirations for the number of years of education to be completed by the son and the number of years of education the respondents' fathers completed is +.24, based upon 271 cases; the correlation with the respondents' mothers' education is only +.17, based upon 324 cases. The correlation between the respondents' fathers' educational attainments and the respondents' own is high: +.39, based upon 263 cases. (The number of cases is reduced when we examine parental educational attainment because many respondents were unable to give this information.)

25. Fathers' occupational socioeconomic status is associated with the husbandless and the married mothers' income and the occupational status of their sons. This indicates the specificity of aspirations in the educational realm, as well as the universality of the valuation of education.

should markedly affect aspirations, and it does. Holding income constant, there is no longer any difference between husbandless and married mothers in aspirations about the number of years of education they want their son to complete. Furthermore, holding income constant, husbandless mothers are more likely than married mothers to aspire for high marks (see Table 9.2), high income, and high-prestige occupations for their children. It is puzzling that income is so strongly associated with aspirations about marks. Income understandably should affect hopes for advanced education, high-status occupations, and high incomes, but school marks do not have this obvious relationship. Perhaps higher aspirations for years of education implies also aspiring for high marks; among all the mothers, the correlation between the two aspirations is moderate.[26] Perhaps relatively high income simply leads to a generalized high aspiration in many areas.

Table 9.2. Per Cent of Mothers Who Would Be Disappointed if Their Children Earned Less than B's by Income and by Marital Status

Mother	*Per Capita Disposable Household Income**	
	Less than $500	*$500 or More*
Husbandless	61.8 (68)	81.7 (60)
Married	46.4 (69)	66.1 (295)

* Per capita household refers to income from all sources in the household minus the annual rent and divided by the number of persons in the household.

Another interpretation is suggested by the earlier analysis of income and work status in relationship to values about education. Perhaps not income *per se*, but the mother's employment status is related to educational aspirations.[27] Among the husbandless mothers, employment is related to aspirations about children's school marks and about the num-

26. The Pearson project moment correlation is +.22, based upon 528 cases.
27. Two-way analysis of variance as well as Chi Squares reveal that mothers' employment is not related to occupational or income aspirations.

ber of years of education desired, but in different ways. Employed husbandless mothers have higher aspirations about marks and about years of schooling than do nonemployed husbandless mothers. More specifically, it is the employed husbandless mothers who are particularly likely to have high aspirations about marks, even compared to married mothers; but it is the nonemployed husbandless mothers who are especially *unlikely* to have high aspirations about the years of schooling for their children, even compared to married mothers (see Tables 9.3 and 9.4).

Table 9.3. Per Cent of Mothers Who Would Be Disappointed if Their Children Earned Less than B's by Work Status and by Marital Status

		Work Status	
Mother	*Full-Time*	*Part-Time*	*Not Working*
Husbandless	82.9 (41)	78.8 (33)	60.7 (61)
Married	61.4 (57)	71.2 (111)	60.4 (235)

Table 9.4. Per Cent of Mothers Who Would Be Disappointed if a Son Did Not Attain More than a High School Education by Work Status and by Marital Status

		Work Status	
Mother	*Full-Time*	*Part-Time*	*Not Working*
Husbandless	34.2 (41)	30.3 (33)	4.8 (62)
Married	38.6 (57)	33.9 (112)	26.0 (235)

This is consistent with our general ideas about husbandless mothers' aspirations for their children. Assuming husbandless mothers displace some mobility concern upon their children and have heightened concern about their welfare, we expect them to be more likely than married mothers to have high aspirations for their children. These aspirations are restrained by difficulties in realizing the desired state. Going beyond high school is more subject to external constraints than attaining high marks in school. Therefore, when we control for income, husbandless mothers only equal married mothers in aspirations regarding years of education; they have extra handicaps in addition to low income. Not being employed also depresses the vision of future extended education. On the other hand, given equal income, husbandless mothers can aspire for higher marks. Being employed, furthermore, gives husbandless mothers a relatively greater range of extrafamilial experience than is true among married mothers. These experiences support higher aspirations in regard to school marks.[28]

Residential areas can directly affect parental desire for their children's educational achievement by the norms and expectations held by the residents in the area. In addition, the residential area is an educational opportunity structure and may influence aspirations by affecting what is believed to be possible. In this study, several questions were asked which bear on these possibilities. The respondents in the cross-sectional sample were asked if they thought it was true or false that, in their residential area, "parents would rather have their children go to work than stay in school." Overall, only 9 per cent of the mothers thought this was true, 79 per cent thought it was false, and the remainder did not know. Respondents were asked how many children in their area "try to do well in school—nearly all, many, or hardly any?" Overall, 41 per cent of the mothers said nearly all, 31 per

28. Since low income and nonemployment are each independently associated with low aspirations, and since income and work status are associated with each other, it is necessary to examine the way they simultaneously affect aspirations. Among husbandless mothers, income and work status each continue to be associated with aspirations when the other is held constant. Among married mothers, an examination of both income and work status in relationship to aspirations about marks reveals that married mothers with low incomes and who are not employed are relatively unlikely to aspire for high marks (only 37 per cent do so). Therefore, among those with high income, work status is not related to aspirations about marks; among those with low income, work status is related. Among those employed full- or part-time, income is no longer associated with aspiration. Among those who are not employed, low income is associated with low aspirations.

cent replied many, 3 per cent said hardly any, and 22 per cent did not know. Finally, respondents were asked if they thought better or worse of people if their children "don't do well in school?" Overall, 21 per cent said worse, 16 per cent said it depends, 61 per cent replied they would not feel any different, and the remaining 2 per cent said they did not know or, in a few cases, said "better." In general, there is little normative pressure on this issue, either because it is considered a private matter or one about which parents cannot be held responsible.

In addition, public housing tenants were asked a series of questions comparing their present neighborhood with their previous area of residence. They were asked, "are the teachers more interested in what the parents have to say" and "are there better schools" where they lived before or now? The distributions for each question by residential area are presented in Table 9.5. The profile for Park tenants is clear. The mothers do not think the schools are good, and the children in the project and in the surrounding neighborhoods are not viewed as trying to do well in school. On the other hand, there is relatively—but not absolutely—high normative pressure upon the parents to make sure that their children do well in school.[29] We expect that mothers in Park project, and particularly husbandless mothers, will try to compensate for inadequacy of peer and school influences upon their children, but are also likely to despair of doing so. We saw in the

29. It is possible that the proportion saying they think worse of someone if their children do not do well in school is not a valid indicator of normative pressure. Two considerations should be noted: (1) there may be a greater sense of privacy in middle-class neighborhoods, making normative judgments of others less likely—but that would not nullify the interpretation of the question; (2) there may also be a tendency for persons of low socioeconomic status to be more readily coerced into choosing one of the forced alternatives posed in the question. Other persons might feel freer to volunteer responses such as "it depends" or "it does not make any difference." Let us combine the responses of "think worse" and "it depends"—which implies normative judgment under certain conditions. Park neighborhood still has the highest proportion indicating normative pressure: 55 per cent of the mothers say they would think worse or it depends. Stern and Grant neighborhoods, however, now have higher normative pressure than Evans neighborhood. Among the projects, normative pressure is relatively high in Stern as well as in Park.

previous chapter that the husbandless mothers in Park are most likely to say that parents are *not* the *most* important determinant of how children turn out. They should be least likely to have high aspirations for their children in regard to years of schooling to be completed.

*Table 9.5. Per Cent of Mothers with Selected Educational Beliefs and Norms by Area**

Beliefs and Norms	*Areas*							
	Projects				*Neighborhoods*			
	Evans	*Grant*	*Park*	*Stern*	*Evans*	*Grant*	*Park*	*Stern*
False that parents rather children work than go to school	86.2 (80)	94.1 (84)	86.2 (80)	81.2 (69)	98.1 (53)	87.5 (24)	80.2 (41)	97.9 (47)
Nearly all children try to do well	49.3 (69)	58.5 (82)	30.9 (68)	46.9 (64)	73.9 (46)	69.9 (23)	31.3 (32)	79.1 (43)
Think worse of people if their children don't do well in school	20.5 (88)	18.8 (96)	31.7 (82)	17.1 (88)	12.5 (56)	25.0 (32)	32.7 (52)	14.6 (48)
Think teachers more interested†	42.9 (28)	30.0 (40)	21.1 (19)	32.1 (28)				
Think schools are better†	41.2 (34)	29.8 (57)	9.1 (22)	61.0 (41)				

* Those with no opinions omitted. Mothers whose children are too young to be in school are included.

† In addition, respondents who are in same school districts as they were in their previous residence are omitted; in Park, naturally, this reduces the base markedly.

The profile for Grant, the project in the other working-class neighborhood, is quite different. The schools are more often thought to be good; children are generally viewed as trying to do well in school and parents are viewed as valuing education; normative pressure upon the parents in regard to their children's education is less widespread than in Park and more like the other projects. Incidentally, the views of the children in the project and in the neighborhood help explain the findings reported in the previous chapter that husbandless mothers in Grant are unusually likely to promote early independence when we examined control over time spent with friends.

Evans and Stern have similar profiles. The neighborhoods are ones in which the parents are universally viewed as valuing education, nearly all the children are generally seen as trying to do well in school, and the schools are considered good. Within the projects, however, the parents and children are less commonly seen to value education and to try to do well in school than in the surrounding neighborhoods. Normative pressure in the projects and in the surrounding neighborhoods is relatively low. For somewhat different sets of reasons, then, the mothers in Evans, Grant, and Stern projects are likely to see greater educational opportunities for their children than the mothers in Park.

Now let us turn to the variation in educational aspirations by area. As can be seen in Table 9.6, there is considerable variation by area—both for married and husbandless mothers—in regard to aspirations concerning years of education. The husbandless mothers' aspirations in Park project are markedly depressed. The husbandless mothers in the other three projects, however, are likely to have high aspirations. Furthermore, in comparison to married mothers, husbandless mothers in Park are much *less* likely to have high aspirations; but husbandless mothers in the other three projects are somewhat *more* likely to have high aspirations. Looking at the neighborhoods, we find a high proportion of high aspirers among complete families and a moderately low proportion among husbandless mothers. This can be attributed to the fact that only about one-fifth of the complete families live in the Park neighborhood while about one-half of the fatherless families reside there. When these area differences are examined, holding constant race, household income, per capita disposable income, or respondents' years of education, the pattern persists despite the small number of cases.[30]

Table 9.6. Per Cent Who Want a Son to Attain More than a High School Education by Area and by Marital Status

Mother	*Area* Evans	Grant	Park	Stern	Neighborhood*
Husbandless	33.3 (21)	31.0 (29)	2.9 (35)	24.1 (29)	13.0 (23)
Married	21.7 (69)	16.4 (67)	22.5 (49)	18.3 (60)	45.4 (163)

* In this table and in Tables 9.8, and 9.10, "neighborhood" refers to the four neighborhoods surrounding each project; there are too few husbandless mothers in each neighborhood to permit separate calculation of percentages.

The panel data provide a further test of these area effects. Analyses of variance were made of the years of education aspired for a son before entering public housing and of the changes between then and a year later. The average number of years aspired for by husbandless and married mothers at the time of the first interview was 12.9 years. Married mothers who later entered Evans had relatively high aspirations (the average was 14.1 years). Among the husbandless moth-

30. In this sample, nonwhites are less likely than whites to aspire for more than a high school education for their sons. Since Park is predominantly nonwhite, we have to consider the possibility that the area differences are attributable to the racial composition of the areas. Married mothers in Park are not particularly likely to have low aspirations; therefore, the depression of aspirations among the husbandless mothers in Park cannot be attributable simply to race. If we control for race, the pattern seems to be maintained, though the number of white husbandless mothers in Park is very small, and nonwhites in Evans and Grant are few. None of the three white, husbandless mothers in Park aspires for more than a high school education for a son. Among the nonwhites, of the ten husbandless mothers living in Stern, three aspire to at least some college; of the 13 living in the neighborhoods, only one aspires for more than a high school education; of the 32 in Park, only one aspires for more than a high school education for a son. In Evans and Grant, however, the nonwhites may be even less likely than those in Park to have high aspirations; the one nonwhite in Evans does not have high aspirations, nor do the six in Grant.

ers, those who entered Grant and Park had slightly higher average aspirations than did other husbandless mothers. Comparing the mothers' aspirations at the time of the first interview with those a year later, we find that the largest change was among the husbandless mothers in Park. As can be seen in Table 9.7, the average years of schooling which would not be disappointing had declined one full year. Although the differences are not statistically significant, the pattern is consistent with the previous discussion and findings.

Table 9.7. Analysis of Variance of Change in Number of Years of Schooling Aspired for, by Area and by Marital Status, Panel Sample

	Area				*Moved, but Not into Public Housing*	*Did Not Move Between Interviews*
Mother	*Evans*	*Grant*	*Park*	*Stern*		
Husbandless						
Average change	0.00	-0.81	-1.06	0.29	-0.71	0.00
Standard dev.	0.00	1.72	2.35	1.94	2.71	2.49
(N)	(9)	(16)	(34)	(14)	(17)	(11)
Married						
Average change	-0.55	-0.14	-0.03	0.38	0.21	-0.22
Standard dev.	2.89	1.51	2.65	1.76	2.29	2.71
(N)	(20)	(28)	(40)	(34)	(47)	(18)

Source	df	ss	ms	F
Columns	5	18.4383	3.6877	0.17182
Rows	1	5.9097	5.9097	1.1510
Rows	5	19.5668	3.9134	0.7622
error	276	1417.0728	5.1343	2.2659

Aspirations about marks, we expect, would be less affected by external circumstances than would aspirations about years of education, though there might be some area effects due to variations in schools and the actual experiences of the children in the schools. Actually, there is little area variation in grade aspirations and the variations which do exist do not follow the same pattern as aspirations about years of schooling. Aspirations about marks are not depressed in Park project, even among the husbandless. The exceptional cells are the husbandless mothers in Evans who are particularly likely to have high aspirations and the *married* mothers in Stern who are particularly unlikely to have high aspirations.[31] The actual marks students receive provide a standard for aspirations which is lacking in the case of aspirations for years of schooling. This additional factor may work in a counter direction to general educational aspirations and thus help account for the low variation among the areas and the particular variations which do appear. The tougher educational competition in the schools of Evans and Stern can lower expectations at the same time that the value of good marks is raised. The panel data reveal that at the initial interview the mothers who later moved into each project did not differ much in the marks they reported for their children. But a year later the marks of the children in Evans and Stern had decreased about a half a grade on the average, while those in the other projects rose very slightly. Consequently, the mothers in Park may still be able to maintain their aspiration for marks while those in Stern have to lower expectations. Presumably in Evans the emphasis upon education sustains high

31. A consideration of occupational and income aspirations for a son fills out the picture. Husbandless mothers are more likely than married mothers to have high occupational and income aspirations in each of the four projects, although not in the neighborhoods as a whole. The differences are statistically significant, using the Chi Square or the Kendall Tau C, only in Grant and the neighborhoods for income aspirations, and only in Evans for occupational aspirations. In addition, two-way analyses of variance were calculated and the pattern is the same, but not statistically significant. As far as differences among the areas are concerned, occupational aspirations vary little among married mothers in the four projects. However, husbandless mothers in Evans, and to some extent in Grant and the neighborhoods, tend to have high aspirations. Occupational aspirations are relatively low in Park for both husbandless and married mothers. Income aspirations are also relatively low in Park. Among the married mothers, income aspirations are high in the neighborhoods and moderately high in Evans. Among the husbandless mothers, income aspirations are high in Evans and Grant. In general, then, aspirations of the husbandless mothers are particularly likely to be high in Evans and low in Park.

aspirations. Furthermore, in the cross-sectional sample, the husbandless mothers in Grant and Evans actually report relatively high marks at the time of their interviews.

All this helps account for the finding noted earlier that working-class children in middle-class schools tend to have higher aspirations than their counterparts in predominantly working-class schools. Apparently, parents of the latter group are influenced by the opportunities and realities of the schools and the prevailing student efforts. Faced with an interrelated set of obstacles, the parents may restrict aspirations for their children, reinforcing the children's own peer influences. Furthermore, socioeconomic origins are *not* related to educational values or aspirations. The relationship between parents' educational attainments and that of their children is largely the result of continuities in social and economic conditions.

Parental Conduct Regarding Children's Education

Husbandless mothers, at least under favorable circumstances, are somewhat more likely than married mothers to value education for their children and to have high educational aspirations. But implementing these desires is likely to pose greater difficulties for husbandless than for married mothers. We will examine parental efforts in regard to children's study time and school marks, parental involvement in school activities, and some indicators of the intellectual climate at home.

Parental effort in regard to the children's school work is not a simple matter. It is impossible to say that one line of action will always have beneficial consequences. For example, the child's own interests and abilities in school, at any given time, markedly affect which line of action is most appropriate. Sometimes attempts at direct control and intervention may be most effective in promoting the child's best efforts. At other times, indirect control, or simply indications of interest and support, may be more effective. Given the husbandless mothers' concerns about their children, the danger to their children's educational achievement may not be lack of interest and support, but rather, too great direct control and too little general and indirect support.

One indicator of parental control of a child's school effort is whether the child or the parent decides upon the time spent on schoolwork. The mothers were asked to report about this, as about the other activities analyzed in the preceding chapter. Parental control is related to the age of the study child; therefore we age-standardized parental control in the same way as for the other activities.[32] There is no difference between husbandless and married mothers in the proportion who report over-control, usual control, or early independence, controlling for age of the study children.

Socioeconomic status origins are only slightly related to type of parental control, holding constant the age of the study child. The direction of the relationships, however, are *not* consistent with the notion of a subculture of poverty. Among the married mothers, those of low status origins are slightly *more* likely to promote early independence than practice control at the usual age, compared to those of higher status. Among the husbandless mothers, those of low status are *less* likely to over-control or under-control, compared to those of higher status. Maternal employment does not affect type of parental control, with one exception. Nonemployed married mothers are more likely to over-control rather than control at the usual age, compared to working mothers. Given the association between non-employment and poverty, it is significant that only among the husbandless is there a tendency for those who are not poor to over-control rather than exercise control at the usual age. Otherwise, however, current income is not related to control of the time the study child spends on

32. Control of time spent on school work is considered only for mothers with study children 8 to 18 years old. Under-control refers to cases in which the parent does not decide and the study child is 8 to 10 years old. Early independence refers to cases in which the parent does not decide and the child is 11 to 13. Usual control refers to cases where the parent decides and the child is 8 to 13, or the parent does not decide and the child is 14 to 18. Over-control refers to cases in which the parent decides and the child is 14 to 18. Fifty per cent of the mothers of 13-year-olds decide, and 32 per cent of the mothers of 14-year-old study children report the parents decide the amount of time the study child spends on his or her school work.

school work. On the whole, these conditions are not important determinants of control over the time a study child spends on school work. Nor is there evidence indicating an intergenerationally perpetuated pattern of conduct inappropriate to educational achievement. Even contemporary poverty does not in itself result in control that is inappropriate for educational achievement, as measured here.

Area of residence does seem to have some effects, but because of the necessity of controlling for the age of the study child, the small number of cases makes interpretation treacherous. Table 9.8 presents the distribution of types of control, age-standardized but not controlling for age of child by area. Taking into account the age of the study children in each area, married as well as husbandless mothers appear to be affected by their area of residence. In Evans, married

Table 9.8. Type of Parental Control of Time Study Child Spends on Schoolwork by Area and by Marital Status

	Husbandless Mothers				
	Area				
Type of Control	*Evans*	*Grant*	*Park*	*Stern*	*Neighborhood**
Under-control Parent does not decide and child is 8–10	0.0	9.5	3.7	5.0	8.3
Early independence Parent does not decide and child is 11–13	30.0	19.1	25.9	5.0	16.7
Usual control Parent decides and child is 8–13 or parent does not decide and child is 14–18	70.0	57.1	70.4	75.0	58.3
Over-control Parent decides and child is 14–18	0.0	14.3	0.0	15.0	16.7
Totals %	100.0	100.0	100.0	100.0	100.0
(N)	(10)	(21)	(27)	(20)	(12)

	Married Mothers				
Under-control Parent does not decide and child is 8-10	15.0	19.4	10.0	17.4	14.1
Early independence Parent does not decide and child is 11-13	10.0	19.4	15.0	8.7	16.2
Usual control Parent decides and child is 8-13 or parent does not decide and child is 14-18	65.0	55.6	75.0	60.9	64.7
Over-control Parent decides and child is 14-18	10.0	5.6	0.0	13.0	5.1
Totals %	100.0	100.0	100.0	100.0	100.1
(N)	(20)	(36)	(20)	(23)	(99)

° See note to Table 9.6.

mothers are particularly likely to report over-control and the husbandless mothers to report early independence, compared to other residential areas. In Grant, the husbandless mothers are particularly likely to report under- or over-control, while the married mothers report allowing early independence. In Park, neither husbandless nor married mothers report over-control, but neither do they report under-control rather than usual control any more frequently than do mothers in other areas. In Stern, both married and husbandless mothers disproportionally report over-control rather than control at the usual age. In the neighborhoods, the husbandless mothers tend to report over-control rather than control at the usual age.

Apparently, in Evans the husbandless mothers can feel that the children's peers and the schools are adequate and there is little need for parental control beyond the usual age. The situation in Park is not immediately evident. It seems that the peer pressures may be so great that the mothers are unlikely to over-control. That the Stern husbandless mothers do not seem to be acting in the same way as those in Evans calls for additional comment. Presumably, the contrast between Stern project and Stern neighborhood, being so great in various socioeconomic characteristics, presents a considerable challenge to the husbandless mothers in the project. Their response in the educational sphere seems to be competitive and not retreatist. These possible interpretations will be developed as other indicators of parental conduct are considered.

I commented earlier that the appropriate parental action in regard to a child's school work varies with the interests and abilities of the students. Possibly, the husbandless mother's concern for the well-being and educational achievement of her child results in less responsiveness to the peculiarities of his school position than is true among married mothers. This might account for the finding that the husbandless, but not the married, mothers are responsive to the circumstances under investigation.

If we examine the relationship between parental control and the mother's satisfaction with the marks the study child receives in school, we find a very high relationship among the married mothers and no relationship at all among the husbandless mothers.[33] When a married mother is very satisfied with her child's marks she is likely to report under-control; when she is not satisfied she reports over-control. The point is made clearer if we look at parental control among mothers with students who are reported to have high marks (A's or B's), compared to mothers with students who have low marks (C's or D's). In the latter case, there is no difference between husbandless and married mothers in parental control. But among mothers of children with high marks, husbandless mothers are much less likely to report under-control.[34] Many husbandless mothers apparent-

33. Satisfaction with the study child's school work was trichotomized: very satisfied, fairly satisfied, and somewhat or very dissatisfied. Among the married mothers, the relationship between satisfaction with school work and control of time spent on school work is high: Kendall Tau C is +.24, based upon 197 cases, p=.001 (Chi Square is 20.27, 6 d.f., p=.01); among the husbandless mothers, the Kendall Tau C is +.05.

34. Among the mothers with study children usually earning A's or B's, married mothers are more likely to under-control than are husbandless mothers. Chi Square is 9.45, 3 d.f., based upon 190 cases, p=.05, Kendall Tau

ly do not relax their pressure for educational achievement when a married mother does.

Another line of evidence supports this interpretation. The mothers were asked what marks the study child usually attained in school and next, how satisfied the mother was with the study child's school work. If the mother said she was satisfied, she was asked if the study child ever had a mark which she thought was too low. If the mother was dissatisfied *or* if the study child ever received a low mark, she was asked if she (or her husband) did or said anything to the study child and what that was. First of all, it should be noted that the husbandless and married mothers report about the same distribution of marks for their children. Nevertheless, among mothers who report that the study child usually earns high marks, husbandless mothers are somewhat more likely than married mothers to say they are dissatisfied or the child has sometimes received too low marks (64 per cent compared to 55 per cent). Even among the mothers with study children receiving low marks, husbandless mothers are slightly more likely than married mothers to say they are dissatisfied or the child has sometimes received too low a mark (81 per cent and 75 per cent respectively).

What the mothers report doing or saying to the child is also significant. In general, although the husbandless mothers seem more likely than married mothers to be concerned about the child's school work and more demanding, they are more likely only to urge the child on, while married mothers more frequently aid the child directly in school work or intervene with the school. The area differences are again complex. As can be seen in Table 9.9, husbandless mothers in Stern and Evans are least likely to be dissatisfied with the study children's marks or, if satisfied, to think he or she never received too low a mark. Furthermore, if the husbandless mothers in Evans say or do anything, it is usually only to tell the child to study more, to urge him on, or talk to him about his difficulties. The husbandless mothers in Stern, compared

---

C is +.14, p=.01. There is a relationship on this item among married mothers, but not among husbandless mothers. This is similar to the findings on the relationship between type of control and satisfaction with school work.

to those in the other projects, are most likely to report helping the child with his school work. Husbandless mothers in Park and Grant are particularly likely to intervene with the school.[35]

Table 9.9 Action Taken if Study Child Does Not Do Well in School by Area and by Marital Status

	Husbandless Mothers				
			Area		
Action	*Evans*	*Grant*	*Park*	*Stern*	*Neighborhood**
Satisfied with school work and never had too low a mark	40.0	15.8	31.3	41.7	23.5
Dissatisfied or has had too low a mark and:					
1. Parent(s) help child with school work	0.0	5.3	3.1	12.5	11.8
2. Not (1), but see teacher, write note	6.7	21.1	9.4	4.2	0.0
3. Not (1)-(2), but punish child	13.3	15.8	15.6	8.3	11.8
4. Not (1)-(3), but encourage child, tell child to study more, talk	40.0	42.1	40.6	33.3	52.9
5. Not (1)-(4), but do something else	0.0	0.0	0.0	0.0	0.0
6. Do or say nothing	0.0	0.0	0.0	0.0	0.0
Totals %	100.0	100.1	100.0	100.0	100.0
(N)	(15)	(19)	(32)	(24)	(17)

35. The panel data can be used only in a limited way in assessing the conduct of parents because many of them had children who still were too young to attend school. Among the husbandless, however, we can observe some patterns to check upon the findings noted. Among the five husbandless mothers who were to enter Evans, none were satisfied with their child's school work and they all simply talked to their child to encourage him to do better. Among the ten husbandless mothers who moved into Stern, the

	Married Mothers				
Satisfied with school work and never had too low a mark	34.5	55.1	48.2	32.3	30.9
Dissatisfied or has had too low a mark and:					
1. Parent(s) help child with school work	17.2	4.1	3.7	9.7	16.4
2. Not (1), but see teacher, write note	3.5	12.2	22.2	0.0	11.8
3. Not (1)-(2), but punish child	6.9	10.2	7.4	19.4	12.7
4. Not (1)-(3), but encourage child, tell child to study more, talk	37.9	10.2	18.5	32.3	27.3
5. Not (1)-(4), but do something else	0.0	2.0	0.0	0.0	0.0
6. Do or say nothing	0.0	6.1	0.0	6.5	0.9
Totals %	100.0	99.9	100.0	100.2	100.0
(N)	(29)	(49)	(27)	(31)	(110)

* See note to Table 9.6.

Apparently the Evans' husbandless mothers are most likely to be content and, if action is felt necessary, to take the minimal kind. The husbandless in Stern, even when they feel action is necessary, are not likely to talk with the teacher or otherwise intervene. The finding that both husbandless and married mothers in Park and Grant are particularly likely to intervene in the schools calls for comment. One might expect that "better" schools would be more receptive to parental intervention than "poorer" schools. This overlooks

proportion who reported helping children with their school work was lower than for the 21 who moved into Park. Intervention in the school was not reported by those who later moved into any of the projects (except for one person moving into Park). These findings indicate that some of the differences noted in the cross-sectional data may be due to selective factors, but only to a limited extent for some ways of handling the child.

two other considerations. Parents of children in schools which the parents do not consider good may tend to feel the school and its teachers are at fault if their children do not do well. They have general and specific reasons for thinking it appropriate to complain. Secondly, parents in low-income public housing projects may well feel at a disadvantage in complaining and intervening in schools with a predominantly middle-class student and parent constituency. Parents in Stern project would feel particularly out of place in relationship to the schools their children attend.

These interpretations can be further considered by examining parental involvement in school affairs. The mothers were asked: Since last September, did you (or your husband) (1) go to school on parent's day to visit a class or a program put on by the children? (2) attend PTA/Mothers' Club meetings? (3) go to a neighborhood meeting about school problems? By asking married mothers about their own and their husband's conduct, comparisons between married and husbandless mothers actually are comparing husbandless mothers to married parents. This distinction is of little analytic importance, however, since husbands rarely go to the school on parents' day without their wives and practically never go to PTA meetings or neighborhood meetings without their wives. In about one-third of the cases, however, a husband accompanies his wife to parents' day events at schools, but only in 5 per cent of the cases to PTA or neighborhood meetings.[36]

Parental participation in parents' day events is most common, followed by PTA meetings, and participation is least at

36. Responses to another series of questions suggest an additional complication. After the questions about involvement in school affairs, the mothers were asked, "Besides any of those things, did you (or your husband) ever go to school to see any of your child's (children's) teachers or counselors?" If a mother responded affirmatively, she was also asked, "Did the teacher ask that you (or your husband) come or did you (or your husband) go on your own?" More than half of the husbandless and the married mothers answered yes to the first question; but the married mothers were more likely to say that they went on their own than did the husbandless mothers. Among those who said they did see a teacher or counselor, about one-third of the husbandless mothers and fewer than 10 per cent of the married mothers said they were asked to come.

neighborhood meetings. For each item, husbandless mothers are slightly less likely to report attendance, campared to married mothers. We will use a summary measure of these items. The three items of parental involvement in the schools are related so that they form a scale.[37] That is, mothers reporting going to neighborhood meetings about schools generally also go to PTA meetings and visit the school on parents' days; if they go to PTA meetings and do not go to neighborhood meetings, they still generally go to school on parents' days. The scale of involvement in school affairs consists of four positions: (1) not involved at all; (2) visit school on parents' days only; (3) visit school and attend PTA meetings only; and (4) visit school, attend PTA, and attend neighborhood meetings. Usually, the involvement is dichotomized into low (scale types 1 or 2) or high (scale types 3 or 4) parental involvement.

This kind of formal involvement in school affairs exhibits a different pattern than does the informal kind indicated by parental intervention with the schools. First of all we should note that married mothers outside of public housing are most likely to have high involvement in school affairs, but this is not true of intervention in the schools as a way of helping children. Involvement in education affairs is generally related to socioeconomic rank. Mothers in Stern neighborhood are most likely to have high involvement (57 per cent are scale types 3 or 4, compared to 40 per cent in Grant, 32 per cent in Evans, and 28 per cent in Park neighborhoods). Among the married, high-income mothers are much more likely to have high involvement than are low-income mothers (34 per cent compared to 11 per cent).

The area differences shown in Table 9.10 are not completely explained by the interpretations and comments presented thus far. In general we expect that mothers in the projects to be less likely than those in the adjacent neighbor-

37. The coefficient of reproducibility is .88, using the method suggested by W. H. Goodenough, as described in Allen L. Edwards, *Techniques of Attitude Scale Construction* (New York: Appleton-Century-Crofts, 1957), pp. 184-188. The minimal marginal reproducibility for the set of items is .77; see Edwards, *op. cit.*, pp. 191-193. Error types were omitted from the analysis.

hood to have high scores; this is true except for husbandless mothers in Park project. If there are any area differences among the husbandless or the married mothers in the projects, we expect them to arise from characteristics of the schools, the normative climate, the example of others, constraints, and opportunities within the projects and in the surrounding neighborhoods. High involvement may stem from concern for the educational achievement of children and attempts to express that concern by active participation. Or it may be an expression of doing the "right thing" according to the social norms of neighbors and friends. Actually carrying out the activity depends upon the resources available.

Table 9.10. Per Cent of Families with High Parental Involvement in School Affairs by Area and by Mother's Marital Status

Mother	*Area*				
	Evans	*Grant*	*Park*	*Stern*	*Neighborhood*[a]
Husbandless	18.8 (16)	14.3 (21)	39.4 (33)	40.9 (22)	17.7 (17)
Married	17.2 (35)	24.5 (53)	25.1 (28)	31.3 (32)	42.7 (110)

[a] See note to Table 9.6.

Before attempting to account for the area variations, we can examine the evidence from the panel phase of the study to further test the existence of any area effects. In the panel analysis, we measured the mothers' participation in the PTA on a four-point scale: (1) do not belong; (2) belong but never go to meetings; (3) belong and go occasionally; and (4) belong and usually attend meetings. Overall, at the time of the first interview, husbandless mothers had a *higher* average score than did married mothers. There was no overall change among either the husbandless or the married mothers after a year, but some variations among them, depending upon the area in which they moved. Among the husbandless mothers, participation increased among those who moved into Park, decreased among those who moved into Grant and Evans, and was unchanged among those who moved into Stern. Among the married mothers, there was a slight increase in the participation score, on the average, among those who moved into Stern and slight decreases among those who moved into Park and Grant. The differences between none of the pairs of areas, however, are statistically significant.

Husbandless mothers in Stern are likely to have high formal involvement in school affairs. The characteristics of the neighborhood around the project and the relationship of the project tenants to the neighborhood apparently account for this finding. Involvement in school affairs among neighborhood parents is generally high. This probably means that there are more opportunities for parents to participate in school affairs, more examples of other parents doing so, and more pressure from children to have their parents participate. The mothers in Stern project, and particularly the husbandless mothers, usually respond by trying to keep up with this pattern. Although the socioeconomic differences between project and neighborhood residents may inhabit informal direct confrontations with the school teachers and officials, apparently it does not inhibit most mothers from formal, if passive, involvement. On the basis of observation, mothers from Stern project sit at the back of the meeting room and do not participate in the discussions. More than one-third of the husbandless mothers in Stern project, seem to withdraw from any involvement—they are in scale type 1 (compared to 15 per cent of the married mothers). Again, there is an indication that the stimulus of Stern neighborhood is a challenge which many husbandless mothers meet while others are defeated by it.

A different explanation is needed for the relatively high proportion of mothers, particularly husbandless mothers, in Park project who show high involvement in school affairs. On the whole, involvement tends to be low in the neighborhood around Park. The mothers of Park project believe that the neighborhood educational influences are not good but they are not particularly likely to try to compensate for this by dealing directly with their children. Apparently, informal and formal involvement with the schools is their way of expressing their concern and desire for the educational achievement of their children. Again, however, more than one-third of the husbandless mothers apparently do not attempt this kind of compensation – they are in scale type 1 (as are 46 per cent of the married mothers).

One other point must be noted in regard to Park. At the time of the cross-sectional survey, a special educational program was underway in the schools serving the area around Park. This program, in addition to trying to improve the education of the students in the area, also attempted to involve parents. This does not fully explain the high participation of many husbandless mothers in Park project, however, since the involvement was not generally high in the neighborhood. It could mean that the interest and concern of husbandless mothers were more readily accepted by the schools or that husbandless mothers were particularly responsive to the appeals.

In Grant project, high involvement in school affairs is relatively rare. The stimulus for involvement from the outside is not as great as in Stern neighborhood nor are project and neighborhood influences viewed as unfavorably as in Park project; thus, compensating for the project and neighborhood influences seems less necessary. They can take the position that the people in charge of the school know best how to administer it.

High involvement is also uncommon in Evans project. Most parents in the surrounding neighborhood, although of moderate socioeconomic status, are not highly involved in school affairs. Even more than in the case of Grant, the Evans mothers believe that the area influences are not unfavorable to the educational achievement of their children – they need not compensate for it by extra effort.

Before concluding the discussion of formal involvement in school affairs, we must consider other possible conditions affecting involvement. As noted earlier, among married mothers, low income is strongly associated with low involvement. Among the husbandless mothers, however, this is not the case. Low-income husbandless mothers tend to show high involvement. This is partly explained by the interpretation made earlier: low income does not denote low social status to the same degree for husbandless mothers as it does for married mothers. Husbandless mothers with low incomes, particularly if they live in public housing, are not as likely as married mothers to feel stigmatized and therefore inhibited from participation in neighborhood or community affairs.

In addition, among husbandless mothers, low income is highly associated with nonemployment. Full-time employment apparently interferes with the husbandless mothers' high involvement in school affairs (see Table 9.11). Thus, employed husbandless mothers are particularly likely to have high educational aspirations for their children and to value education, but they are less likely to express their attitudes by being highly involved in school affairs, compared to nonemployed husbandless mothers. Finally, husbandless mothers of high socioeconomic status origins are somewhat more likely than those of low origins to have high involvement, while this is not true among the married mothers. Again, we find that intergenerational processes related to the idea of a culture of poverty do not seem to be operative for all mothers; only among the husbandless does there seem to be some effect.

Table 9.11. Per Cent of Families that Have High Parental Involvement in School Affairs by Mother's Work Status and Marital Status

Mother	*Work Status*		
	Full-Time	*Part-Time*	*Not Work*
Husbandless	20.6	28.0	33.3
	(29)	(25)	(54)
Married	30.3	35.7	31.7
	(43)	(70)	(142)

In addition to the direct involvement of parents in the education efforts of their children, the intellectual climate of the home is an important condition affecting the educational achievement of children. On the whole, husbandless mothers are just as likely, or unlikely, to say that reading is their most preferred leisure-time activity, to read books, to read magazines, or to have an encyclopedia at home, but are less likely to go to concerts, plays, and museums. Having an encyclopedia in the home varies little by area among the husbandless mothers, except that husbandless mothers in Stern project are most likely to report having one. In each project, however, husbandless mothers are slightly *more* likely than married mothers to have an encyclopedia; but in the neighborhoods the situation is reversed. Going to concerts, plays, and museums does not vary much by area among husbandless mothers, although again, it is slightly higher in Stern project than in the other areas. The proportion of mothers who read books and magazines and read books of a relatively serious nature is particularly high in Evans.

Conclusions

On the whole, educational values, aspirations, and parental conduct relevant to the children's educational achievement are only *partially* explained by the circumstances and general background factors we are investigating. One reason for this is that the children themselves are an important circumstance. A child with high educational ability and interest will affect his parents' wishes, hopes, and conduct toward him, as well as vice versa. Thus, in the cross-sectional sample there is a moderate correlation between the study child's school marks and the number of years of education which the mother would want her child to complete.[38] In the panel sample, too, there is a relationship, but it is less marked and not always consistent. The causal direction of the relationship, however, is not obvious. Do parents aspire for more education because they see that their child is doing well in school or does a child do well in school because the parents have high aspirations for the child? Or, perhaps, the relationship is

38. The Pearson product moment correlation between the study child's school marks and the number of years of formal education aspired to for a son of married and husbandless mothers is +.21, based upon 366 cases.

spurious and both are affected by a variety of other determinants.

The panel data can throw some light on these possibilities. Among the married mothers, there is no relationship between the grades reported for the child at the time of the first interview and the mother's aspirations for educational attainment a year later. Among the husbandless mothers, however, there is a moderate positive relationship. Similarly, among the married mothers, there is no relationship between the years of education aspired for at the first interview and the grades reported a year later, but among the husbandless mothers there is a strong positive relationship.[39] Apparently the married mothers' aspirations are not as related to the conduct of the child as is true of the husbandless mothers. Earlier we had noted that husbandless mothers seem less likely to relax pressure upon their child regardless of how well he was doing in school. That is not necessarily inconsistent with the present findings. The concern of the husbandless mothers may result in continuing pressure, but they are sensitive to obstacles to their children's educational attainments—including the children's own school achievement. Furthermore, husbandless mothers who do have high aspirations presumably try to implement them by pressure upon their children; now we see some evidence that this is positively related to the school marks the children later attain.

Even aside from the relationship between the child's school marks and his mother's educational aspirations and efforts, how well the child does in school affects his later educational attainments. Therefore, we should note how the circumstances under study may affect the child's marks. In the cross-sectional sample, among married mothers, low income is associated with low school marks; but among hus-

39. Among the husbandless mothers, years aspired for at the time of the first interview are strongly related to marks reported a year later: Kendall's Tau = .30, statistically significant at the .001 level; marks at the first-wave interview are moderately associated with years of education aspired for at the second-wave interview: Kendall's Tau = .17, statistically significant at the .05 level.

bandless mothers, those with low income are just as likely to have a study child with high marks as are those who are not poor. Among married mothers, employment is not related to school marks, but it is among husbandless mothers. The pattern for married mothers is the one found in many studies of socioeconomic rank and school achievement: those who are poor have lower aspirations and are less likely to participate in school affairs; their children do not do as well in school as the children of married mothers of higher income; and maternal employment does not make any real difference. All this seems to be an accommodation to current circumstances rather than the result of intergenerational processes. Among the husbandless mothers, however, the relationships are not so obvious. Low income depresses aspirations for years of education, but is not related to how well the child does in school nor the mothers' involvement in school affairs. Maternal employment is associated with higher aspirations and marks, but it seems to depress involvement in school affairs. In short, among married mothers the several aspects of educationally relevant attitudes and conduct are mutually consistent, and even consistent with the academic achievement of the child. This is not as true among the husbandless mothers. It is as if they cling to what they can and even compensate for difficulties, but some obstacles are so great that they affect particular attitudes and actions. The subjective result must be considerable tension.

School marks vary somewhat by area, and this variation should be taken into account in drawing conclusions about area effects upon attitudes and conduct. Marks are relatively high in Grant and relatively low in Park and Stern among the study children in the sample. The husbandless and married mothers do not differ in the school marks they report for their study children, with the exception of Stern project. Here, husbandless mothers are more likely to have study children with high marks (especially A's), compared to married mothers in the housing project.

In Stern project many husbandless mothers are particularly likely to engage in behavior which is supportive and conducive to their children's achievement. Neither the values nor aspirations of the Stern mothers seem to explain this. Normative pressures from inside or outside the project do not seem to account for this conduct, since the generally low normative consensus and social integration makes this unlikely. It appears that responding to the models available in the surrounding neighborhood, perhaps communicated by the children in the schools, is one of the major processes by which the effect occurs. In addition, the accommodation process probably plays a major role. The surrounding neighborhood imposes a challenge: the schools have a student composition and style that fosters some academic competitiveness but the surrounding area also includes children and parents who are not part of this academic competition. For example, the observations of the group of adolescents from Stern and the surrounding neighborhood revealed that nearly all the members of the group were uninterested in academic subjects and had only vague aspirations even about employment. In such circumstances, a concerned parent might be expected to put extra pressure upon the child or otherwise try to structure his situation to encourage school achievements and fend off possible adverse peer influences. In some cases, of course, and particularly as the child becomes older, such efforts may be abandoned as futile.

In Park, the husbandless mothers face much more severe educational obstacles for their children. Those who try to overcome these obstacles do so by various supportive activities rather than by direct control or aid. Again, neither the values nor aspirations of Park husbandless mothers seem to account for this. Although normative pressure is relatively high in Park project and neighborhood, it is in an absolute sense not very great. The conduct of the husbandless mothers is quite possibly an accommodation to the difficulties of the area—an attempt at differentiating themselves and overcoming the obstacles. This is quite a different kind of challenge, and the models are not positive but negative. There is also less consistency and faith in the outcome—witness the low aspirations.

In Grant, the husbandless mothers feel less challenged by the neighborhood, either positively or negatively. They can feel more relaxed. This helps explain the findings noted in the preceding chapter; although the area is considered almost as dangerous as Park, mothers are not likely to see educational obstacles arising from widespread academic disinterest among parents and their children. The children can be allowed freer rein than in Park. Some husbandless mothers in Grant, as we noted in the last chapter, seem to respond to the threat of delinquency by over-controlling the decision about the time a study child can spend with his friends.

Finally, in Evans the challenge is least threatening and the husbandless mothers can most easily relax efforts to push their children. But they are also not stimulated to exert themselves in efforts which are educationally relevant for their children. Nevertheless, the generally supportive educational climate of the schools, neighbors, and the children's peers, as well as the general level of educationally relevant activities makes compensating parental effort unnecessary.

On the whole, the husbandless mothers are very concerned about the educational achievement of their children. Low income depresses their aspirations for years of education as it does those of married mothers. Employment is associated with higher valuation of and aspirations for educational achievement.[40] Employment among the husbandless mothers, however, makes it less likely that they will be high participators in school affairs. In general, the husbandless mothers find it difficult to act in ways which will implement their goals. For example, as can be seen in Table 9.12, husbandless mothers show no relationship between aspirations about years of school for their children and participation in school affairs. They are as likely to be high participators if they have low aspirations as high ones.

Our analysis of the relationship between control of study time and school marks of the study child shows that husband-

40. In one English study it was found that children of working mothers were better adjusted in school than children of nonworking mothers. The author suggests that the mothers who are robust in health and temperament can work and care for the children; the children of such mothers are healthy due to congenital factors, and this accounts for the children's better adjustment. See D. H. Stott, "Do Working Mothers' Children Suffer?" *New Society*, August 19, 1965, pp. 8-9.

less mothers do not relax the pressure for academic achievement when married mothers do. This is probably related to the findings and interpretations of the preceding chapter. Lacking some of the indirect and informal supports and influences upon their children, and also lacking the secure base for future support and encouragement, husbandless mothers try to push hard where they can. This pressure may sometimes even be excessive, despite the motivation. Again we must add that the differences and associations we have noted, even if statistically significant, are not very large. Being without a husband does not change these values, beliefs, and behavior for most mothers.

Table 9.12. Per Cent of Families Having High Parental Involvement in School Affairs by Mother's Aspirations for Years of Education for Son and by Marital Status

	Educational Aspirations	
Mother	*12 Years or Less*	*13 Years or More*
Husbandless	28.6 (91)	27.8 (18)
Married	29.1 (179)	40.3 (77)

10. Conclusions

THROUGHOUT this book we have noted the limitations of explaining the way of life of the poor or the perpetuation of poverty in terms of a subculture of poverty. In the first chapter we observed that a cultural or situational approach might each have validity, depending upon the question being asked and the way in which crucial terms were defined. Clearly, if we define the poor simply in terms of income, their way of life is not accounted for by a subculture of poverty intergenerationally transmitted. The poor in America are too heterogeneous in age, region, race, and way of life to make such an explanation tenable.

Even if we restrict the category of poor to those who are of child-rearing age and who live in an urban center in one region of the country, the subcultural explanation does not seem adequate. The way of life itself is not sufficiently integrated, homogenous, and distinct from the nonpoor to make a subcultural explanation appropriate. The same is true even if we further restrict the category to husbandless mothers living in enclaves of poverty. If we ask how poverty is perpetuated the subcultural explanation has even greater limitations.

If we define the poor in terms of income and some particular aspect of their way of life, then we might begin to find a subcultural explanation having greater relevance. But that easily leads to tautology. It may be that some segments of the poor live in such isolated, closed communities that a subcultural explanation is appropriate and valid in accounting for the perpetuation of their way of life. To some extent, the blacks, the Indians, and persons living in physically isolated poverty-stricken communities in the U.S., meet some of the conditions necessary for a subcultural explanation to be more relevant. Even in such cases, I would argue, the relevance of such an explanation for their continuing poverty is limited.

Some of the ideas which make up the subcultural approach, nevertheless, contribute to our understanding of the life of the poor and its perpetuation. Undoubtedly people facing common problems develop some similar ways of accommodating. With communication and shared identity, the similarity will be recognized and take on additional collective qualities. Various aspects of the responses will tend to become integrated—if they are sufficiently stable. Children growing up in families embedded in such a setting will develop values, beliefs, and habits which have some lasting consequences, again insofar as the setting remains the same. But at each stage of this argument the heterogeneity of responses and of conditions and their varying rates of change must be recognized.

It is these latter considerations which are emphasized in the situational approach to the study of the poor. According to this approach, each condition associated with poverty has a particular set of consequences. Further, different aspects of the life of the poor are differentially affected by each condition. From the perspective of the individuals involved, the situations appear as given; they live in circumstances not of their own making. From a larger perspective, the circumstances themselves are problematic. Basic changes in the way of life of the poor depend upon the alteration of the circumstances in which they live.

These assertions call for more detailed defense and some elaboration of the situational approach. In the first chapter of this book we discussed some of the issues underlying the differences between the cultural and situational approaches to the study of the poor. The second chapter presented hypotheses about the relationship between poverty, various conditions related to it and the relationship between those conditions and different kinds of social characteristics. We can now consider the issues between the two approaches in terms of the hypotheses and the evidence presented.

Conditions and Consequences of Poverty

What is a cause, or a condition, or a consequence of someone living in poverty is partly an empirical issue. But it also depends upon the analytic perspective used. Presumably, various background characteristics of a person make it more or less likely that he will live in poverty. Living in poverty may be associated with various conditions and each of those conditions may help perpetuate characteristics making life in poverty more likely.

The characteristics, conditions, and consequences may constitute a vicious cycle of poverty. This may be true in two senses. First, the various characteristics, or the set of conditions, or the many consequences may reinforce each other in the perpetuation of poverty. Second, the background characteristics, conditions, and consequences may be linked over time in the life cycle and intergenerationally so that poverty is perpetuated. We must now examine these possible vicious cycles of poverty. Insofar as they are cumulative and time-linked, intercession is more difficult. Where we discover noncumulative elements and weak time-links, promising points of intercession are indicated.

I will first discuss some of the conditions associated with poverty and later in the chapter turn to some consequences of those conditions. In this work we have examined the poverty-associated conditions of broken families, welfare dependence, and residence in low-income neighborhoods. I will now reconsider the findings relevant to these conditions as they bear on the basic issues set forth in the beginning of the book.

In Chapter 2, I discussed the qualities of social characteristics which affected their vulnerability to different kinds of determinants, particularly contemporaneous compared to intergenerational ones. Those ideas are relevant for the general issues which concern us. I argued that insofar as characteristics were dependent upon others to be carried out, received clear feedback, were not central to a person's self-conception, and were serially independent, the characteristics would be vulnerable to contemporary circumstances.

On the whole, the conditions studied have these qualities. Certainly, whether or not one lives in a low-income neighborhood or more particularly, in public housing, is not simply a matter of personal taste, independent of the constraints and opportunities of other persons. Living in one rather than another neighborhood has many palpable consequences. It is not central to one's self-conception, although some dimensions of residential area have symbolic meanings which may be related to important self-conceptions. Finally, on the whole, where one lives is not very dependent upon previous residence in the city.

Being dependent upon welfare also has qualities which make it relatively susceptible to contemporary conditions. The availability of alternative sources of income, certainly for husbandless mothers, is very largely affected by others—from the former husband to government agencies and programs. There are many clear and immediate consequences of choosing one rather than another alternative. The choices have considerable serial independence if we consider only employment *per se* and not employment in a particular occupation. On the other hand, some aspects of the alternatives undoubtedly have implications for a mother's self-conception, since working and mothering activities have special meanings in a woman's socialization, and the activities are often viewed as somewhat competing in this society.

Finally, marital disruption is also relatively susceptible to contemporary conditions, although not to the same degree as the preceding conditions. A broken marriage is not simply and often not at all within the mother's control, even aside from disruptions caused by a spouse's death. Some of the consequences are clear, but the opportunities to try out being married and not are limited. Certainly many aspects of maintaining a marital relationship involve basic self-conceptions, but a wide variety of the conceptions are relevant to both maintaining and disrupting a marriage. Once a marriage is entered, its disruption is hardly serially independent of events in that marriage, but it is relatively independent of events prior to the marriage.

Given these qualities of the three conditions, we would not expect them to be part of an intergenerationally transmitted subculture of poverty. We *would* expect them, however, to be highly associated with current poverty. To some extent, this is necessarily the case. To receive welfare benefits in this country means that one is living in poverty. Depending upon how broad the stratum of the poor is drawn, a proportion of the poor will not be receiving public assistance. About half of the fatherless families live in poverty, a larger proportion than of complete families; but most poor adults are not in fatherless families. Most poor families live in low-income neighborhoods, but usually not as homogenous ones as public housing. Even these conditions, then, are not perfectly associated with poverty. Some nonpoor persons are husbandless mothers and some live in low-income neighborhoods. In short, even these conditions are not distinctive for the poor compared to the nonpoor. It must also be remembered that these conditions are not permanent. Most families receiving public assistance do so for only a few years and most husbandless mothers remarry.

One of the major issues underlying the differences between a subcultural and situational explanation of the way of life of the poor is the extent to which that way of life is intergenerationally maintained. Even if many components of the life style of the poor are not directly passed on, the conditions which re-create that style may be. To what extent are these conditions intergenerationally transmitted?

In Chapter 7, we saw scant evidence that growing up in broken families increased the probability of having one's own marriage disrupted. The immediate socioeconomic conditions are more determining of the disruption. We also saw that growing up in families which had been on welfare increased the probability of being on welfare as adults. But most families receiving public assistance did not have parents who did. We have no data on the extent to which growing up in low-income neighborhoods is related to living in low-income neighborhoods as adults.

Several matters of interpretation and explanation are important. First, even if the direct transmission of particular conditions is not very marked, perhaps several conditions are cumulative so that there is a vicious cycle of poverty which is self-perpetuating. Second, it may be that the conditions are linked over time and those links are more important than the direct relationship between the same conditions in the family of origin and the family of procreation. Third, we are interested in the nature of the links: perhaps the conditions in the family of origin result in values and beliefs that then affect the choice of such conditions. This is related to another issue underlying the differences between the subcultural and the situational approach: the relative importance of objective circumstances and subjective orientations.

We will consider these matters in accounting for welfare dependence among husbandless mothers, relying largely on the data presented in Chapter 6. Some conditions are cumulative in affecting the likelihood of being poor and thus dependent upon public assistance. We cited some evidence in Chapter 7, that coming from poor and broken families is handicapping for educational and occupational achievement. These effects are true for each condition and the effects are greater when both conditions exist together. In the sample studied here, however, there is no relationship between the marital status of the mothers' parents and the mothers' poverty or nonpoverty. Interestingly, among married fathers, there is a small relationship: of fathers who grew up in complete families, 7 per cent have annual per capita disposable incomes under $400, compared to 9 per cent and 16 per cent for those who grew up in families disrupted by death and divorce, respectively; broadening the poverty stratum, 14 per cent of the fathers who grew up in complete families have per capita incomes under $500, compared to 18 per cent of those of families broken by death of a parent, and 24 per cent of those who grew up in families disrupted by divorce, separation, or desertion. The mothers' current income is largely determined by current circumstances, particularly those relating to her marital relationship, while the men's income is more directly related to their own educational occupational attainments and those are related to their own social origins.

Turning directly to the choice of welfare dependence by husbandless mothers, we can examine the possible intergenerational links. First of all, the husbandless mothers' socioeconomic origins are only moderately related to the amount of money they receive from public assistance (zero order correlation is -.15). Some of the effects of the family of origin are mediated through the amount of education the mother attains and the socioeconomic status of her former husband, which is also positively related to her education. The former husband's socioeconomic status is moderately and negatively related to the size of the welfare benefits (-.20). Taking into account all the other variables, the relationship between socioeconomic origins of the husbandless mothers and welfare received is reduced (from -.15 to -.11).

The linkages discussed thus far have more to do with objective constraints and opportunities than with values. Let us consider possibly relevant values for which we have indicators. Disapproving of someone accepting welfare benefits is moderately related to socioeconomic status of the family of origin (.19), and that in turn is related to the amount of welfare received (-.21); but once the other variables are taken into account, disapproval of accepting welfare is no longer related to the amount received (-.06). Another value is related to the welfare received, even taking into account all other variables. Mothers who disapprove of a mother working instead of taking care of her children tend to receive public assistance (.15) and this is not reduced much when all other variables are simultaneously considered (.13 is the beta coefficient). But this value is not related to the socioeconomic status of the family of origin. It is not even related to whether or not the husbandless mothers' own mothers were employed. Nevertheless, employment by the mother of the husbandless mother is inversely related to the husbandless mother's receiving welfare benefits; but this seems to operate independently of other variables (the zero order correlation is -.16, and that is also true when all other variables are considered).

The two major determinants of the amount of welfare received are the number of children and the amount of secure income (the beta coefficients are .45 and -.43, respectively). But neither of these variables is related to any other of the significant determinants we have been considering. In other words, the husbandless mother's dependence upon public assistance seems to be affected largely by two circumstances which themselves are not determined by her personal background. Values and beliefs related to a mother's employment contribute to accounting for welfare dependence, but these seem to operate independently of social origins.

In short, this poverty-associated condition, among husbandless mothers, does not appear to be intergenerationally transmitted in any major way. The links to the prior history of the husbandless mothers are not strong and where they do exist do not seem to be part of a subculture of poverty. Similarly, we have not found that coming from a low socioeconomic status family or from disrupted families of origin markedly affect marital status, the husbandless mother's poverty, or her residence in public housing.

It might still be possible that the current conditions are highly related to relevant current values and beliefs. In that case, one might argue that the same current circumstances determine pertinent values and beliefs as well as the choice of conditions. Consequently, there is an integrated system of actions and subjective evaluations and beliefs. Even in this regard, however, we found either no relations, weak ones, or even negative ones. Thus, among the husbandless mothers, we did not find any relationship even between wanting to work and actually working. The analysis of the choice of public housing, in Chapter 5, indicated that this was a constrained choice and that the lack of viable alternatives seemed to account for the choice rather than any positive valuation of public housing tenancy. We found no evidence that a conventional marriage was unwanted by the husbandless mothers.

Discrepancies between the conditions associated with poverty and presumably relevant values and beliefs should not be unexpected. We have seen that the choice of conditions is often constrained by other circumstances. Yet the values and beliefs pertaining to those choices are affected by a wide variety of other experiences and circumstances, even ones shared with the nonpoor. We will discuss the relationship between the mothers' values and beliefs and their actual conduct in more detail later in this concluding chapter.

Thus far, we have considered some conditions associated with poverty focusing on the possibility that they are chosen in expression of subcultural values that were developed while growing up in low socioeconomic strata. This intergenerational link, among husbandless mothers, was found to be very weak. We now turn to examine another way of considering this link. Does living in poverty with its associated conditions result in mothers' rearing children in ways which perpetuate values, beliefs, and conduct associated with poverty? Are children reared in these conditions likely to develop patterns of thought and conduct that will, in turn, constrain their choices and keep them in poverty? We examined a variety of child-rearing values, practices, and beliefs which presumably affect the children's later independence, general achievement, and particularly educational attainments.

In the light of the ideas outlined in Chapter 2, the parental child-rearing patterns of thought should be more resistant to contemporary circumstances than the conditions I have been discussing. The values, beliefs, and patterns of conduct related to child-rearing are less dependent upon others; the feedback from them is less clear, although the opportunities for variation are greater; they are more central to the mothers' self-conceptions; and they are not as serially independent. Nevertheless, we also expect some variation in susceptibility to contemporary influences among the particular values, beliefs, and patterns of conduct analyzed. These observations will be elaborated in the discussion of the issues underlying the differences between the cultural and situational approaches to the study of the life style of the poor.

One underlying issue is the degree to which the poor do have a distinctive way of life. The major focus of the analysis has not been on noting the differences between the poor and nonpoor, but upon accounting for whatever differences were observable. Nevertheless, on the whole it should be clear that in the values, beliefs, and patterns of conduct regarding child-rearing, the differences between the poor and the nonpoor mothers are not large. For example, consider the responses to the question about agreeing or disagreeing that parents should try to make a 10-year-old boy do what he is told without talking back. About two-thirds of the poor mothers and slightly more than half of the nonpoor said they agreed very much with the statement. Among the various items examined, this percentage difference is relatively large, but after all a majority of both the poor and nonpoor did agree very much with the statement. Again and again, the same point can be made: we are dealing only with differences in proportions. We have no evidence that in this area all or even nearly all the poor have one value, belief, or pattern of conduct while the nonpoor have another one.

Since many, if not most, of the poor and nonpoor have similar values, beliefs, and patterns of conduct regarding child-rearing, we cannot expect to find that the conditions associated with poverty fully account for these thoughts and actions. Nevertheless, we want to know how and to what extent various conditions associated with poverty independently and jointly affect them. One basic issue underlying the differences between the cultural and situational explanations of the life style of the poor is the relative importance of intergenerational processes or, more particularly, of growing up in poverty. We will consider those effects first.

In Chapter 2, I argued that, generally, values more than conduct were resistant to contemporary conditions and therefore tend to be more strongly affected by intergenerational processes. Usually in our analysis we have examined the consequences of having grown up in families of low socioeconomic status. Presumably that indicated a whole set of experiences in early life associated with poverty. It is possible that intergenerational processes are operative, but are not revealed by this mode of analysis. Thus, if a particular value or pattern of conduct is not related to socioeconomic rank in the parental generation, we would not find any relationship between the parental values or patterns of conduct and those of the mothers studied, even if on a family basis there is some intergenerational transmission. For example, we noted that the mothers' belief in spanking as a way of disciplining a child was not related to social origins, but it was highly related to the beliefs of the mothers' parents (see Chapter 8 and Table 8.6).

In regard to intergenerational processes, aside from socioeconomic origins, we do find evidence supporting the ideas set forth in Chapter 2. In order to make these points clearer, I will also refer to other characteristics analyzed in this study—neighborly relations, leisure-time activities, and organizational participation. These are reported more fully elsewhere.[1] Thus, as may be seen in Table 10.1, husbandless mothers whose own mothers went to meetings tended to belong to voluntary associations.[2] The degree of association for this pattern of conduct, however, is much less than was found in regard to thinking spanking was very important. The degree of association in regard to organizational participation by husbandless mothers is about the same as the correlation noted between husbandless mothers' employment and whether or not their own mother worked. The relationship

1. Louis Kriesberg and Seymour S. Bellin, "Fatherless Families and Housing: A Study of Dependency" (Syracuse University Youth Development Center, 1965; offset).

2. Whenever the data made the comparison possible, we saw that among the female respondents the relationship was higher between their current attitudes or behavior and those reported as characterizing the mother as compared with those characterizing the father. Although mothers may be the major channel for the transmission of values and beliefs, what they transmit is affected by their relationship with their husbands. The absence of a husband means greater intergenerational continuity for some characteristics and less for others, compared to complete families.

between voting in the gubernatorial election and whether or not the mothers' fathers were interested in politics is also of the same magnitude.[3]

Table 10.1. Associations Between Number of Organizations to which Mothers Belong[a] and Frequency with which Mother's Parents Went to Organizational Meetings[b]

Kendall Tau C	*Mothers* Husbandless	*Mothers* Married
Between respondent's organizational participation and frequency of mother going to meetings	.18[c] (128)	.05 (374)
Between respondent's organizational participation and frequency of father going to meetings	.09 (108)	.03 (333)

a The numeer of organizations to which the mothers belong is based upon responses to a series of questions. The respondents were first asked, "Do you belong or take part in . . . (eight different kinds of organizations were asked about, including church and union organizations)?" Then the respondents were asked, "Altogether, how many organizations do you belong to or take part in?"

b The respondents were asked about their mothers and about their fathers: "When you were 11 or 12 years old, how often did your mother do each of the following things? First, go to meetings of social, church, neighborhood or other organizations? Did whe do that at least once a week, many times a year, rarely, or never do that?" The respondents were asked the same question about their fathers going to "meetings of his union, lodge, church, or some other organization."

When we assess the relationship between social origins and various thoughts and actions in regard to child-rearing, then, we cannot directly test the ideas about the relative vulnerability of different characteristics to intergenerational processes. These ideas, however, should help in interpreting the findings; moreover, the ideas about variations in the degree of intergenerational transmission among married as compared to husbandless mothers can still be assessed.

One of the most striking findings of the study is that none of the values, beliefs, or patterns of conduct studied pertaining to child-rearing were found to be even moderately associated with socioeconomic origins for both poor and non-poor husbandless and married mothers. At least in the area of general values, we might reasonably have expected to find that growing up in families of low socioeconomic status

3. Kriesberg and Bellin, *op. cit.*, p. 264, n. 20.

would have some general, enduring, and direct effects. That it does not indicates the lack of distinctiveness in child-rearing thought and action in the parental generation between those of low and high socioeconomic status. This is no artifact of the analysis. In some areas we can find such general direct effects; for example, in the area of general style of life, including leisure-time activities. Thus, even in a pattern of conduct such as dining out, there is a clear difference between those who grew up in low-status families of origin and others, holding constant marital status and current income (see Table 10.2). The same pattern, although not as marked, was found for going out to watch sports events.

Table 10.2. Per Cent Ever Dining Out by Father's Occupational Status and by Mother's Income and Marital Status

	Husbandless Mothers Per Capita Disposable Income		*Married Mothers Per Capita Disposable Income*	
Father's Occupational Index	*Less Than $500*	*$500 or More*	*Less Than $500*	*$500 or More*
18 or less	30.3 (33)	64.3 (28)	28.6 (35)	62.6 (131)
19 or more	54.5 (22)	88.5 (26)	61.1 (18)	77.0 (122)

* The data are from responses to one item in a long series. The question was: "Do you sometimes do things in your spare time such as . . . (go to dinner in a restaurant)?" If the respondent replied "yes," he was asked, "Do you usually do that about every day, once a week, two to three times a month, once a month, or less often?"

This does not mean that socioeconomic status origins have no relevance even in the area of child-rearing; it does mean that those effects are mediated by other circumstances. Before reviewing some of the consequences of differences in social origins, in interaction with being poor and husbandless, it is worth noting that for some characteristics studied there is no relationship with socioeconomic origins even within each category of persons studied. Thus, we found no or very small relationships between various measures of valuation of education and socioeconomic origins. Presumably, high valuation of education is so widespread today that everyone is subject to many contemporary influences supporting it. The general societal shift largely overcomes whatever differences may have existed in the parental generation.

Having a husband facilitates certain kinds of social activities, and married mothers can implement predispositions acquired earlier that are relevant to such activities. For example, having a husband facilitates going to parties and visiting other families. A mother without a husband is less likely than one with a husband to engage in those activities even if predispositions to do so were acquired earlier. Consequently, the degree of association between participating in those activities and relevant family-of-origin patterns is higher among the married than among the husbandless mothers (see Table 10.3). Compare the variations in the degree of association with those noted in regard to organizational participation as

Table 10.3. Associations Between Frequency of Mothers' Going Visiting or to Parties[a] and Frequency with which Their Mothers Took Them out as Children and Frequency with which Their Parents Went out Together[b]

	Mothers	
Kendall Tau C	*Husbandless*	*Married*
Between respondent's going visiting and to parties and frequency of mother taking family out	-.04 (125)	.14[c] (379)
Between respondent's going visiting or to parties and frequency with which parents went out together	.05 (103)	.12[c] (328)

a The data are from a question series: "Do you sometimes do things in your spare time such as . . . visit or go to parties?" and "Do you usually do that about every day, once a week, two to three times a month, once a month, or less often?"

b The data are from a question series: "When you were 11 or 12 years old, how often did your mother do each of the following things?" The first item is based on the question item: "Go out with you and the rest of the family to visit someplace or see something; did she do that at least once a week, many times a year, rarely, or never do that?" The second item is based upon responses to the following question item, asked only of respondents living with both parents or parental surrogates: "Go out with your father to a party or a movie or something like that?"

c Significant at .01 level.

presented in Table 10.1. Similarly, we noted that socioeconomic origins are more related to whether or not children play at home with friends among the married than among the husbandless mothers.

On the other hand, a husband is also a source of contemporary influence. He can induce or inhibit his wife's behavior; he can urge, suggest, or simply model different values and beliefs. All this competes with influence from the past. If a particular pattern of thought or conduct is not dependent upon a husband for expression, then husbandless mothers are more likely than married mothers to show high associations between such patterns and their family-of-origin experiences. Thus, in Chapter 8 we saw that the relationship with social origins was higher for husbandless than married mothers in values and beliefs such as valuing obedience and thinking planning is not possible.

The intergenerational transmission of thought and conduct is not a simple, mechanical persistence. Predispositions acquired in childhood may affect the responses persons make to their circumstances. A husband, thus, is not only a competing influence or a facilitating condition; his presence or absence results in other conditions which interact with previously acquired predispositions. Thus, as shown in Table 8.1, husbandless mothers of high socioeconomic origins who were not in poverty were much less likely to value obedience than similarly situated married mothers. The nature of the relationship with the children may be altered by the absence of the husband-father, but the way in which it is altered depends upon the mother's previous background as well as her current circumstances.

All this has important implications for the subcultural explanation of the life style of the poor. In many, but not all, respects, husbandless mothers are more subject than married mothers to intergenerational influences. But this interacts with current circumstances in a complex manner. Those current circumstances associated with poverty, however, are more determined by still other current circumstances than by the mother's socioeconomic origins. Consequently, neither among the married nor the husbandless mothers do we find an integrated set of previous and current conditions perpetuating patterns of thought and conduct which would be conducive of their children acquiring the orientations and skills that would perpetuate the life style and conditions of their own poverty.

Each condition associated with poverty does not uniformly tend toward the perpetuation of values, beliefs, and skills among the children that are conducive to poverty. We have noted this in regard to growing up in a fatherless family. The same may be noted in regard to avoiding poverty by the mother working. We have noted that employed husbandless mothers, in many ways, have values and beliefs conducive to their children's upward mobility; but in other ways their activity has some consequences which may be contrary to their upward mobility. In general, there is no reason to believe that everything that a child experiences in growing up in poverty is handicapping for later educational and occupational achievement. The motivation for striving, the skills acquired in a less comfortable environment in some ways are useful for later achievements.

This brings us to another basic issue underlying the difference between a subcultural and situational explanation: the role of particular influence processes. That is, what is the relative importance of objective conditions and subjective orientations, of social and nonsocial conditions, and of learning through the inculcative efforts of others or by accommodation to circumstances. We have noted that some orientations acquired in the family-of-origin have continuing effect in interaction with other circumstances. But many of those circumstances have their effects as conditions to which people accommodate. Thus we have reported various residential area effects; upon examination, these effects were operative not through normative processes as much as by posing problems with which the mothers must contend. This does not necessarily mean that the residential areas have the same consequences for everyone living in the same area; the area has differential effects depending upon still other conditions, such as marital status.

Another basic issue in understanding the life style of the poor is the extent to which the values, beliefs, and patterns of conduct constitute a consistent, integrated system. More particularly, we are concerned with the degree to which the values and beliefs people hold are consistent with their actual conduct. Of course we have found that usually there is some degree of association between those values and behavior that an observer would expect to be related to each other. Since the attitudes and behavior are both ascertained from the respondents' verbal reports to an interviewer, there is even less reason for being struck by such findings than would otherwise be the case. But what is revealing is the variation in the degree of association for different pairs of attitudes and behaviors and among husbandless as compared to married mothers.

First of all, we should note the general reason why there may be little relationship between attitudes and behaviors an observer might reasonably expect to find. Each attitude and behavior pattern is subject to a somewhat different set of determining conditions. Attitudes, for reasons developed in Chapters 1 and 2 and as indicated by several findings in the study, are less vulnerable to contemporary conditions than is conduct. Consequently, despite any psychological tendency for congruence or dissonance reduction, some discrepancy is inevitable.

It is also necessary to keep in mind that many different attitudes are relevant to any particular conduct. As research analysts we may examine one pair—but for the subjects, other attitudes may be more relevant. For example, we saw in Chapter 9 that among married mothers there was a marked association between being dissatisfied with a child's school marks and controlling the time he spends on his school work; but among the husbandless mothers, there was no relationship at all. The husbandless mothers' concern about the educational achievements of their children makes it less likely that they will relax pressure when a married mother would. Attitudes such as desire for excellence, belief in the effectiveness of parental control, and general anxiety about school achievement can all be related to the same conduct; but which attitude is most associated with the conduct can vary among people in different circumstances.

We have noted two other ways in which being husbandless

affects the likelihood of congruence between attitudes and behavior. One involves the ability to implement and act out the conduct which would be related to the attitude. High educational aspirations may not be associated with involvement in school events if there are obstacles to the activity. Thus, participating in school affairs is less highly associated with such presumably connected values among husbandless than among married mothers. The same patterns of association were found in regard to enjoying and participating in sports activities. The second way in which congruence is affected by being without a husband involves the ability to be free from engaging in activities a mother has no interest in conducting. Thus, political interest and voting are less highly associated with each other among married than among husbandless mothers.

These findings have an important implication: If attitudes are less subject to contemporary conditions than are behavior patterns, and if there is a tendency for attitudes and behavior to be subjectively consistent or congruent, we would expect that changes in attitudes usually follow rather than lead changes in behavior.

One final observation about the possible intergenerational links between the way children are reared and their later economic conditions is necessary. We have examined ways of rearing children that presumably have some later effects upon the achievement motive, autonomy, intellectual ability, and educational attainments of the sons and daughters of the mothers studied. We must not forget that those later effects are probably not very large. Many other factors, aside from personal qualities affect a person's avoidance of poverty. The chances for a child of an affluent family to maintain his position are greater than for an equally endowed child of a nonaffluent family to attain a comparable position. The differences in these chances are probably greater when the children are equally inadequately endowed.[4] Certainly, a

4. A study of high school youth who were followed for a seven-year period (1957-1964) provides data on parental education, youths' intelligence, and perceived parental encouragement to go to college, plans to go to college,

wide range of skills, energy, and discipline are compatible with filling every occupational category. The resources of affluent parents *can* compensate for the intellectual or personal failures of their children to secure employment that at a minimum avoids poverty.

In summary, we have not found an integrated subculture of poverty with a distinctive set of values, beliefs, and patterns of conduct that are intergenerationally transmitted. Rather, we have found a variety of conditions associated with poverty, each having a somewhat different set of determinants. Each condition, moreover, has varying effects upon different aspects of the way of life of the poor. The conditions have some joint effects, but not merely to produce a vicious cycle of poverty. There are many paths into and out of poverty. The findings of this study have many implications for social policy, and we turn to them now.

Policy Implications

Some governmental programs were the subject of this study insofar as they are conditions associated with poverty. Thus the findings have particular pertinence to low-income public housing policy and public welfare programs for fatherless families. The findings, however, have implications beyond these two programs. In order to assess the implications for reducing poverty among female-headed families, it is advisable to consider a wide range of possible policies.

Let us assume it is desirable to eliminate the dependence

---

college attendance, and college graduation. The ratio between youths with fathers having high education compared to youths with fathers having low education in reports of parental encouragement is greater among youths of low intelligence than among those of high intelligence. The same is true for planning to go to college, attending college, and graduating from college. Moreover, the differences in ratio are greater for each successive step. All this indicates that parents with high education are more able and in fact do push their less able children on more than do parents with low education. Data are from William H. Sewall and Vimal Shah, "Parents' Education and Children's Educational Aspirations and Achievements," *American Sociological Review,* 33 (April, 1968), pp. 191-209. Also see Louis Kriesberg, "The Relationship Between Socioeconomic Rank and Behavior," *Social Problems,* 10 (Spring, 1963), n. 22.

of fatherless families upon public welfare. This can be accomplished in two ways: (1) by preventing the establishment of fatherless families or quickly converting them back into complete families or (2) by preventing fatherless families from becoming and remaining poor.

This may sound facetious, but there is a point in taking such a broad perspective. It encourages thinking of a wide range of possible solutions and indicates some basis for evaluating particular programs. Let us note the general solutions before turning to some specific programs that may lead to their attainment. The occurrence of all fatherless families cannot be prevented, but their number could be lessened by policies that reduce divorce, separation, desertion, and adult mortality and that increase remarriage. Fatherless families can be prevented from being poor if the former husband-fathers are sufficiently wealthy to provide the necessary income for the families or if the mothers work and earn enough to place them beyond poverty. Their poverty could also be ended by various combinations of expanded social security programs, more generous public assistance programs, negative income tax programs, or family allowance programs.

The poor are a heterogenous category that disproportionally includes the aged, the disabled, the blacks, the irregularly employed, and those in economically depressed areas, as well as fatherless families. Programs to reduce the poverty of one segment may have little relevance for other segments. In this discussion the concern is with female-headed families. Some of the programs discussed have relevance to other segments of the poor, but their consequences for other segments will not be assessed.

The fundamental implication of this study is that the life style of the poor and the movement out of poverty by parents in their own life or by their children depends upon the circumstances in which they live. It is unreasonable to expect people to stop acting like they are poor as long as they are poor.[5] Values, beliefs, and patterns of conduct interfering

5. Lee Rainwater, "The Lessons of Pruitt-Igoe," *The Public Interest,* No. 8 (Summer, 1967), pp. 116-126.

with moving out of poverty will persist if the conditions supporting such thoughts and actions continue; if those conditions are altered, so will the thoughts and actions. In the discussion that follows, then, the emphasis is upon policies affecting the conditions of life of persons in poverty and vulnerable to it. But we have also seen that every condition has diverse effects.[6] Altering one condition to attain one objective may interfere with the attainment of other desired goals. A discussion of policy alternatives, then, should consider the wide range of values and empirical relationships involved and the possible paradoxes of pursuing any given policy. I shall try to do that as I discuss the government programs for which this study's findings have particular relevance.

Public housing. The evidence of this study demonstrates that low-income public housing projects, even as traditionally built, can vary in ways that inhibit or facilitate remaining in poverty and maintaining a style of life associated with poverty. Public housing projects need not take the form of huge projects in the midst of slum neighborhoods that perpetuate if not intensify the deliterous consequences of poverty.[7] Projects can vary in size, composition, physical ar-

6. For both basic research and applied sociology concerns, it should be kept in mind that the findings reported in this study are based upon an investigation of the effects of particular conditions, but the range of the conditions is fixed. If one condition has a relatively large range, it will appear more important than when other determinants do not vary as significantly. Of course the degree of variation in a condition depends in part upon the research design and the treatment of the data. By design, one can insure small or large variations in a condition. The extent and nature of the variation of each condition in this study were described in Chapters 3, 4, 5, and 6. I noted, for example, that I was using gross categories of employment in the analysis of possible effects of maternal work status. This may, therefore, obscure the effects of maternal work status. Although the variation in each condition is fixed, the significance of the variation can still differ depending upon the characteristic being explained. Income is particularly relevant for engaging in many kinds of leisure-time activities. Consequently, we found that variation in income was more highly related to engaging in various leisure-time activities than it was to many other kinds of activities. Nevertheless, in a study of a population with a greater range of income, large income effects might be found for other kinds of activities.

7. For documentation of the current status and operations of the low-income public housing program, see Alvin L. Schorr, *Slums and Social*

rangements, neighborhood setting and other characteristics that affect the quality of the tenants' lives. It is possible, if politically difficult, to build projects that provide more than physically improved residential conditions.

The contributions that low-income public housing projects can make to the solutions outlined earlier are undoubtedly small, but they do exist. Just because they have not solved many of the problems of the poor or basically altered the conditions associated with poverty, they should not be written off as a huge error. Until more basic policies in regard to poverty are implemented, some form of subsidization of housing for the poor is necessary. Otherwise the poor, and particularly the poor fatherless families, will be condemned to live in substandard housing and devote a very high proportion of their meager income to housing costs.

Consider some of the implications of simply living in minimally adequate dwellings as provided by public housing. A detailed and careful longitudinal study of one public housing project in Baltimore found only limited changes resulting from a move into the project.[8] The project was located in the same neighborhood as the one in which the tenants previously lived. Consequently, the social environment was not radically altered. There were some consequences, however, of living in relatively sanitary and safe buildings: there was a reduction in illnesses and perhaps mortality. This alone has pertinence for the previously outlined solutions. Fatherless families are less likely to be created if the husband-father is alive and healthy enough to maintain steady employment. Furthermore, the children do better in school if they are not frequently absent due to illness. Achievement in school is associated with the attainment of an education that will facilitate earning a stable and decent income and maintaining a marriage.

The consequences of varying social compositions and

Insecurity, U.S. Social Security Administration, Division of Research and Statistics, Research Report #1 (Washington, D.C.: U.S. Government Printing office, 1963).

8. Daniel M. Wilner, and others, *The Housing Environment and Family Life* (Baltimore: Johns Hopkins Press, 1962).

neighborhood settings are more complex and more mixed. On the whole, most husbandless mothers living in the small projects of Syracuse derive social support from residing there. They are more likely to have extensive neighborly relations and engage in mutual aid than are those living outside.[9] Depending upon the social characteristics of the projects, this encourages involvement in a wide variety of extrafamilial activities. We need to consider some of the determinants of social support in different projects and the variety of possible consequences in order to make specific recommendations in regard to public housing.

The mothers' integration into a network of neighbors and friends and of mutual aid in a project is facilitated by prior acquaintance with another tenant, by previous residence in the neighborhood near the project, and by project homogeneity. These are maximized when projects are located in predominantly low-income neighborhoods. Consequently, the integration and support furthers the maintenance of low-income life styles. Nevertheless, extensive neighborly relations and mutual aid were found in the two projects in middle-income neighborhoods more than in the other two projects studied. The smaller size of the projects in the middle-income neighborhoods is probably an important factor accounting for the extensiveness of neighboring and mutual aid.

The social support available from friends and neighbors may have diverse consequences for the establishment and maintenance of fatherless families. On the one hand, social support and extensive relations can facilitate finding and holding jobs and a new husband. Also, insofar as living in public housing offers adequate housing at a financially bearable price, a married couple may be able to lessen some of the marital strains otherwise arising from poverty, and maintain a marriage. On the other hand, the support and aid low-income public housing provides husbandless mothers may make the alternative of being husbandless seem more acceptable, and the clinging to a distressful marriage less

9. Kriesberg and Bellin, *op. cit.*, pp. 157-208.

necessary.[10] Furthermore, a husband may feel less sense of responsibility if he sees husbandless mothers managing well with the assistance of many formal programs and the support of informal networks. These consequences are more likely where the proportion of fatherless families is high, where being a husbandless mother is almost expected, even if undesired.[11] In short, the social composition and neighborhood setting of public housing projects can indirectly affect marital disruption and remarriage rates; the contribution of the projects to affecting these rates, however, is certainly small.

There are value issues at stake here, as well as empirical ones. My own values lead me to feel that it is better to have mothers feel they have a real alternative to a distressful marriage than to make the alternative so unpalatable that even a marriage that damages the marital partners and their children will be endured. The preference for a happy, stable marriage is sufficiently strong for most adults that if conditions are constructed to make it likely, that alternative will be chosen over a comfortable fatherless family and male bachelorhood.

Aside from the possible effects of public housing upon the adults' marital status, we should consider the possible effects upon raising children who will themselves be able to maintain a stable marital union. On the whole, the evidence from this study does not indicate that growing up in a broken family increases the likelihood of oneself having a broken marriage. Other evidence from this study, however, indicates the special strains that a husbandless mother has in raising children and the relative importance of the neighborhood and its influences upon her children. A husbandless mother can, within appropriate conditions, raise children who are as capable of maintaining a stable marital union as are children of complete families. But a slum neighborhood, whether pub-

10. This issue is discussed in Helen Icken Safa, "The Female-Based Household in Public Housing: A Case Study in Puerto Rico," *Human Organization*, XXIV (Summer, 1965), pp. 135-139.

11. This sample has been studied most intensively in regard to the Caribbean . See, for example, William J. Goode, "A Deviant Case: Illegitimacy in the Caribbean," *American Sociological Review*, XXV (February, 1960), pp. 21-30.

lic or private, is not an appropriate environment. In addition, a high proportion of fatherless families in the area, although easing some strains and stigmas for the children of such families, may make the possibility of disrupted marriages too readily expected by all children.

Public housing may also reduce the chances of the mothers' continuing poverty and welfare dependency. The social support can facilitate the mothers' employment—both by providing child-care arrangements and by word-of-mouth information about jobs. But whether or not the facilitation is accompanied by encouragement or discouragement of employment depends upon characteristics of the projects and its neighborhood setting, as well as of general housing policy.

As regards the raising of children who will be economically independent, the evidence, again, is inferential. The schools play a particularly important role for fatherless families. The quality of the schools in slum neighborhoods is usually below that of schools in neighborhoods with higher socioeconomic status families.[12] Husbandless mothers are even more handicapped than married mothers in providing an educationally supportive home to compensate for inadequate schools and adverse peer influences. The schools in middle-income neighborhoods present opportunities for their children that are consistent with husbandless mothers' high aspirations. The mothers can and do support their children's efforts. For some husbandless mothers, however, the challenge may be too great for their children and they are unable to provide the additional efforts that middle-income schools require of the students' parents.

In the light of these observations, I venture the following recommendations regarding public housing. Since even traditional low-income public housing helps alleviate the strains of fatherless families, and some projects facilitate movement out of poverty, the construction of low-income housing projects should be continued and even increased.

12. Patricia Cayo Sexton, "City Schools," in *Poverty in America*, L.A. Ferman, and others, eds. (Ann Arbor: University of Michigan Press, 1965), pp. 234-249, reprinted from *The Annals of the American Academy of Political and Social Science*, March 1964.

Some housing projects may also help perpetuate the social conditions that are obstacles to stable marital unions and to employment. Therefore, the new projects should be located, constructed, and managed in ways that maximize the possible benefits.

Government regulations should be designed to insure that public housing projects reduce and not increase the economic and racial segregation of American cities. For example, it is possible to limit the size of new public housing projects and to avoid the proliferation of housing projects built side-by-side. Rehabilitated housing and newly constructed housing for middle- and low-income families should be interspersed. In addition, some new public housing projects should be required to be built outside of low-income areas. The extension of city housing authorities to cover metropolitan areas would aid this development. There could be an additional benefit: the construction of projects for the elderly near their friends and former homes in the suburbs. Construction of projects for low-income families in middle-income residential areas could be required to constitute between 30 and 70 per cent of new public housing units. This could be required in initial plans, to be implemented within a fixed number of years for each building program. The lower percentage figure is to insure a minimum number of units outside the slum areas of the city; this may also require construction on open land rather than the destruction of existing housing units. The upper percentage figure is to insure that at least some units are constructed near the present residence of potential tenants, and thus preserve some opportunities for maintaining neighborhood relations and organization.

Limited in size and scattered in the metropolitan area, projects outside of low-income neighborhoods would make it likely that eligible poor families who now exclude themselves from public housing would avail themselves of it. This could even be the base for some political support. In any case, it would improve the social composition as well as the neighborhood setting of public housing projects. Furthermore, reduction of residential segregation in the cities would reduce the fundamental impediment to the equalization of educational facilities.

Existing projects could be made better social environments by some changes in administrative policy. One desirable change would be to raise the income limits for continued residence. If families that have managed to increase their income—even to middle-income levels—are allowed to stay in public housing, the residential stability of the projects would be higher, the increase in the proportion of socially and economically handicapped families living in each project would be slowed, and the emergence of indigenous leadership would be more likely. Employment by additional family members and the seeking of better-paying jobs would also be encouraged by this policy. The housing authorities could also expect increased rental revenues (since rents would bear some relationship to family income). This, in turn, would make it easier for housing authorities to rent more units to the very poorest families, who are often excluded at present. This policy must be introduced in conjunction with the construction of additional units for low-income families; otherwise, the number of housing units for low-income families will decrease as more are retained by families with higher incomes.

Many issues also surround the deliberate social organization of public housing tenants. Tenant councils or other organizations can improve the services available to the tenants, aid the integration of new tenants, and improve the general spirit of the project. It is also possible that the internal cohesion increases the barrier to the external environment, but this need not be the case. Organizations and facilities for meetings can be constructed to increase tenants' relations with the neighborhood residents. One issue in these matters is the degree to which the housing authority should directly try to organize and direct the tenants. On the whole, it is best for the authorities to allow the tenants to organize themselves, and then channels for discussion, negotiation, and collaboration can be created as demands arise.

Recommending the construction of low-income public housing projects does not mean that other forms of providing low-income housing, such as rent subsidies and individual houses operated by a housing authority, should not be carried forward. There are unquestionably advantages to such arrangements. But one of the points emerging from this analysis is that fatherless families can derive extra support from residence in small housing projects under appropriate conditions. We have not studied the effects upon complete families in equal detail, and their interests must also be weighed. It is safe to say, however, that the provision of alternative housing arrangements for low-income families would provide the possibility of families choosing the arrangements that will be most beneficial to their own and their childrens' independence. All forms of subsidization of housing have some disadvantages. In the long run, the solution to the problems of providing decent housing to the poor must be found in insuring that everyone has sufficient income to pay for minimally adequate housing.

We turn next to a consideration of policies to reduce poverty among fatherless families. I will discuss some aspects of existing programs affecting the income of fatherless families. The recomendations will be based, if only inferentially, upon the analysis reported. The analysis has dealt with some of the concommitants of welfare programs affecting fatherless families. Thus, AFDC, by providing minimal subsistence, frees the mother from the necessity of working. We have examined some consequences of maternal employment and of income above the poverty line.

In regard to remarriage, we have no evidence that a husbandless mother's employment decreases her chances of remarrying. On the contrary, the expansion of relationships beyond the family and neighborhood network and the circumscribed leisure-time activities of the nonemployed may even increase the opportunities and therefore the likelihood of the employed husbandless mother remarrying. Thus, 35 per cent of the working husbandless mothers expect to remarry, although they say they do not want to, compared to 15 per cent of the nonworking husbandless mothers.[13] About the

13. Kriesberg and Bellin, *op. cit.*, p. 279.

same proportion say they want to get married. The nonworking mothers are particularly likely to say they want to get married but do not expect to do so.

The critical issue surrounding employment is its possible detrimental effects upon the children under the mothers' care. We certainly have found no evidence that employed husbandless mothers withdraw concern about their children. Rather, they seem particularly concerned about the future well-being of their children and, if anything, have higher aspirations and are more likely to value independence of the children. A husbandless mother's employment does seem to interfere with some direct interaction with her children and participation in their school activities. On the other hand, the greater involvement in the political community and certain leisure-time activities can provide a more stimulating home environment than would otherwise be the case. The total effects must in part depend upon the nature of the other sources of influence upon the children—from peers, schools, and other formal and informal relations. In a national study, it was found that among both Negro and non-Negro men raised in female-headed families the heads' employment contributed to the sons' occupational success.[14]

Income level, given the generally low levels among the husbandless mothers, was not found to have a marked relationship with many of the attitudes and behaviors of interest in this study. Income is associated with many leisure-time activities and certain values, beliefs, and aspirations for children. Income, however, is also related to area of residence. Poor husbandless mothers are restricted to housing for low-income families and, with the segregation of housing by income as well as by race, this means differential access to many public services, notably good public schools.

In Chapter 7, we discussed the evidence concerning the extent to which poverty and welfare dependency was intergenerationally transmitted. Although we noted much movement into and out of poverty and welfare dependency, the handicap which growing up in families dependent upon welfare entails cannot be denied. This can be seen if one consid-

14. Beverley Duncan and Otis Dudley Duncan, "Family Stability and Occupational Success," *Social Problems*, 16 (Winter, 1969), pp. 282-284.

ers the occupational mobility of sons of fathers who had white-collar occupations. If the sons were in families that received ADC benefits, despite the presumed cultural advantages of white-collar background, their mobility is handicapped. In a national study of terminated ADC cases, the occupations of ADC children 20 years of age and over were ascertained.[15] About 20 per cent were in white-collar occupations, 18 per cent in skilled trades, and the remainder were skilled and semi-skilled operatives and unskilled workers. If we consider the relationship between the ADC children's occupations with those of their fathers, we see that upward occupational mobility is less than is the case for the nation as a whole. Thus, of ADC sons with fathers who were skilled and semi-skilled operatives and unskilled workers, only 16 per cent were in white-collar occupations; of those with fathers in skilled trades, 21 per cent were in white-collar occupations; and, even of those with fathers in white-collar occupations, only 39 per cent were themselves in white-collar occupations. In the nation as a whole, about one-third of the sons of fathers in manual occupations are in nonmanual occupations, and about two-thirds of those whose fathers were in nonmanual occupations are themselves in nonmanual occupations.[16]

Present-day public assistance for children in fatherless families does not provide the experiences and resources which give them an equal opportunity to compete economically. Subsistence maintenance is an inadequate base for most persons to rise above subsistence. This is true even in states with relatively high assistance benefits; in many states the benefits are very much lower than those provided, for example, in New York. The problems arising from limited educational attainment and other skills and resources are aggravated by the general decrease in the demand for unskilled labor and the rising educational requirements.[17]

15. Gordon W. Blackwell and Raymond F. Gould, *Future Citizens All* (Chicago: American Public Welfare Association, 1952), pp. 142-150.

16. Seymour Martin Lipset and Reinhard Bendix, *Social Mobility in Industrial Society* (Berkeley: University of California Press, 1960), Fig. 2.1.

17. The potential for the growth of poverty in the United States follows from these conditions. See Michael Harrington, "A Social Reformer's View

In the light of the findings of this study, some suggestions can be made to reduce the poverty and dependence of female-headed families. First, I will consider possible modifications and extensions of current welfare and antipoverty governmental programs. Later I will refer to more general governmental and nongovernmental policies. As in the case of public housing, it is easy to point out the failures and limitations of current programs. The evidence from this analysis indicates that nevertheless many people manage to escape from poverty. In a sense it is the success of the general policies developed in the past that creates demands for further improvements. As the poor become a smaller segment of the population, their relative deprivation becomes greater, more of a public scandal, and less amenable to the same old methods of easing. As expectations and skill requirements rise generally in the society, so do new problems; for example, although the proportion of students who complete high school continues to rise, the concern about high school drop-outs rightfully increases.

Welfare regulations should be devised to permit maternal employment without the penalty of an equal reduction in public assistance. This means that earnings should not be subtracted dollar for dollar from welfare allowances. In the case of children's earnings, recognition of the value of allowing earnings to be an increment to family income is now being made. Permitting a mother to earn a minimal amount of money without reducing assistance benefits would also simplify the administration of assistance programs and avoid the effects of possible cheating and collusion that may otherwise occur. Furthermore, a formula which permits a mother to retain a significant proportion of her earnings as an increment to public assistance payments would have several advantages. The family income could be increased for at least some families on AFDC. A mother could experiment with employment and increase her chances of financial independence when the children no longer need her care. In addition, the widening experiences her work activity entails can

of Poverty," in *Poverty in America*, Margaret S. Gordon, ed. (San Francisco: Chandler, 1965), pp. 27-37.

stimulate her children's educational and occupational achievement.

To maximize the benefits and minimize the disadvantages of such changes, adequate day-care centers should be established. Of even greater benefit would be an extensive pre-school educational program, as signaled by Operation Head Start. In addition to the direct benefits for the children, it would facilitate mothers' employment. Knowing that their children are well taken care of may not only relieve mothers of some of the concerns which inhibit employment but may also reduce some possible adverse effects of employment. Feeling guilty and anxious about employment may make the mother act in ways which harm the child; if she is free of such feelings, the effects of employment would be quite different.[18]

Finally, the poverty and dependency of fatherless families might be reduced if the wage differential between males and females were ended. This is difficult to accomplish by any single governmental action, but governmental and nongovernmental programs directed to this end could effect some changes. If women received equal pay for equal work, employment would be more worthwhile and economically rational for them. This is particularly true for husbandless mothers who have the extra expenses of child care and the alterna-

18. Increasingly, women appear to be entering the labor force out of choice rather than necessity. See Sanford Dornbusch and David M. Heer, "The Evaluation of Work by Females, 1940-1950," *American Journal of Sociology*, LXIII (July, 1957), pp. 27-29. Lois Hoffman has shown that different attitudes toward work have different implications for a mother's relation with her children. A mother who enjoys working is "relatively high on positive affect toward the child, uses mild discipline, and tends to avoid inconveniencing the child with household tasks; the child is relatively non-assertive and ineffective. The working mother who dislikes working, on the other hand, seems less involved with the child altogether and obtains the child's help with tasks; the child is assertive and hostile." She speculates that the presence or absence of guilt in the mother may be an important intervening variable. For example, mothers who enjoy working may feel more guilty about leaving their children and may react by overprotecting and overindulging them. Of course, an important contingency is the mother's belief about the consequences of her absence from the home during the day. The author cautions, however, that several alternative interpretations are also possible. See Lois Hoffman, "Mother's Enjoyment of Work and Effects on the Child," in *The Employed Mother in America*, F. Ivan Nye and Lois W. Hoffman, eds. (Chicago: Rand McNally, 1963), pp. 102-103.

tive of welfare dependency if employment does not yield enough money. It might be argued that if women received equal pay, their marital dependence would be reduced and marital disruptions increased. But, aside from the right of free choice and valuing positive rather than negative alternatives the actual effects upon marriage and remarriage rates are not likely to be great. Men are still likely to enter and hold higher-paying positions. Equal pay might even result in opening more jobs for men since the competitive edge that women have as lower-paid workers would be lost.

All these programs, which directly deal with the problems of poverty and dependency of fatherless families, can make only limited contributions to the solutions outlined earlier. In many ways, it is men's earnings and job security which fundamentally affect marital disruptions, remarriages, and the poverty and dependence of fatherless families.

In a national study of terminated ADC cases, the occupational distribution of fathers of ADC recipients was analyzed.[19] In the Northeast region of the United States, only 8 per cent were in professional, managerial, clerical, or sales occupations, while 29 per cent were unskilled laborers; the distribution for the employed males in the general population in the same region is quite different: 31 per cent were in such white-collar occupations and only 8 per cent were unskilled laborers. Clearly a husband in a low-status occupation, lacking an adequate income and job security, is unlikely to maintain or to leave his family economically independent if he divorces or dies.

The inference is also supported by the extraordinarily high relationship between the unemployment rate of nonwhite males and the number of AFDC cases opened (for the period between 1948 and 1962, the correlation is .91); the relationship between the per cent of nonwhite married women separated from their husbands and the unemployment rate of nonwhite males age twenty and over is also remarkably high (for the period between 1953 and 1964, the correlation be-

19. Blackwell and Gould, *op. cit.*, pp. 33-37.

tween the deviations of the two series from their respective trends is .81).[20]

Policies which improve the employment possibilities of men, particularly those with limited education, should be actively pursued. More specifically, efforts should be increased to create additional jobs for men with limited training, reduce racial and ethnic discrimination, and upgrade the income security of low-status occupations. These efforts can take a variety of forms. One of the most fundamental is the maintenance of full employment. More particularly, the expansion of public services, such as returning to two mail deliveries a day and an expansion of construction of low-income housing would be helpful.[21] The insistence upon formal credentials—such as high school graduation or college completion—for jobs that require skills that can be learned while working or that an applicant may already have should be reduced. More regular employment in particular occupations should be encouraged, for example, by the thoughtful scheduling of government contracts for construction. In addition, union and governmental efforts should be made to extend the units of time for which an employer assumes some responsibility for the payment of his workers.

There will always be some female-headed households with and without children. The facilitation and encouragement of female employment is one of the major ways in which the poverty of such households can be prevented. In addition to policies directed at reducing sex discrimination in employment, the provision of child-care services, and specific job-training for women, more general changes are needed. Recognition that women are generally employed for some portion of their life and often become the sole support for their children or themselves should result in the encouragement of women to consider an occupational role as part of their whole life.

20. Daniel Patrick Moynihan, "Employment, Income, and the Ordeal of the Negro Family," *Daedalus*, xciv (Fall, 1965), 745-770.

21. Leon H. Keyserling, *Progress or Poverty* (Washington, D.C.: Conference on Economic Progress, 1964), especially pp. 127-33, 138.

Overall, greatly expanded educational efforts are needed. These must range from pre-school training, to retraining of adult women and men, and should include increased opportunities for higher education. The elementary and high schools in low-income neighborhoods need much improvement if they are to equal those in higher-income neighborhoods. Even more must be done to compensate for the less educationally supportive home and peer relationships in such areas. Unless students can expect that jobs appropriate to their educational attainments will be available to them, however, the incentive for educational achievement will be checked. Thus, it is essential that racial discrimination in employment end so that Negroes have the same access to jobs as whites with the same educational attainment.

To help implement such programs and to help insure that the programs reach, with maximum effectiveness, the people for whom they are intended, those who are to be affected must be able to influence the directions and operations of the programs. This means the development of political and organizational strength among the poor. Such efforts, in themselves, probably also aid in developing skills and confidence for occupational and marital stability.[22]

In addition, other government programs should be maintained and expanded. The Social Security program and its provisions for survivors' benefits has made an important contribution to preventing the dependency of widows and their minor children. The expansion of this and other forms of insurance in coverage and size of benefits can make further contributions.

Finally, serious consideration should be given to a guaranteed minimum income program and particularly to a family allowance plan.[23] Under a family allowance plan, families

22. See, in particular, Warren C. Haggstrom, "The Power of the Poor," in *Mental Health of the Poor,* Frank Riessman, Jerome Cohen, and Arthur Pearl, eds. (New York: Free Press of Glencoe, 1964), pp. 205-223.

23. See Edward E. Schwartz, "A Way to End the Means Test," *Social Work* IX (July, 1964), pp. 3-12, reprinted in Ferman and others, *op. cit.* pp. 481-496. Robert J. Lampman, "Approaches to the Reduction of Poverty," *American Economic Review,* (May, 1965), as reprinted *ibid,* pp. 415-421; Daniel P. Moynihan, "Where Liberals Went Wrong," in *Republican Papers,*

would receive a fixed amount of money for each child in the family. At present, income tax deductions are available for each child but are used only if the family has sufficient income to be taxable. A family allowance system would provide some secure income for every family, broken or not. This should reduce some of the strains facing poor complete families and reduce divorce and separation. It should also encourage the remarriage of husbandless mothers, since the remarried couple would not lose benefits otherwise lost through other programs as presently constituted. Furthermore, the secure income base provided by family allowances would encourage employment by husbandless mothers, since the possibility of their earnings placing them above poverty would be greater. Such a plan would not increase birth rates, unless the increased marital stability would slightly increase the chances of a couple having children. (In any case, information and means of birth control should be made more widely available). The basic way to attain the solutions outlined earlier is to provide more income to the poorest stratum in our society, and family allowances are a good means to do so.

A wide variety of governmental and nongovernmental programs and efforts are relevant to the reduction of poverty and dependence of fatherless families. We have considered policies that bear on the conditions studied and others deemed relevant to the life style of the poor and the perpetuation of poverty. The findings from this study indicate that variations in each of the conditions studied have some effect upon the life style of the poor. Pessimistically, this means that no single program will resolve all problems nor reduce only the undesired consequences of living in fatherless families. Optimistically, this means that some incremental advantage will accrue to some people from each improvement in the programs.

On the whole, the husbandless mothers hope and strive

Melvin R. Laird, ed. (Garden City: Anchor Books, 1968), pp. 129-142; Milton Friedman, "The Case for a Negative Income Tax," *ibid*, pp. 202-220; and Richard Lee Strout, "Paying for the Right to Life," *The New Republic*, 159 (Nov. 23, 1968) pp. 15-16.

to escape poverty themselves and have their children avoid it. But people cannot continue to maintain hope without some experiences to support the hope. Without that support, some mothers finally despair. Even before despair crushes hope, there is anguish. All this is not inevitable. There are many ways in which the fatherless families' circumstances can be eased. Many conditions can be modified so that families do not become poor and disrupted. These conditions and circumstances are subject to change by governmental and nongovernmental policies. Herein lies the hope and the challenge to government, to business, to organized labor, and to each American.

Appendix A. Sampling and Data Collection Procedures for Cross-Sectional Survey

The Sample

THE CROSS-SECTIONAL phase of the study required a representative sample of residents within each of four Syracuse public housing projects and the neighborhood surrounding each project. In order to obtain a minimum of about 100 families in each project and neighborhood without collecting an immense number of interviews, it was necessary to use different sampling ratios. In the smaller projects and less dense neighborhoods, a high percentage of the residents were selected for interviewing than in the larger projects and denser neighborhoods.

We excluded all persons who were interviewed in the panel phase of the study from the cross-sectional phase. Wherever possible we did this by utilizing our records and public records of tenant residency. In addition, the interviewers were instructed to exclude from their assignment any respondents who had been interviewed in the panel phase.

We have given pseudonyms to each of four Syracuse public housing projects: "Evans," "Grant," "Park," and "Stern." At the time the study was designed, these four projects were the only ones in operation in Syracuse; since then, one additional public housing project has been completed and is in operation.

Public Housing Sample. The Syracuse Public Housing Authority maintains a roster of continuous numbers by which tenant accounts are identified. Numbers are assigned to housing units (apartments) rather than families, so that a new tenant assumes the account number of his predecessor. The account numbers are continuous within multiple dwelling structures or single courts, depending on the geographical layout of the project. Certain structures are specifically reserved for occupancy by the elderly (either single individuals or couples aged 60 and over). These units are predominantly, but not exclusively, occupied by the elderly. Similarly, an occasional elderly tenant may at any given time be found to occupy an apartment which is not specifically reserved for the elderly.

In the Evans and Stern projects, the number of apartments occupied by the elderly is sufficiently small (6.5 per cent reserved, 7.7 per cent occupied for both projects combined) to warrant sampling without regard to the elderly/non-elderly distinction. In each of these projects a two-thirds random sample was drawn, using a table of random numbers. Three-digit random numbers were matched with the continuous tenant account numbers until the sample quota was met.

The Grant project reserves 53 per cent of its 528 units for the elderly, and of these one-eighth was randomly selected. Here there are four separate series of account numbers for the inhabitants of the reserved units, and one-eighth of each series was drawn. Of the remaining number, a 50 per cent random sample was selected. In the Park project there are 216 units for the elderly, and fifth of them was selected. For the remaining units, a one-fourth sampling ratio was used.

The available pool of dwelling units, sampling ratios, and resulting sample N's are shown in Table A.1.

Table A.1. Population, Sampling Ratios, and Sample Size by Project

Project	Elderly			Non-elderly			Total Sample
	Population: N units	Ratio	Sample N	Population: N Units	Ratio	Sample N	
Evans*				200	2/3	134	134
Stern*				213	2/3	142	142
Grant	280	1/8	35	248	1/2	124	159
Park	216	1/5	43	461	1/4	115	158
Total			78			515	593

* Not stratified on an elderly/non-elderly distinction.

Since the tabled N's represent dwelling units rather than the tenants themselves, the sample N totals serve only as an approximation of the proportion of elderly to non-elderly tenants selected in the sample. Once sampling was concluded, each project sample was treated as a *whole* and no attempt was made to maintain the stratification in the process of collecting data.

Substitute tenant account numbers, drawn in exactly the same manner as for the original sample, were used to replace units that were randomly selected but found to be occupied by tenants who had already served as respondents in the panel phase of the study and to replace dwelling units that were discovered to be vacant at the time the interviewer called. If a housing project apartment was found to be vacant, there was then a good probability that the next tenant would be a panel-phase respondent. Thus it would have been uneconomical to wait for a new tenant to move in. Substitute units were used in the order in which they were originally selected.

Neighborhood Sample. Each neighborhood around a housing project was defined as a sampling area by delineating approximately four to five city blocks in each direction from the housing project. Fewer blocks were included in some directions if a "major artery" would have had to be crossed to maintain the count. For example, a main boulevard one block north of Stern project was used as the northern boundary for the area around Stern. There are generally three criteria of a sampling area: (1) number of blocks included; (2) major arteries or natural boundaries such as a creek or boulevard; (3) the size of the resulting area and its distribution in all directions from the project.

For each of the four neighborhoods, all visible or identifiable dwelling units were listed giving an address or unique description of each. The accuracy with which this was done can be judged in terms of the appropriateness of the method for purposes of the study rather than by comparison with a published standard, of which two were available: the *Syracuse City Directory* for 1962 and *U.S. Census Reports, 1960.*

The city directory was used occasionally to clarify building addresses, spellings of names, and similar questions that arose. However, it frequently fell short of completeness. By listing, it was possible to identify a great many dwelling units for addresses where the directory listed only one or two occupants. In addition, one of the sample neighborhoods extends beyond the city limits into a relatively new developed area for which published data were not available.

Once the neighborhood listings were completed they were edited to eliminate entries which were not eligible for the sample, such as student dormitories or commercial establishments. The edited listing sheets were then paginated beginning with a randomly selected sheet and the eligible entries numbered in order of listing. This yielded the population N's shown in Table A.2, where the corresponding sampling ratios and final sample sizes are also shown. The

Table A.2. Population, Sampling Ratios, and Sample Size by Neighborhood

Neighborhood	*Population N: Dwelling Units Counted*	*Sampling Ratio*	*Sample N*
Evans	662	2/9	146
Grant	1467	2/19	152
Park	1023	1/5	212*
Stern	867	1/6	144

* Sample N was relatively large because it was known that many dwelling units were vacant.

samples were selected by counting and identifying every *N*th dwelling unit beginning with page 1 of the listing, thus obtaining the desired sample size, counting over all pages in the listing.

In Evans neighborhood, two-ninths of the population was drawn by alternately selecting the fourth and fifth listed dwelling. Similarly, in the Grant neighborhood, two-nineteenths was drawn by counting alternately the ninth and tenth dwelling. In the Stern area, one-sixth was the needed ratio, and every fifth and seventh listing was alternately selected. The Park neighborhood required a one-fifth sample; but due to the urban renewal process, two steps in drawing the sample of dwelling units were taken. First, from 1,023 listings, a one-seventh sample was drawn; this yielded 152 households. Then, when vacant, condemned, and abandoned units were judged to be so many that too few cases would result, 60 more units were drawn by selecting every 14th listing, this time *not* counting listings reported vacant at the time of listing and not counting units already selected.

Selection of Respondents

The interviewers were assigned a list of households in which interviews were to be obtained. The interviewers secured from a household informant a complete list of all the persons in the household and their relationships to each other. The interviewer then chose the proper respondent or respondents according to a set of instructions. We wished to obtain interviews with a married couple, both husband and wife, and preferably the parents of a minor child. A minor was defined as someone eighteen or younger who was not married nor was the parent of any children. The interviewers were instructed, therefore, to select respondents in the following order of preference:

1). If a male head is in the household, he and his wife, if any, are the preferred respondents. A male head is defined as an adult male who is the father or father surrogate of a minor child.

2). If no male head is present, the female head is the ireferred respondent. A female head is defined as an adult female who is the mother or mother surrogate of a minor child.

3). If two or more male heads are present, their names (beginning with the first name) are placed in alphabetical order and the first person in the list and his wife are the preferred respondents.

4). If several individuals or couples of the same generation are in the household, the respondents are chosen in the same manner as stated above.

5). If there are two couples in the household, one of which has minor children, then the husband and wife with minor children are the preferred respondents.

Once the selection of the preferred respondent was made, no substitutions were allowed.

Data Collection Procedures

The work schedule in the four project areas was planned so that interviewing would begin in one area and then move on to the next, except for a few of the staff who would conclude work in the preceding area before moving on. Letters introducing the study were mailed to the selected addresses according to a staggered schedule that would make the receipt of the letter and the arrival of the interviewer fairly concurrent events for the respondents. According to interviewers' reports, the interviewer's arrival within a few days of receipt of the letter seemed to facilitate rapport.

Since Negro interviewers worked almost exclusively in the predominantly Negro area of Park project, and since they constituted between about 15 per cent and 25 per cent of the staff, work was begun in the Park area concurrently with Stern and carried on throughout most of the interviewing phase. Work in Park neighborhood was begun and ended somewhat later than in Park housing project, and white interviewers were assigned to this area as need arose. Work in the Stern area was begun first, then Evans was added, and finally Grant. Some interviewing in each area continued after the bulk of the effort shifted to the next area, since we continued with some assignments as long as time permitted.

Generally, each assignment was handled individually when difficulty was encountered in completing it. If an interviewer had been refused but felt that someone else on the staff would be more likely to be granted an interview, he was encouraged to make such suggestions and an effort was made to make the suggested arrangements. For example, younger male interviewers occasionally asked to be replaced by an older female interviewer and Negro interviewers suggested that a white interviewer be sent.

In several cases a second letter was written to a reluctant respondent explaining the specific necessity of obtaining an interview with him and offering more information about the study. This was generally useful in that such respondents would reconsider and grant an interview without requiring numerous further calls.

The general success of the data collection procedure is presented in Table A.3. The percentage of completed assignments is computed on the basis of the number of possible completions. Vacant dwellings were not considered as potential completions.

Table A.3. Sample, Vacancies, and Assignments Completed by Area

Area	*N Total Sample*	*Vacant Dwellings*	*Non Complete Assignments*	*Percentage Complete*
Projects				
Evans	132	–*	104	77
Grant	159	–*	122	77
Park	159	–*	123	78
Stern	142	–*	113	80
Totals	595	–*	462	78
Neighborhoods				
Evans	146	4	95	67
Grant	152	16	98	72
Park	212	71	109	77
Stern	143	6	104	76
Totals	653	97	406	73

* Vacant apartments were dropped from the sample and substituted.

Table A.3 represents assignments where *at least* one respondent was interviewed, regardless of whether one or two respondents *should* have been interviewed in that household. Table A.4 shows completed assignments where (1) both husband and wife were interviewed; (2) only one spouse was interviewed and an unsuccessful attempt was made to interview the other spouse; (3) there was only one eligible respondent in the household.

Table A.4. Completed Interviews with Both Spouses, with One of Two Spouses in the Household, and with Single Respondents by Area

Area	*Both spouses in Household*		*Single Respondent in Household*	*Total "Complete" Assignments*
	Interviewed Both	*Interviewed One*		
Projects				
Evans	62	19	23	104
Grant	63	17	42	122
Park	41	18	64	123
Stern	40	32	41	113
Totals	206	86	170	462
Neighborhoods				
Evans	63	18	14	95
Grant	36	19	43	98
Park	48	15	46	109
Stern	53	24	27	104
Totals	200	76	130	406

Very few potential respondents clearly refused to be interviewed and categorically turned the interviewer away. The overwhelming majority of people who did not welcome the interviewer failed to make their intentions clear. Thus the interviewers for the most part dealt with various degrees of reluctance. For example, respondents said they were busy now, had appointments, were on their way to work, were not feeling well, or would perhaps talk some other time. Many would set up appointments with the interviewer, a large number of such appointments subsequently being broken by the respondent. Usually refusals were accepted as final only after one of the more persuasive interviewers had called upon the respondent, acting in the role of a supervisor to ascertain that the refusal was not merely a brush-off. There were many cases that the supervising interviewer managed to salvage. Such considerations account for the small numbers of failures due to refusal, shown in Table A.5.

Table A.5. Types of Assignments Not Completed at the Conclusion of the Interviewing Phase by Area

Area	*Refusals*	*Possible Completions*	*Total Incomplete*
Projects			
Evans	17	14	31
Grant	11	26	37
Park	4	32	36
Stern	12	17	29
Neighborhoods			
Evans	12	35	47
Grant	7	31	38
Park	2	30	32
Stern	5	28	33

We have no basis for estimating how many of the "possible" assignments could have been completed eventually, but the experience of our most "successful" interviewers indicates that, given time, more completions could have been obtained. People who chronically fail to answer their doors or who continue to set up and break appointments can, with continued effort and at great expense, be interested in giving an interview.

Our interviewers' efforts did not seem to be inversely related to the quality of the interviews. This is particularly true of people who failed to understand what was being asked of them until after they had consented to, and given, the interview. Interviewers often reported that a reluctant respondent became quite enthusiastic about the study and their part in it once the interview was *completed.*

Possible completions can be classified into three types: (1) respondents who broke appointments, offered temporary excuses and delayed completion of an interview but who did not refuse the interviewer; (2) addresses where numerous calls were made but no one was found at home on any call by the time the interviewing phase was completed (these include some homes where the interviewer did find children alone or where neighbors offered some clues as to when or how to contact the residents); and ((3) respondents who were uncooperative or refused the interviewer but who could have been approached again.

Appendix B. Sampling and Data Collection Procedures for Panel Survey*

A MAJOR OBJECTIVE of this inquiry was to determine ways in which people change or do not change as a result of moving into a housing project in one kind of a neighborhood as compared with projects in other kinds of neighborhoods. The panel study was limited to families with at least one minor child and focused primarily upon implications of family structure. The sampling plan called for stratifying the study population in each of four projects by conjugal intactness (both parents present/ one parent present) and by race (white/ non-white).[1] A quota of 10 families was established for each sampling cell, yielding a total of 160 families (240 respondents, including both husband and wife in the intact families) for whom interviews would be available at two points in time: at the time of application for public housing while still in their neighborhood of origin and after 12 months of residency in public housing. The original sample

* Prepared by Seymour S. Bellin.

1. A fifth public housing project was subsequently built and opened. The study, however, was restricted to the original four projects.

design allowed for oversampling in anticipation of attrition. Since there could be a time lapse between time of application (and the initial interview) and an offer of a vacancy, some families might withdraw prior to such an offer. Still others could be expected to move out before the full minimum year of housing occupancy.

The Problem of Selectivity

Early in the history of this inquiry, it became evident that marked selectivity occurred in the allocation of families among the four public housing developments. Applicants differed not only in their project *preferences* but in their *willingness* to even consider a vacancy in the various housing projects. Characteristics of the projects themselves as well as the larger neighborhood context affected their choices. Applicants appeared to prefer the housing project closest to the site of their residence at the time of application. A strong racial consideration also was evident: few white families were willing to accept a vacancy in the predominantly nonwhite Park project. While nonwhite families were less selective as a group than the white families, many were unwilling to consider residency in the Evans project which, of the four projects, is most remote from the present Negro community and the downtown urban center. Both white and Negro families tend to avoid Stern because of dissatisfaction with its architectural design: it consists of three-story walk-ups.

Superimposed upon applicant preferences is selectivity which results from eligibility criteria as they are interpreted and applied by the Housing Authority. The Authority gives consideration both to preferences and needs of applicants in the assignment of housing projects and apartments within each project. It was their stated policy that applicants for public housing should enjoy at least as much free choice as exists in the private housing market. Applicants were free to reject a vacancy offer without prejudice with respect to any other vacancy that subsequently might become available. While this policy had the probably unintended effect of further reinforcing de facto racial segregation, it also minimized vacancy and apartment turnover rates. Ultimately, actual project and apartment assignments are greatly constrained by the economic, statutory, and administrative realities as interpreted by the housing authority.

The need became paramount to randomize the assignment of families to the four projects in order to minimize selectivity. Procedures were developed in cooperation with the Housing Authority that maximized the chance for equal consideration for all projects to which an applicant was willing to accept placement.[2] All applicants, however, were free to reject a vacancy without penalty. Clearly, despite randomization, some noncomparability can be expected to persist which must be taken into account in the analysis.

Procedures for Assigning Families to Vacancies

The housing management furnished the research staff with a list of families eligible for public housing who met the study criteria.[3] These families had been assigned to one of two priority classifications on the basis of need and statutory considerations. Priority II families were to be offered a vacancy only when the priority I list had been exhausted.[4] These lists were periodically updated (about every two weeks) to include families accepted for housing since the previous list was established.

An order in which the families were to be offered a vacancy was established independently for each of the four

2. The Evans project was an exception to the rule. Housing management was reluctant to relax the stricter standards it applied in screening applicants for the Evans project which, it was stated, presented minimal administrative and maintenance difficulties. There probably was concern also about the possible consequences of a sudden substantial increase in the number of nonwhite families, given the racial tensions that were beginning to surface then.

3. In addition to elderly individuals and couples, a small number of families, by prior agreement, were exempt from the randomization process on the basis of extenuating circumstances, e.g., emergency need for immediate residency in the case of a family burned out of an apartment.

4. Priority status was periodically reviewed and could be altered. An excessively long wait by a priority II family could be the basis for reassignment to priority I.

projects. Each family received a rank order number for each project in which it would accept a placement. A family might be first in line for the next vacancy in one project but last of a group of families interested in a vacancy in another one. A separate rank order was established within each priority classification. If an applicant changed his mind about a project, his card for the project was withdrawn without affecting his order number for other projects.

When vacancies occurred simultaneously in more than one project, they were to be filled in a fixed order of rotation among the four projects.

Since eligibility status of a family conceivably could have changed from the time of application to the availability of a vacancy, and a family might fail to reply or delay in responding to the letter of inquiry, the housing management contacted several families at a time. Thus, despite the procedures, some discretion could be exercised in practice in assigning a family to a vacancy.

The Interval Between Interviews

At the outset, 12 months was established as the maximum feasible interval between admission to public housing and the reinterview. As the study neared a conclusion, the minimum period of residence was reduced to 6 months to enlarge the sample, particularly in undersized sampling cells. The great majority of panel families, however, were in residence for the full 12-month period. The actual time that elapsed between the initial interview and the second interview was longer in many instances, since a majority of families experienced some delay in gaining admission to public housing. But in few instances did the delay amount to more than 3 months.

This period of time was expected to be sufficient to reveal detectable effects of neighborhood influences in many domains of attitude and behavior. It was also recognized, however, that the full effects of neighborhood impact on residents might require a much longer period of time and that our findings would afford a conservative estimate of neighborhood influences.

SAMPLING RESULTS

Of families eligible for public housing who met our study criteria, about 9 in 10 were successfully interviewed. Some families had withdrawn interest in public housing and others had already gained admission to public housing apartments before they could be interviewed. Because the list of qualified applicants was relatively shallow at times, the local

Table B.1. Interview Status at Wave I of Household and Individuals Making up the Panel Sample by Sex, by Race, and by Marital Status

	Men	*Women*	*Total Number of*	
			Individual	*Households*
Total All Persons				
Conjugally Intact				
Interview status				
Both hu/wife	222	222	444	222
Wife only	—	21	21	21
Conjugally Broken				
Women	—	135	135	135
Grand Total	222	378	600	378
White Persons				
Conjugally Intact				
Interview status				
Both hu/wife	85	85	170	85
Wife only	—	10	10	10
Conjugally Broken				
Women	—	46	46	46
Subtotal	85	141	226	141
Nonwhite Persons				
Conjugally Intact				
Interview status				
Both hu/wife	137	137	274	137
Wife only	—	11	11	11
Conjugally Broken				
Women	—	89	89	89
Subtotal	137	237	374	237

Housing Authority did not always allow much lead time for our interviewers from the time eligibility was determined to the offer of a vacancy.

The initial panel population consisted of 600 persons, 222 men and 378 women, who were interviewed between July 7, 1962, and May 15, 1964 (see Table B.2).

These persons represent 378 households, 243 of which were conjugally intact, 135 of which were husbandless. Of 243 married couples, in 222 instances interviews were completed with both marital partners. In nearly all of the 21 instances in which we failed to interview husbands, this was attributable to our inability to reach them before they moved into public housing. The wife was interviewed in all conjugal households. Unless an interview was completed with the wife, the household was not included in the study.

Of the original panel population, 546 (or 91 per cent) were successfully reinterviewed: 88 per cent of the men and 93 per cent of the women (see Table B.2). The reinterview completion rates were little affected by marital status or changes in marital status between the two interview waves. Of 378 households in the original sample, a change in marital status occurred in 35. Eighteen of the 243 conjugally intact households were disrupted by separation, divorce, or death. Of 135 women who were husbandless at the time of the first interview, 17 had remarried. In all marital status categories, at least 9 of 10 persons were reinterviewed, except for a small number of husbands who had separated or divorced their wives or who had died in the interim.

Of 225 conjugal households that remained intact throughout the study period, interviews were completed with *both* marital partners at both points in time in 186 instances.

In addition to the 546 of the original panel respondents who were reinterviewed, 26 men were interviewed for the first time in Wave II (see Table B-3). Thirteen were husbands who had been missed at the initial interview; the remaining 12 were husbands of husbandless women who had gotten married; the remaining person was the new husband

Table B.2. Reinterview Status of Panel Respondents Interviewed at Wave I by Sex, by Marital Status, and by Change in Marital Status

	Interviewed at Wave I	
	N	%
	600	100.0
Interview status at Wave II		
Reinterviewed	546	91.0
Not reinterviewed	54	9.0

Marital Status and Marital Status Changes from Wave I to II

Marital status:

	Wave II–Married Married *Wave II–No Change*				*No Spouse Change**		*No Spouse Married*		*Total No Change*	
	N	%	N	%	N	%	N	%	N	%
Men	205	100.0	17*	100.0	0		0		222	100.0
Interviewed at Wave II										
Yes	186	90.7	9	52.9	—	—	—	—	195	87.8
No	19	9.3	8*	47.1	—	—	—	—	27	12.2
Women										
Interviewed at Wave II										
Yes	206	91.5	16	94.1	17	100.0	118	94.4	357	93.0
No	19	8.5	1	5.9	0.0	7	5.6	27	12.2	

* Includes one family in which the wife divorced and both remarried; the *new* husband was interviewed at Wave II

of a woman who had remarried. Thus, at Wave II there are a total of 572 completed interviews.

Approximately two-thirds of the original panel population was nonwhite. The completion rates by marital status and sex characteristics for both the initial and follow-up interviews were approximately similar for both white and nonwhite.

In a total of 294 households, marital status remained unchanged as of the follow-up interview. A total of 200 house-

Table B.3. Interview Status at Wave I and II of the Panel Sample by Sex and by Change in Marital Status

	Men Interviewed at					Women Interviewed at				
Marital status at Wave I & II	*Wave I Only*	*Wave II Only*	*Both I*	*Tot. II*	*Neither I nor II*	*Wave I Only*	*Wave II Only*	*Both I&II*	*Tot.*	*Neither I nor II*
Married, No Change	19	13	186	218	7	19	—	206	225	—
Married, Remarried	1*	1*	—	—	—	—	—	1	1	—
Married, Broken	7	—	9	16	1	1	—	16	17	—
Broken, Married	—	12	—	12	—	—	—	17	17	—
Broken, No Change	—	—	—	—	—	7	—	111	118	—
Grand Total	27	26	195	248	8	27	—	351	378	—

TOTAL BOTH SEXES

I Only	II Only	I & II	Total	Neither I Nor II
54	26	546	626	8

holds, 124 married and 76 husbandless mothers, gained occupancy in public housing (see Table B.4).

Quotas for the planned sampling design were not fully met. Whites are underrepresented in Park; nonwhites are underrepresented in Evans. This holds true for married as well as husbandless women.

Although several other cells are a few shy of their intended quotas, the numbers are such that comparisons among three projects may be possible for whites as well as nonwhites. Comparisons between white and nonwhite persons by marital status appears possible for Grant and Stern.

Table B.4. Women Whose Marital Status Remained Unchanged and Who Were Successfully Interviewed at Both Wave I and Wave II by Housing Outcome, by Marital Status, and by Race*

	Public Housing Projects					*Did Not Enter Public Housing*			
	Park	*Grant*	*Stern*	*Evans*	*Total*	*Moved*	*Did not Move*	*Total*	*Grand Total*
Married									
White	1	14	7	18	40	22	10	32	72
Nonwhite	40	15	27	2	84	26	8	34	118
Total	41	29	34	20	124	48	18	66	190
Husbandless									
White	0	9	7	9	25	5	4	9	34
Nonwhite	36	7	8	0	51	12	7	19	70
Total	36	16	15	9	76	17	11	28	104
Total By Race									
White	1	23	14	27	65	27	14	41	106
Nonwhite	76	22	35	2	135	38	15	53	188
Grand Total	77	45	49	29	200	65	29	94	294

* In residence in public housing a minimum of six months prior to reinterview.

Name Index

Subject Index